D0186097

JESSIE'S JOURNEY

AUTOBIOGRAPHY OF A TRAVELLER GIRL

JESS SMITH

BIRLINN

First published in 2002 by Mercat Press Ltd
Reprinted 2002, 2003 (three times), 2004, 2005, 2006
New edition published 2008 by
Birlinn Limited
West Newington House
10 Newington Road
Edinburgh
EH9 1QS

www.birlinn.co.uk

Copyright © Jess Smith 2002, 2008

The story 'A Natural Love' was first published in *The Scots Magazine*,
September 2000.

The moral right of Jess Smith to be identified as the author
of this work has been asserted by her in accordance with the
Copyright, Designs and Patents Act 1988

All rights reserved. No part of this publication may be repro-
duced, stored or transmitted in any form without the express
written permission of the publisher.

ISBN-13: 978 1 84158 702 8
ISBN-10: 1 84158 702 8

British Library Cataloguing-in-Publication Data
A catalogue record for this book is available from the British
Library

Digital restoration of cover photograph: Howitt Imaging Ltd, Edinburgh

Set in Bembo and Adobe Jenson at Birlinn

Printed and bound in Great Britain by Antony Rowe Ltd

JESSIE'S JOURNEY

JESS SMITH

was raised in a large family of Scottish travellers. She is married with three children and six grandchildren. As a traditional storyteller, she is in great demand for live performances throughout Scotland. This is the first book in her autobiographical trilogy, which continues with *Tales from the Tent* and concludes with *Tears for a Tinker*. She has also written a novel, *Bruar's Rest*.

Contents

ILLUSTRATIONS

Between pages 54 and 55:
Jessie's mother's birth certificate
Four generations of the Power family
Granny Riley
Granny Power
Granny Riley and Auntie Maggie
Jessie's father aged 15
A gathering of relatives at 'The Berries'
Jessie's mother and father in 1940
Jessie's mother and Uncle Charlie
Jessie's father

Between pages 150 and 151:
The Devil's Elbow, Glenshee
Jessie's mother with her older sisters
The bus and the 'wee Fordy van'
Jessie's mother and father with three of her older sisters
Jessie, eight months old
Jessie's mother and Uncle Wullie
Mona, Chrissy, Shirley and Janey
Jess in her school uniform
Jess with her mother, Jeannie
Jess with her father, Charlie

To the bus driver Charles Riley (Daddy),
I dedicate this book.

Acknowledgements

I would like to thank my husband Dave for his love and constant support.

Also my precious children and grandchildren.

My beloved mother, Jeannie. Always with me.

Shirley, Dave and family for believing in me.

My dear friends Maimie, Sonja, Mona, Alison, Kay, Donald, Malcolm, Harry and the Writers Group.

Maurice Fleming and John Beaton, who set the word in motion.

Tom, Catherine and Seán.

And to those too numerous to mention—thank you all, from my heart.

PROLOGUE

*T*he ways of my people, their language, culture and livelihoods, are with each passing moment vanishing off the face of the earth. I am not learned enough to give you a history of the travelling life in its entirety. Nor do I wish to burden you with the 'ethnic cleansing' story others have written so passionately. 'But' I hear you ask, 'just what is a traveller?'

Well, my friend, in complete honesty, I do not know. Ask me further, 'Where do you belong?' I say to you, 'Wherever the feather falls or the seed is blown.'

Without feathers, there is no nest, and without seeds, there are no flowers.

We are the storytellers. Wandering minstrels, respecters of the soil, lovers of family and friends. Once we were your heritage, now we blot your landscape. Soon we will be gone and you will have no culture. I will be a ghost of Scotland's colourful past, but before I fade, let me tell you about my life on the road with my seven beautiful sisters, protective parents and the mongrel dog called Tiny.

I have stories to tell—sad, humorous, outrageous, aye, even unbelievable, but tell them I must. Why? Because with our leaving we take with us to the grave our greatest gift—'the spoken word'.

The art of storytelling, with which so many travelling folks are gifted, seldom finds its way through the pen. I am grateful to my parents for giving me the ability to do this, and to the many hardy souls we met on the road, for without their taking time for tales I would find it impossible to write this book.

Every person born is a story; from womb to grave we live a tale. Parents tell stories of the time we were babies, then how we grew into teenagers, and so it goes on, a rich tapestry of life.

Although regarded by many as Scotland's outcasts, travelling people are as true to her soil as the roots of the heather. I proudly cleave to these roots, and preserve her culture and traditions.

And through these pages I claim my rightful place as one of Scotia's Bairns.

Come with me, reader, and share a traveller's campfire. I promise we won't steal your children or fleece your pocket. You might even get a wee bit closer to understanding us.

1

I AM A SCOTTISH TRAVELLER

I start my life story at the age of five, in the year of 1953, and I will finish it in the spring of 1963, when I was fifteen. The reason for such a short span, I hope, will become clear in the telling of my tale.

Both my parents were from travelling backgrounds. Charlie Riley, my father, was the eldest son of Wullie Riley and Margaret Burns, who had eleven of a family (nine survived to adulthood). Grandad's mother's name was O'Connor, and I believe she came from Ireland. Although they travelled extensively through the north and west of Scotland, they chose Perthshire as the favoured place to settle down. When all but four of their family had left them, they put down roots in Pitlochry, north of Moulin, in a bonny wee cottage called Lettoch Beag. All of the Riley clan (except Daddy) eventually integrated into the settled community and gave up the travelling life for good.

My mother was Jeannie Power; she was the daughter of Nicholas Power, whose people came from Kilkenny in Ireland's south. Her mother was Margaret Macarthur from Kintyre. They had a large family of ten. Grandad's mother's surname was McManus.

Like my father's family, they settled in the Bobbin mill at Pitlochry, eventually spreading throughout Perthshire, Fife, Angus, Argyll and England. They too went into the 'scaldy' (settled folks') life, all except Jeannie, my wee Mammy.

Not many folks can say this, but I have all through my life found my relations to be honest decent people, rich in kindness to everybody, never judgmental and always a smile to the stranger. And fair enjoying o' the 'crack'. They will pop in and out of my tales as I go along.

My parents between them gave the world eight girls. The four eldest were born before the Second World War, the four youngest, after the War; Mona, Chrissie, Charlotte (Shirley), Janey, Jessie (me), Mary, Renie and Barbara (Babsy).

Our mother had a difficult childhood. Every day from birth until she married was on the road; horse, cart, a father seldom sober and too fond of his fists. Although proud of her roots, she had foreseen that the ways of the traveller were changing, and not, sadly to say, for the better. She told our Daddy many times that the summer was the time to go back on the road.

'The lassies must have a decent education,' she reminded him often. Therefore a house for the winter was paramount. He verbally agreed, but his heart was yearning for the open road with the old ways.

The family settled in a fine house in Aberdeen—it went on fire; then to a large spacious dwelling house in Aberfeldy—it was flooded. Daddy even bought a plot to build his own house at Finab, Pitlochry, but was refused planning permission.

'Sorry, Jeannie, my bonny lamb,' he finally told my mother, 'but it looks awfy like us travelling folks are just what the label says—"born to the ways of the road".'

People said it must have been the shell-shock he suffered during the War that unsettled him—rubbish! He was a 'thoroughbred', my father. Born to travel.

So after a brief spell living in an articulated wagon, Daddy purchased our new home—a 1948 Bedford bus! My bus was created in the same year as myself.

Mammy was far from happy at the thought of her proud lassies crammed like sardines in a bus. The older girls were horrified, and the wee ones were neither here nor there. Except me!

There was Baby Babsy newborn, two-year-old Renie, three-year-old Mary, then me. I was five years old, and even as I write I remember well my feelings of excitement at living in a BUS.

A forever holiday. I was going home, something way deep in my young soul knew; here was my destiny, the road ahead had already been made for me by generations of travelling folks. I was about to be reborn into the old ways.

To me, my Daddy was the inventor of do-it-yourself. No matter what—building, electrics, plumbing, you name it—he could do it. Cleverest pair of hands in the whole of Scotland, I kid you not. We were living temporarily in a converted wagon at Walkers field outside Pitlochry. It was September 1953, and Mammy had just that very month given birth to my youngest sister—Barbara, her eighth child, and all girls.

I remember that day so well, the day he drove off Finab road end and onto the field with the bus, he looked so small inside it. My first memory of the inside of the bus was neat rows of seats covered with Paisley-patterned material. I watched as my Dad unbolted every seat and piled them outside, leaving an empty shell. What fun I had jumping up and down on those springy benches with the flowery purple covers.

'Mammy, it's going to look terrible, living in that thing, Daddy's lost his senses.' My oldest sister Mona had been used to living in houses; she thought of the travelling life as a way of the past, and a touch below her! 'And you can just tell him I'll be biding with Granny Riley from now on.' Our Mona, nineteen at the time, was as refined as gentry.

'Give me over another nappy, this wind will have all the washing dry in no time,' said Mammy, ignoring her daughter's haughty remarks and reminding her at the same time that Granny had had her full share of teenagers in her life and needed a bit of peace.

Her turning to see me leaping high in the air on her future furniture brought a volley of curses.

'Jessie, get you off those bloody seats, your father's putting some of them back into the bus, and look at the state you've got them in with your guttery shoes! Now do something useful and play with your wee sisters.'

Mona stormed away in the huff, as I took Mary and Renie by the hands over to the bus door and said, 'this is our new home, braw isn't it?' My two wee sisters looked at me in total bewilderment. What did a three- and two-years-old know about anything, I ask you?

The long seat at the back of the bus was left in place, with bolts and brackets added, allowing it to be converted into a double bed. They christened it 'the master bed', and it was the courie doon of my parents. Next a sideboard was placed at the bottom right-hand-side of the bus. This took all dishes, pots, pans and cutlery. Our bed was placed lengthways on the left, and like the big one it had brackets fitted so it could be doubled up during the day into seating. But if ill health like measles or mumps visited then the big bed was left down. Of course in such times it became quite a squeeze to get past us. The two seats at the front were left in place, along with the one for the clippy, and as Mammy said jokingly she was the equivalent of a bus conductor she bagged this one. It was really so she could be navigator for Daddy, but we knew fine it was the seat with the best view. My father had other plans for our dear Mum though, she would have to learn to drive herself, and I'll tell you why later.

Luggage racks were left in place, and into these narrow shelves went all our worldly goods.

What amazed experts who saw the finished product was 'how did he manage to change the fixed windows so that they wound down?' He never said. Like I told you earlier, cleverest pair of hands in the land. He laboured the best part of a week to get the bus liveable—not just that, but pleasing for his fine lassies. Well he knew, by the long faces, they would take a damn lot of coaxing.

Most important of all to convince was Mammy. She had to feel comfy, clean and secure in her new home. So next day, leaving us wee ones in the care of the older lassies, he took her to the town of Pitlochry, where she chose curtain material and a good quality carpet.

What a right bonny bus it was when Mammy finished hanging up those bright blue gingham curtains with matching tiebacks. Lastly, the Paisley-patterned Axminster runner, almost identical in colour to the seat-covers, was laid neatly on the floor. 'To keep your wee feet warm in winter, bairns,' she said.

'One thing left to do, Jeannie,' said Daddy, 'I'll be back later.' He waved cheerio as he set off that warm September morning in his old lorry, accompanied by his younger brother Wullie.

It was suppertime before he eventually came back, minus the lorry. In its place was a wee green Ford 10 van. I remember thinking it looked like a frog with a swelt head!

Our father opened the van's back door and revealed, sitting like old Queen Victoria when she was right fat, a wee three-legged Reekie stove! 'Why mention that?' I hear you ask. Well, through the coming years I hope to share with you the warmth from its coal-stapped body. Winters in the bus were to be a mite cold, I can tell

4

you. Of course, the family pots of soup and the morning porridge were another blessing, thanks to our wee Reekie. Summertime cooking was done outside on the open campfire, but if the nights were damp and wet the wee stove couldn't be beat.

Daddy positioned the stove behind the driver's seat. With him being the driver, that made sense; he was not so silly, my Dad liked his heat.

Bolting the stove securely to the floor, he made a partition around the back, protecting the wall from the heat generated by the chimney that protruded out of the bus roof. I wouldn't mind, but of all things that partition was made of dangerous asbestos! Thank God, none of us suffered any ill health as a result.

'Now, Jeannie, can you ask for a better home than that?' asked Daddy, admiring his handiwork.

'Aye, lad, you've worked wonders, but something bothers me,' answered Mammy.

'What's that, then, lass?' A look of concern spread across his face.

'Who do you have in mind to drive the van?'

He laughed, then took the breath from her with his answer: 'Jeannie, there is nothing easier.'

'For God's sake, man, I've just had a baby, I wouldn't say I was fit.'

'Rubbish, you're the picture of pure health, sure I don't know a stronger lass than yourself!'

So, several driving lessons from Daddy later, and a provisional driving licence, the necessary bit of paper needed, she became a rare sight for those days—a woman driver!

Mona was still protesting at living in the bus. After a while Chrissie had joined in her disapproval. Daddy had his work cut out trying to convince them. So when supper was over he sat them down to talk it out.

'Now, lassies, fine I know your lives are about to change. But travelling ways are not like they used to be; those days are well gone. You don't have to see life from a tent mouth like your mother and I did. This braw bus with all its modern ways will make sure you want for nothing.'

My big sisters hummed and hawed, but they knew Daddy was the boss and no amount of moaning faces would change his mind. Nevertheless, our Mona still had to get her tuppence worth: 'Modern, huh! We still have to fetch water from the burn, hang kettles and pots from an iron chittie over an outside fire. Washing, now, it will still be hung from tree to tree. And worst of all, God help me, washing my tender face in a cold burn. Modern, what difference is that from your and Mammy's days?'

'Come now, lassie, a bit of country living did nobody any harm.' He attempted to put an arm round her shoulder and she instantly brushed it away.

'I'll be old and wizent before my time!' she shouted. 'Long before it.'

Daddy laughed at his oldest daughter's remarks, then walked off, saying, 'make sure you don't keep that frown on your bonny face for much longer, the wind will change and you'll stay that way!'

We all laughed. She tutted, reached inside her skirt pocket and took out a nail-file. Storming outside she sat on the dyke by the side of the road, and the more she thought about the life ahead of her the harder she shaped her fingernails into talons.

'You could do with a pair of wings now, seeing as you've the claws of a hawk on yourself Mona,' mocked Shirley.

'It wouldn't bother you if you stayed on a dung heap, so shut your face or I'll rip it off!'

'If you try that, lady, then I'll turn your backside into a sieve when I ram those talons up your arse!'

'That will do with the foul tongue,' said Mammy, pointing a finger sternly at Shirley.

Then she whispered to Daddy, 'Perhaps she would be better staying with Granny after all.'

'Definitely not, she's our daughter, and until a suitable lad comes along then she'll stay with the family!'

2

A VERY LONG DRIVE

Protests ignored, we were on the road, and you'll never guess where to—of all places, over the Border, our feet were to travel to England! In those days a distance like that was seldom contemplated.

Perhaps sitting behind the wheel of a grand bus made Daddy feel like 'King o' the Road'. Have castle, will travel. One with wheels, that is. Maybe it was the sense of freedom he felt after six war years; especially the last three spent fighting from a tank. He never told us, but I think it made him claustrophobic. By God, though, he didn't half eat up those long tarred miles as we trundled down to England.

Mammy adapted no bother to her wee Fordy van (as she christened it). And a mite too fond of it she became. Because, at the brow of every hill, her insistence to stop and give the wee green van a rest, then check if it needed a drink of water, had her and Daddy shouting at each other more than once, I can tell you.

After several days on the road, everybody began to think the land went on forever. Mammy asked Daddy, 'Where do we stop, Charlie? My bum's gone past the point of rigor mortis.'

'I mind chumming an English lad during the War,' he answered, 'who sang the praises of his home town—Manchester, he called it.'

'Manchester, where in heaven's name is that?' She looked at him as if he had mentioned a far outpost on the moon.

'Lancashire,' he answered, putting a reassuring arm round her waist. 'The county o' the Rose.'

'Dad, that's where Glasgow is!' shouted Shirley, who was reading a 'true romance' comic on the back seat of the bus.

'No, that's Lanarkshire,' said Janey, 'and hurry up with the comic, you've been reading it for days.'

We spent a few weeks getting acclimatised to the shire, stopping at Lancaster, Preston and several towns round about. Best place was Blackpool. 'It would have been nice to live there for the winter,' I heard the older girls say. But Manchester was where my father had set his sights, and he wouldn't be swayed.

Everybody settled back as we travelled the last few miles to our destination.

Soon it was time for tea, and after eating and tidying up Daddy smiled, saying we'd soon be there, adding when we came into the town that Mammy had best stay close behind the bus. 'If you get lost, lassie,' he warned her, 'I'll never find you.'

We all laughed, imagining our Mother driving wee Fordy round in circles.

'Is there a place to pull on, in this Rosie-shire town?' she asked.

'Jeannie, there's miles of houses, surely a wee corner can be found to winter on. When we get there we'll have a drive round in the Fordy and find some place suitable.

He added, 'there will be a lot of waste ground, because the brave folks who live here have seen the worst of Hitler's flying bombs flatten whole streets.'

'I just hope the polis give us the freedom to settle, then,' she said.

'Oh, I hardly think we'll cause any difference to the landscape,' he reassured her.

'Another thing, I hope this town isn't too big, I don't like the idea of my lassies living in a place where I can't keep an eye on them!'

It was easy to sense our mother's fears. She had seldom been in a place any bigger than Aberdeen.

'Everything will be fine, wife, never fear, just think on the hawking you can do among so many folk. When we go home in the spring you'll have plenty to crack to the folks about, it's not just anybody who can say they travelled so far, now is it?'

Little did our father know just what a tale she would tell! Oh my, if we but knew what Manchester had in store for us, the bus would have been put in reverse there and then. Ochone! Ochone!

I can't recall much of the actual journey down to England; being only five I played with my toys and my wee sisters. One thing I do remember thinking was how much like Scotland the bonny welcoming hills of Cumbria were. Great rolling giants clothed in green and brown velvet.

I conjured up a friendly monster with wings who followed us from the midst of the hills, all the way to the smog-shrouded county of our destination, then disappeared as quickly as he came. I named him Greenwing. My imaginary friend.

Not like home ground, though, was the thick grey smog of Lancashire!

Smoke from a million reekit factory coal fires lifted itself up to meet the sun then fell back and covered the whole of the otherwise bonny countryside. Like a shroud, it was terrible stuff, filled lungs and brought early death to the weakest of folk. Aye, a shroud indeed!

Thankfully the use of that so-called fossil fuel has all but gone, replaced by healthier alternatives. I feel a fraud saying that, though, because nothing can ever replace the welcome one got from a coal-fire on a winter's night.

As young as I was, one thing I do remember was Mammy saying to Daddy and the older lassies that she wasn't feeling very well. Given that this was late October, and wee Babsy, her eighth child, was born in September past, she put her state of health down to natural weakness and the upheaval of the bus life. The War itself left its mark on many a wife, especially those left holding the fort. Her state was no different than that of many another woman in the country in those days. That thought consoled my Mammy, so she put her health to the back of her mind and got on with things in hand.

Things being Manchester, for here we were at last in the smog-shrouded city. The first thing—where to winter settle?

The journey had been a difficult one, especially when Mammy insisted on resting the wee Fordy at ever hill's brow and refreshing it with a drink of water. Before I leave the road for this chapter, I would like to mention that when we came upon the notorious Shap Fell (an extremely steep hill on the old Cumbria A6 road), Mammy point-blank refused to put her van through such torture. This resulted in Daddy towing it while she walked behind, to make sure it was all right!

3

MANCHESTER ✦ SAVING JEANNIE

Daddy found a scrapyard, and got permission to pull on at the rear for the night. We hardly slept for the noise of lorries coming and going. After breakfast our parents headed off to find a suitable wintering ground, leaving us wee ones in the firm hands of the older girls. By the time they eventually came back, Chrissie had skelped me three times for spitting at Mary.

'Mammy,' I cried, shoving my legs up so she could examine them, 'look at the welts on the back of my legs with her leathering me!'

'You must have been a bad bairn to deserve that,' she answered, hardly glancing at the very visible red stripes across my poor wee limbs.

You see, if any of us wee ones got walloped by our older sisters, then without question we had most likely been bad! No why, or how, we must have been misbehaving. I remember many a time being the innocent party, but getting punished because of the mood my big sister was in (whichever one was taking care of me at the time), and Mammy always believed her, because she was the elder. Some justice, but it never did us any harm, and certainly, on this occasion, I was guilty! Well, she did stand on my big toe did our Mary, and it was right sore because Dad cut my toenail the night before and snipped it too far down 'to the quick', I think it's called. It bled, and ached. So I spat, for I wasn't allowed to slap her.

Mammy ignored us, drank her tea, then said they'd found a smashing place in an area called Cheetam Hill. An acre of waste ground, with a water tap and next door to public lavvies, you couldn't ask for anything better. Next day we pulled on.

It was here for the first time we came across English gypsies. We had heard many a tale about our southern neighbours, and here they were in the flesh.

Beautiful floral painted bow-wagons, a dozen of them sat in a half circle. Massive shire horses grazed close by, tethered to metal poles embedded in the earth.

There were wicker baskets filled with paper flowers, red, yellow, purple, green, pink: all the colours of the rainbow came from those baskets. I remember thinking, 'Wish I could do that,' when I saw the women folks, hair braided with colourful ribbons, winding crepe paper into flower heads.

Our arrival by bus seemed to cause quite a stir, and they gathered in a crowd wondering who we were, uncertain about our presence. Several men approached at the bus door. When they saw we were all female with no big burly brothers, they softened and began introducing each other.

Mammy knew she'd need eyes in the back of her head. There were plenty handsome young men, who were already crowding round, eyeing up her lassies; but it was only curiosity, if any fancying was done, then it certainly wasn't noticeable.

Mind you, being so young I hardly noticed anything like that—it's with the passing of time listening to my sisters round a campfire I learned enough to slip such comments into the writing of those past times.

Within a week we had settled, and the gypsies treated us like kin. That was, after all, exactly what we were, their Scottish cousins.

We were on the site for a week or two when our first frightening experience with the Manchester police left this incident vivid in my mind.

Daddy had been cracking round the dying embers of the fire with one of the older men. He stood up and, stretching his back, said, 'It's a cold night for sure, and this damnable smog fills my lungs, so I'll say goodnight to you, lad.' That said, he pulled seats and stools back from the hot ashes and doused the fire. Once, as a boy, he witnessed an old man burn to death after a fiery stick set his trouser-leg ablaze, and had ever since been vigilant where campfires were concerned.

'Yes, Charlie, it's bed for me too. I've ten dozen clothes pegs need whittling first light, so I'll be a busy man tomorrow.'

Closing the bus door tightly behind him, Daddy came over and unfolded the top of the blanket covering my face, whispering, 'Jessie, don't do that, you'll smother yourself, lass.' I had a bad habit of lying under the bedclothes. I moaned that it was cold, so he tucked the blanket under my chin, saying, 'Only the dead have covered faces'.

'Charlie,' whispered Mammy, 'before you bed yourself, bring me a drop water from the can, I've an awfy headache. I'll take a powder then hopefully get some sleep.'

'You'll turn into a powder, Jeannie, that's the third one today.' He was becoming more and more concerned with her daily headaches.

'Just give me the water, will you, man!' she retorted as she sat up in bed and shivered.

As young as I was, I can still remember my dear mother constantly complaining about her health the whiles we stayed that winter in Lancashire.

The night grew colder. Mary had lodged her knee under my ribs, and Renie had removed half my blanket, and claimed it for her own chin.

Now, had my mother not been sore-headed I'd have wakened her, but that would have been selfish. So, unable to sleep, I sat up, pulled back the curtain and—Lord roast me if I lie—the ugliest face in God's kingdom was staring at me through the window from the smog-shrouded night. It was a police raid! They banged their fists on the windows and rattled the sides of the bus with rubber batons. I began screaming.

My screams, coupled with the awful din, wakened everyone. Daddy was groping in the dark for the matches to light the Tilley lamp, when suddenly the thump, thump, thumping on the door added to the state of terror we were put in that night. It was the first time we had had any bother from the law.

'You in there, come out now,' a man shouted through the darkness.

Daddy found the matches and calmly pumped up the light until its welcome glow shone through the bus. Like moths we gathered round it. Baby Babs had wakened and Mammy held her tight into her breast. We were whimpering and shaking with fear, eyes staring from sockets like frightened owls. What was happening, for God's sake?

Daddy slowly opened the door, not knowing what manner of awfulness stood on the other side. 'It's all right, Charlie lad,' said a familiar voice. The old gypsy man my father had bidden goodnight to earlier on stood in his shirt-tail and bare feet, surrounded by several fearsome-looking men dressed in black.

'It's the hornies,' said the old chap, 'they say we've to move on.'

My father leapt down from the step, buttoned up his trousers, clumsily slipped his braces over each shoulder and shouted at the nightmare visitors closing round him.

'Have you bastards got nothing better to do than frighten in-nocent folk in the dead of night? I've a puckle wee bairns in here.' He pulled on his jacket and stood face to face with a big policeman, made six inches taller by a ridiculous pot-hat perched on his head, and waited on a response.

'Arrest this one,' the man ordered.

'He's from Scotland,' pleaded the old gypsy man, 'He don't know this be common practice in these 'ere parts, sir.'

'We'll arrest him, then, and maybe in future he'll remember.'

Daddy had no time to answer, as two policemen bundled him away in the back of a shiny black van. I can still see his bewildered face staring out at us, and all I could think was, how strange it was seeing my Dad in a motor car without his bunnet on.

We huddled round our mother completely dumbstruck, shivering with fear. Eventually Janey broke the eerie silence. 'What if they come back and murder the lot o' us!'

'There now, pet, that doesn't happen these days.' Mammy gently held her close. 'You've been taking far too much of those Suspense Comics to heart,' said Chrissie, draping a tartan rug round her shoulders.

'The polis are wicked in England, Scottish ones wouldn't do a bad thing like that, now would they Mammy?' asked Shirley, peering out at the darkness through the half-open curtain. At that moment I'm sure the whole bunch of us wished we were home in Scotland.

'Polis are the same the world over, some bad, some good. Give me my cardigan, it's getting cold in here. Mona, put some coal on the fire while I make the bairn a bottle.' Her milk had dried up; she hated 'false milk' (her description of dried milk), but the baby was belly-greeting and she was more than eager to calm her.

'I hope my Da is all right,' said Mona, stapping extra coals on the fire and hoping he'd be home any minute.

'They big polis will have kicked half the shite out o' him before we see him again.' Shirley's words sent a shiver through the bus.

'You better pray they don't or else we'll never see Scotland again,' said Mona.

Mammy told them not to think like that, then added, 'I'm right angry with your father for coming this far down the country, at least if we were nearer home the folks could help if we were stuck.' Then she ran a hand over her head and said, 'God, these powders are rubbish, I'd be as well taking the wee one's dried milk for this headache!'

A knock on the door had us clinging onto each other in total fear, thinking the polis were back to finish us off.

'Lassies, come now, you're working yourselves into a state', said Mammy. 'Chrissie, put the kettle on the stove. Shirley here, put Babsy to bed, I'll get the door.'

It was the friendly old gypsy who had tried to speak up for our father. 'Jeannie, don't worry about your man, they'll let him out early morning, but what is more important, we have to move on now.'

The usual procedure with gypsy harassment (and this is the same today as it was then), was that when the police came with orders to move on, that meant—move immediately, right then and there!

'But it's the middle of the night, they took my man away. Who do they expect will drive the bus and where will we go?' For our sake, Mammy tried to disguise the worry in her voice, but without success. 'This is bad doings right enough,' she said.

Our kindly neighbour, though, soon set her at ease by saying, 'My eldest son will drive it for you, pack your things away, dress the children, just a couple of miles along the way there's a nice bit of waste ground will do us all. Come on now, Jeannie, you have no choice: the police will drive your home onto the road then charge you with obstructing the King's Highway.'

She smiled, took the kindly man's hand and gave it a gentle squeeze. Thanking him from the heart, she said, 'God will see that you and yours want for little. The kindness you show us this night will be rewarded.'

'We stick together, us wanderers, and one day you may return the favour if we come to Scotland.'

Shirley took no time in telling the man that in Scotland only God and Mother Nature determined where and when travellers lived. Not big bullies with cosh sticks and pot-hats.

He laughed, and said England had its free countryside too.

Mammy told Shirley to mind her manners, then said to the man, 'You'll find a grand welcome among us, that's for sure.'

Soon we had everything secure. The old man's son came and said the caravan was hitched up to the horses and ready for the road. Before leaving he said to Mammy, 'I think it wise if you stay with your girls. I'll get my cousin to drive the van, will that be all right?'

She gladly accepted his offer; the last thing she wanted to do was drive through the smog-thick streets of Manchester in the middle of the night.

As our replacement driver trundled slowly the two miles towards the new campsite, I thought of Manchester as a place of menace, where in every dark corner a polisman with a pot-black hat was lurking, and began whimpering. My sisters joined me, and before long hysteria was taking hold amongst us. Mammy recognised the signs and quickly worked her magic on us. 'Did any of you lot ever see a bigger nose on a man than the one on the polisman who arrested Daddy? Fancy the disappointment of his poor mother the first time she set eyes on that. The nearest I can think to compare it with would be a rhino's horn. Yes, the biggest honker in England, wouldn't you say girls?'

We looked at each other, and within no time thoughts of menace were replaced by giggles and laughter, as we pictured in our mind's eye the policeman's big red hooter.

This was our Mother's way of avoiding mass hysterics amongst her brood, change the subject quickly. It worked. A clever woman, my mother.

For the rest of the night I worried dreadfully for my father's safety. It was then my imagination conjured up Greenwing, the wee Cumbrian flying monster. He told me children shouldn't worry. Instead they should play. So off on his wings I went, as he flew me over the velvet hills of his home ground. After playing all kinds of fun games he took me back to bed, where I slept soundly.

In the morning weary Daddy came home, muttering to himself

about keeping his big trap shut next time. Thankfully, though, that was the one and only time we had to go through polis night visits. They left us in peace for the duration of the winter on the waste ground at the far end of Cheetam Hill.

Mona asked if the polis hurt or manhandled him in the jail.

'God, no, they were a fine bunch o' lads; we played cards all night long, won myself twenty-three bob.'

'The last time I worry about you, then,' snapped Mona as she huffed out the door.

If she'd taken the time, as Mammy did, she'd have noticed at his hairline an ugly, bruised swelling. Or if she'd looked closer at his face she would also have seen a dark red trickle of dried blood round his nostrils.

After another week passed, the three eldest girls found work at a hamburger canning factory in Sale, on the outskirts of the city. Janey, although only twelve, didn't go to school that winter; she and Mammy took turns ragging and watching after the wee ones, Renie and Babsy.

Ragging consisted of handing round big brown paper bags containing six washing pegs and a sample-size packet of Rinso (older readers may remember this washing powder). Included was a note saying 'we are not begging, please accept the contents for the filling of the bag with rags, preferably woollens.' The ragman gave more money for woollens.

Most folks were grateful for a free box of washing powder with pegs, and took the contents before filling the bags with cast-offs, but there were dirty, vile people who, after helping themselves to the pegs and Rinso, left the fillings of their bowels as payment instead. I won't tell you what my father called these creatures. Thankfully they were few and far between.

Mammy washed and pressed the best of the rags, selling them at the local open markets, which were common in English cities, even up to the present day.

Mary and I went to the nearest school, a convent. Not because of our religion, but because it was the nearest to the site, a mere half mile away. That doesn't seem far, but in the thick smog on a freezing morning it felt like miles and miles.

Let me tell you about our nun-run school, and I promise you this, it certainly wasn't the proper way to start an education. Mary was four years old in the December. This was when we both started at the school. The Mother Superior, after a visit from Daddy to say he didn't want Janey taking care of three little girls, said there were plenty under-fives at the school and she'd be happy to take us both.

As we walked hand in hand to school that morning, the cold December wind blew smog into our eyes. Mary cried that she wanted Mammy. I reminded her that I too was frightened going to a new school, after all I was not yet six. But I pretended to be brave for her sake.

We gathered in the playground: a crowd of pitiful-looking children with running noses and sad faces. Some had thin, torn coats and bad-fitting shoes. Others didn't even have coats, only flimsy woollen jerseys with darned elbows. Several hadn't even the luxury of shoes. Instead they wore plimsolls on their wee feet, and it winter time too! I think they were from the poorest run-down areas, ones the gypsies called slums.

A loud bell rang, not like a school bell, more akin to what you'd hear from a church. We all rushed in together like ewe-less lambs and huddled close for warmth. Perhaps we totalled thirty in number, not much more. A woman dressed in black and white, I heard kids say she was the Mother Superior, led us in. Other women in grey and white followed; they were called sisters. Then it was us, into a hall with a ceiling so high I could hardly see the long thin flex the yellowed light bulbs were suspended from.

Silently everyone knelt down: a thin arm belonging to a tall lad yanked me onto my knees, and Mary did as I did.

'Bow your head. If *she* sees you, you'll get the Jesus Box!' said the lad, glancing swiftly over in the direction of a nun who I later was told went by the name of Sister Alice.

One whole hour later we left the assembly hall. Prayers were said for the morning, the lessons, and the poor little 'black babies of the world, the food in our bellies, the clothes on our backs'.

Prayer followed prayer and finally, when we got down to lessons, prayers were said at the start and finish. If we needed to go for a pee, we had to pray.

We were the ones who needed the prayers. Our wee knees were lumpy and sore. My head felt like a rain-soaked tennis ball, having hung it down for so long!

There weren't classes as such, because we were all taught together, and our ages ranged from as young as three up to ten. Three nuns took turns teaching, with the Mother Superior taking morning prayers. The only named nun I remember was Sister Alice, because she took an instant dislike to my wee sister and me. She never missed an opportunity to let us know how she felt. Being so young, the words 'dirty heathen gypsy' meant nothing to me.

At playtime I asked the tall laddie what he meant by the Jesus Box.

'You'll find out soon enough,' he said. 'Even if you're saintly they'll still find a reason to put you in it!'

He ran off to join a small band of lads congregating over by the school wall.

That night my wee sister and I had very little to tell the family about the school, except we could now recite several prayers.

'What did lessons consist of?' they enquired. So far not much, but that was understandable; after all nothing much happens on the first day.

As I lay in bed that night it was freezing, but I didn't feel the cold. My mind had visions of a big box with something scary in it, a thing named Jesus! Not my mother's precious Christ. He didn't punish little children. No, this must be someone else.

As the night grew darker my fear grew with it. I floated in and out of one nightmare then another. So awful were my fears that Greenwing stayed away from my dreams.

The school day began at seven. Sister Alice stood like a sentry at the door. As we walked in she ticked each of our names on a notepad. 'Bow your head, gypsy,' she called out at someone, then added: 'Have you no respect for a holy place?'

I looked around, feeling sorry for the poor soul who was being addressed, whoever it was, before realising *I* was the unholy offender! I felt my sister's fear as she held my hand so tightly the tips of my fingers went white.

The day went by with the same rigorous form of religion, and by the week's end we had learned nothing but prayers and more prayers.

For reasons known only to herself, Sister Alice had by now shown her dislike by using me as an example of 'how not to be'. I was, she told everyone, disobedient, unwilling to learn, full of cheek and, oh yes, a heathen gypsy!

After I told my parents, they said they were disappointed in me for being a wee midden. It was as if nuns were superhuman. Scolding me, my mother said, 'Nuns are next to God, they would never harm a child, Jessie. You must be misbehaving. Stop it or you'll get a right leathering, my lass.'

Daddy tried to lighten the issue by saying, 'Why don't you get the gypsy lassies to show you how to make paper flowers, then you can take a bunch to the sister?'

That sounded a good idea, it was something I'd wanted to learn since first seeing the pretty gypsy girls. So after breakfast I sat amongst yards and yards of coloured crepe paper, learning the art of flower-making, gypsy-style. An old woman with steely blue eyes braided my hair, then tied a floral apron with a big pocket round my waist. Little cuts of fuse wire were held in the pocket.

Take a yard of the crepe paper, cut in two-inch widths, push thumbs gently into the paper making wee dents, and roll into flower shapes resembling roses. Then tie these using the wire to privet hedge cuttings of twelve inches in length to produce the lifelike flower that English gypsies were so famed for in days gone by. 'Six red roses and a blessing!' was the hawker call of these gentle nomads.

I made six for Sister Alice, and was glowing with pride when I tied them together with one of my tartan hair ribbons reserved for Sundays and visitors.

The strictest law in the convent school was Sunday worship. To miss the seven a.m. call was blasphemy! It was six-thirty on that particular Sabbath, and Mary didn't want to go. I pleaded with her to hurry. Half-eaten jammy sandwich hanging from her mouth, I pulled her, half-running, half-dragging, along the still, dark road towards the chapel. We could hear the bell as if demanding we hurry up or else. I was forcing my poor wee sister to run faster, the chapel was in sight the last gong of the bell trailed away, when suddenly Mary went all her length, badly grazing her knee. Blood poured down, filled the crumpled sock and disappeared into her tiny brown shoe.

'Oh pet, I am so sorry. Look, forget the chapel, your wee leg needs a clean. I'll explain to the nuns in the morning, it will be alright, they'll forgive us.' Mary nodded through her tears as we turned and went off home.

I won't say I wasn't frightened to go into school that Monday morning, because I was terrified, but perhaps my peace offering of coloured flowers would smooth the waves?

Who was I kidding? Sister Alice took one look, then screwed my gift into a crunched-up ball between her fists before throwing it into the big dustbin at the playground gate.

I bit my lip. Her actions made me angry and confused. Looking back I am certain the woman had been verbally cursed by some rough gypsy body in her past, and it was fear made her act the way she did. We were marched along to the Mother Superior's room.

Our punishment for being absent from Sunday worship would soon be known.

'You shall both go in for punishment this morning. Mary, you will go first.'

'No, that's not fair, it was my fault we missed chapel! Please don't put my wee sister in,' I cried. 'Look, she cut her leg yesterday. We went back home and were too late for your stupid chapel,' I screamed. 'She did nothing wrong, I tell you!'

Completely ignoring me and determined to rid the devil from our innards, the elder woman took hold of my sobbing sister and repeated her judgement. 'Sister Alice, please put this child in for her punishment.'

As the nun grabbed my sister by the arm, I lunged at her fingers, sinking my teeth into her thumb. She screamed, instantly letting go of Mary's wee arm.

'You touch her and I'll chew the hand off you,' I warned.

'To the boxroom, sister, at once,' repeated the Mother Superior.

For a moment I was rigid with fear, but then, grabbing hold of my sister firmly by the coat sleeve, we ran as fast as we could, out of the wood-lined study, down the long corridor and we didn't stop until halfway home!

Mary's face was blood-red with running, poor wee cratur. I wet the edge of my cardy with my tongue and wiped it across her tear-streaked face. That's what my mother usually did.

'Blow your snottery nose, pet, it's filling your mouth, you'll be sick.' Mary pulled a flannel square from the fold of her own cardy sleeve and did as I asked.

'God,' I thought, 'I'm for it now. I'll get killed for doing this.'

Daddy hadn't yet left for ragging, when we ran into the bus, panting. Like two gurgling turkeys we unsuccessfully tried to explain why we were not at school!

'Jessie, what is it?' he asked, sitting me down. 'Take your time now, tell Daddy.'

I did the best I could to explain our absence from the convent school. 'The Jesus Box, Dad, they were putting us in the Jesus Box!'

'What's that?' he asked.

'A punishment, Daddy. A place where you meet a monster called Jesus!'

'Better not let your Mammy hear you say that. Now, while she's at the shop getting bread, we'll go back to the school and sort out this carry on.'

Holding each of us by the hand, he walked into the Mother Superior's room. Surprisingly she smiled and held out her hand, saying 'A misunderstanding, Mr Riley, let me explain.'

We were ushered out to stand in the cold corridor flanked by Sister Alice, while my father sat listening to the saintly-looking head-covered nun.

In no time he came out smiling and said, 'Jessie, wee Mary will not be punished, but I've heard you've been a little madam, so you will have to take yours.'

Kneeling beside me on one knee he smiled, then winked, saying, 'Now, lass, I don't know where you got the idea that Jesus was a monster in a box, but someone has told you fibs. Be a good girl and take your punishment.' Those words said, he walked off down the long passageway, leaving me to my fate.

Sister Alice walked Mary into the classroom while the Mother Superior marched me off. At the farthest end of the school we climbed a narrow, winding, metal stairway that clanked noisily with every step. Reaching the top she opened a heavy dark wood door of the smallest room I had ever seen, though I'd never been in a house apart from Granny Riley's. Perhaps this was normal. I peered in, only to see a wee three-legged stool and nothing else.

'This, my dear, is where we teach children that disobedience is wrong. Our Lord Jesus will decide if you are forgiven or not,' said the holy lady.

She motioned me to sit down. I did as I was told. Before closing the door she said, 'Always keep your head bowed. Do not look up, understand?' I nodded as the door creaked shut, leaving me alone, and I remember thinking, 'This isn't so bad, that tall lad must have been pulling my leg right enough'. Perhaps I'd misjudged these saintly ladies of the cloth. 'I'll say a few prayers. If I say them loud and she's standing listening behind the door, that'll surely please her.' So I closed my eyes, clasped my hands and prayed for everybody in the school. Parents, poor folk, sick ones, old ones, dogs, cats, on and on I went, finishing only when I'd totally exhausted everything worth praying for, or, come to think about it, everything I could think of whether worth it or not.

I opened my eyes, unclasped my little hands and sat quietly counting the cracks in the stone floor. Surely I'd soon hear the latch open and hear her call me out. But no! I could hear the big church clock ring out hour upon hour. All this time I sat with bowed head until my head became heavy and my neck sore. So, disobeying my superior, I stretched my neck up towards the ceiling. The sight froze my body. I grasped the wee stool beneath me for fear I'd fall onto the stone floor.

Suspended directly above my seat, the Crucified Lord hung from a wooden cross! From his thorn-crowned head to his nailed feet, painted blood trickled down his body like a river of red. So lifelike, so tortured. To go by my memory of it, whoever the artist and sculptor were, I can only imagine they must have been on Calvary and witnessed the Crucifixion themselves.

As if drawn by a magnet my gaze was forced further upwards. I stared deep into his crucified eyes. He stared down at me through the painted tears, and I swear it was as if he spoke to me, saying, 'Bad child, wicked child. Hell for you!'

I closed my eyes tight. In my head I called in silence for wee Greenwing to take me away, and he did in a magically vivid dream. We flew over the smog-filled city, up and away from the Jesus Box. On and on we flew, over Manchester, Cumbria, the Borders, on and on until the smoking chimney of my Granny's white cottage in the north of Pitlochry at the foot of Ben Vrackie came in sight. We sat on her rooftop until the pounding in my heart subsided. I had left the evil statue with the staring eyes far behind me.

Greenwing held my hand telling me it would soon be over, this fearful punishment, because he heard the bell ring for school's out. 'Open your eyes, Jess,' he said, 'the nun comes. I'm away now, be brave.'

'Don't leave me, wee friend,' I pleaded.

I tightened my eyelids even more. I knew the statue would get me if I saw it.

My imaginary friend was gone. I was now vulnerable. Instantly I was back sitting petrified on the three-legged stool in the cold convent. Granny's Heilan' Hame was far, far away, and I was at the mercy of the Jesus Box. Here was the Lord of the bloodied cross who frightened children. Mammy never knew this Jesus.

'Well, child, have you discovered the beauty of your Lord?' The Mother Superior's voice brought me back to the world as she pulled open the heavy door.

Keeping my eyes shut tight, I nodded my head vigorously.

'Good, then that will be the last time we see the bad side of you, my dear.'

Yes, the Jesus Box was a dreaded punishment, because from that day until my little sister and I left, we were, to say the least, angelic!

The tall lad came up to me as we were going home that unforgettable day, and pushed something into my hand. When the school faded into the smog I opened my fingers. There, all crumpled up, was my wee tartan ribbon. He had seen Sister Alice throw it in the bin and retrieved it for me.

On reflection I can say now that that place would have been better suited to a gang of criminals rather than innocent children. Make no wonder that the playground was an unnatural place, it was more like a graveyard with all those sad, silent, little bairns. Not a bit like how they should have been—skipping, playing, loud, happy, healthy children. I have never forgotten them. Even to this day I find my thoughts wandering back. Where are they now, all in holy service maybe, or perhaps not? Who knows? I still believe that was the wrong way to teach religion.

It took me a long time to find a different Jesus from the one a sculptor and an artist had fashioned to frighten little children in the convent in Manchester all those years ago. I would further like to say that as an adult I've discussed that place with many nuns, priests and convent-educated people, who assured me that my experience was the exception, not the norm.

Before I leave this tale, I would like to add that there was something else in the box-room with me all those years ago, a strong smell. One of urine.

In the meantime the smog became more of a hazard as cars and buses crept along the streets. Mammy worried night after night waiting on the older lassies coming home from the factory.

'That thick smog had the clippy walking in front of the bus with a torch, showing the driver the way,' exclaimed Mona, coming home one night from work two hours late.

'Good God!' said Daddy, 'fancy a bus with its powerful lights needing to be guided by a wee torch!'

'The street names, the driver couldn't make them out, the poor soul didn't know where he was going,' added Chrissie.

'He must have been new to the job, that's all I can say,' answered Dad.

As the month went on, Mammy's concern for her girls, plus the ragging, then standing for cold hour upon hour selling freshly washed and ironed clothes from the ragbags at the open market, took its toll.

Daddy stayed at home to watch after the wee ones that day. Our Janey was needing a change from babysitting, so she went with Mammy to the market. Two hours into the morning, Mammy asked Janey if she'd fetch some hot tea from the wee café. When she came back a terrible sight made her drop the tea, because Mammy was lying across the stall clutching her stomach.

'Help, somebody, please!' she cried out.

'God sake, Mam, what's up?' sobbed Janey, trying to hold her up.

'Take my lassie home,' was all she could say, before collapsing in a crumpled heap on the freezing concrete.

By the time an ambulance arrived, a dark pool of blood had formed round her feet, and within minutes she was lying in a Manchester hospital. Her body had had enough. She was at death's door. Our nightmare had begun!

Chrissie asked first. 'Is she going to be all right, Daddy, when is she getting home?'

By the pale frightened look etched across his face it was easy to tell things were far from right. He looked round at each of us and said, 'I don't know.'

'Influenza with standing all day at the market,' Mona gave her answer, the one she'd convinced herself of. 'They'll keep her a fortnight with that.'

'Bloody big smoggy town, she's not used to this way of doing, she needs Scottish air, does my mother.' Shirley was frightened. She feared ill health, worried for Mammy. 'No wonder she was always swallowing pills and powders!' said Janey, before covering her face with her hands, then adding through floods of tears, 'All that blood, my Mammy's precious blood. It was pouring from her.'

'Oh my God, she's only five feet in height,' cried Shirley, 'she needs all the blood she's got.'

This brought us all to tears. We were frightened, confused and turned to Daddy for the answer. 'Lassies,' he said, removing his bunnet and running a hand through his thick black hair. 'You know I'm not a man for prayer, but if there is a time for it, then this is the time.'

Those few words told us just how sick our mother was. Silently we gathered round our father's feet, bowed our heads and prayed. I prayed with hands clasped so tightly my wee knuckles went white. But not to Jesus. No, my pleas were to my wee Cumbrian monster Greenwing. He came immediately into my head and sat behind my eyes. I felt instant comfort from his velvety invisible wings. I needed my friend more than ever. I was very afraid.

The Jesus Box with its terror wasn't a patch on the fear that made its presence felt right inside my very heart. Somehow life without Mammy had never entered my head. At my tender age the possibility that she and I would be parted by death was unimaginable, and unthinkable!

Mammy needed major surgery. For a start her womb was removed. She lost a large part of her stomach. Her right lung was weak with infection. However, she was made of stern stuff, our mother, because against all the odds she slowly began to recover. Each time Daddy came home with the news, 'She's a wee bit better', it brought a warm glow to our hearts.

Christmas came and went, but there was no sign of it in our wee home. No toys or talk of turkey, Santa and his reindeer or fairy lights on pine trees. All we thought of was her getting well and heading home to Scotland, for us to be a whole family again.

I always imagined that because of the closeness of us living in such a tiny space, we became as one body. Let me put it simply for you: our parents were the head. Then, according to the age of my sisters, we were joined into limbs and so forth, one living body! If one took sick, then we all felt the symptoms, so think how we were feeling when the sick part in Manchester was the most important part of all, the one who gave us life!

On New Year's day we all piled into wee Fordy. We were going to see her. Up till then only Daddy was allowed in. How excited we were. I even took Greenwing, who'd now become a permanent member of the family. But only I saw him.

'Mr Riley, we've a bit of a setback, come with me please.' The nurse looked concerned.

'Girls, if you could stay in there, please, Dad won't be long.' She pointed to a half-shut door. Without a word, we followed each other into the room and sat close together.

Daddy came in several minutes later, as white as a sheet!

'Mammy's taken a turn for the worse, she's losing blood, the doctor told me she needs a lot more! Without it...' He stopped himself saying the inevitable in case we became hysterical. Instead he drew in a heavy sigh and said, 'Let's leave her sleep.'

But now came the frightening realisation, something he never knew before, that she had a very rare blood group. The only person the hospital had on their list who was a match was a captain in the Merchant Navy.

Would this man come and save her life? Thanks be, he did, all the way from Singapore!

I believe the hospital paid for his flight, plus several weeks' accommodation while he donated his precious blood, saving our mother's life. And all that for Jeannie, a simple little traveller woman from Scotland!

Daddy needed to shake this man's hand, to say thank you, but he wanted anonymity. So not one of us got to meet him, let alone thank him in person. Mammy later told us that sometimes, through hazy eyes, she saw a tall man standing at her bedside, and wondered who he was. Once her sight was clear enough to define a bearded face, but she wasn't sure. When she began to gather her strength, she asked the doctor if her saviour would visit. He said the good man had left the country, his task complete. So she never did get to thank the tall, bearded navy captain who gave so much.

If you are out there somewhere, sir, know this, that you have the thanks of a very grateful family. With your gift a woman lived to see eight sons-in-law, twenty-one grandchildren, and eight great-grandkids.

It was mid-February before Mammy was finally allowed home. She had lost half her body weight and her hair saw its first grey. Daddy wouldn't let her lift a finger. Mona and Chrissie were more than pleased to give up the factory work and help at home.

To see her sitting cracking away with the gypsy women was a treat. Just looking at her was a gift for my eyes. She had spent too long away from us. I stroked her hair and simply touched her apron, as if assuring myself she wasn't a dream.

After she came home my friend Greenwing came less and less to visit me. One night, while everybody slept, he told me there was a sad little girl who needed him more than I did. He said she was a shepherd's child who'd lost her rag doll, and he had to find it for her. I was sad to let him go, but it didn't matter all that much. After all, did I not have my precious Mammy back? So we parted, my imagined friend and I.

The middle of March saw little openings in the clouds, revealing a blue sky with the odd bird or two. Daddy was becoming restless; if he'd been under the bonnet of the bus checking the engine once then he'd done it a dozen times. A wee touch oil here, a wee bit water there; yes, soon it would be time to go. But who would drive the Fordy?

'I'll drive my wee van,' said Mammy.

'Never, you're not well enough,' said Daddy.

'If we take our time, say twenty miles a day, maybe a day's rest here and there, we'll get home before the summer.'

Mary and I were more than glad to leave school; the older lassies said their farewells to friends made. The gypsies gave us a wee going-away party with promises to come and visit us at the Berries, but as is the case so many times, we never saw them again. The concerns Mammy had for her lassies being courted away by the handsome lads came to nothing, they were all spoken for. It seems they seldom marry outwith their own kind.

Next day we parted with the rosy city of Manchester, the place that saved our Mother's life. She later told folks that, had it not been for the list of blood donors kept by that particular hospital, she might not have survived.

The journey home was, as Mammy said, 'slow but easy'. We arrived in Crieff, Perthshire, for the start of June, with another bit mishap to report to our friends.

4

I CAN FLY!

Before leaving Manchester, Mammy had written to Granny Power and Granny Riley, letting them know all about her illness and her saviour, adding that we were coming back to Scotland, so to look out for us in Crieff, Perthshire, round about apple-blossom time. The two Grannies had no idea she'd been so ill. The news was spread, and when we arrived in Crieff they were eagerly awaiting to pamper her. Not only them, but most of our relatives as well. Enough to fill the green!

It was great seeing my cousins. We played in the woods, swam in the river Earn and built a wee hidey-hole in the yellow broom with sticks and branches. This is where I told them all about the English gypsies, Sister Alice and the Jesus Box, and, most important of all, my Mammy's illness and how she nearly died. I was the 'most important person', for I had heaps of things to tell.

Soon though, apart from Anna, the rest of my relatives went on the road, but because Mammy was still weak we stayed in Crieff awhiles longer. The site we were on had been, during the War years, a prisoner-of-war camp. Crieff had hundreds of war prisoners, and Cultybraggan outside Comrie had at one time over six thousand of them.

The concrete bases of the huts made a fine solid stance for the bus and caravans. This meant no guttery feet in and out the bus, mucking up the Axminster runner. It also meant the wash-basin didn't get knocked over on uneven ground. Mammy would often say, 'Would it not be braw if all the sites were like this one. Oh, and a great luxury into the bargain, toilets!' (I'll bring this wee house to your attention quite soon.) Today the caravan site no longer exists. In its place is a chicken hatchery.

Years before, Mammy, when in Crieff, would visit with certain women. She told their fortunes, you see. One of them saw my sister Chrissie up town and recognised her; she asked if Mammy might return to see her. My sister told the woman that she'd had been ill and she didn't think she could come. On hearing that, the woman decided to visit her instead. She took some friends with her.

So there, in the shade of a large elm tree, my dear mother told their fortunes. To this day I can picture her tenderly holding one of their hands and reading from the palm that which was pleasing to the ear. To watch the look of worry turn to a smile of quiet relief was indeed worth the seeing.

'Do you really see into the future in the folks' hands?' I once asked of her.

'Now, pet, what I think you're asking is, do I see bad news for them.'

I nodded, awaiting enlightenment. Knowing my mother as I do, her answer did not surprise me. 'When you've enough worries to fill the days, a wee bit good news goes a long way, lassie. These people know fine what worries have went by them. Thinking the future will be better does no harm, none at all, now does it?'

'Jeannie, dear, you're far too nice for this world.' I'd heard Granny say that to her many times. And never a truer word was spoken. She had a heart of gold did my Mam.

§

If there's one thing Crieff had plenty of in those days, it was 'characters'. Let me tell you about two of them. Jenny Ford and her giant of a brother, Wull. 'Midden-rakers' of the finest first class!

In my young life you'll see, if you read on, how I gained the ability to determine the value in scrap metal. It is not to dealers or travellers that I owe this skill, but to my very own 'coupies', Jenny and Wull. No fancy lorry or horse and cart contributed to the wealth this duo amassed. Wull wielded a bogey, while his sister wouldn'tsee past her big green pram.

As soon as the bin cart finished tipping, the pair of them were at its back. Pulling and tearing, routing out among the week's rubbish, keeping this, keeping that. Laying aside old bits of wood, iron, wheels; endless useless-looking bits were thrust into the bogey and pram, then wheeled away to be added to piles already filling their yard. This fine yard was situated along the aptly named Ford Road.

I remember Jenny once let me see round the place. A privilege, believe me, because this honour wasn't bestowed on just anybody. To the left of their yard was the river Earn, to the right the grave-yard. Jenny would point down to the burial ground and say, 'Do you see those craturs lying beneath the ground? Well, lassie, they are all dead. Useless! Not like the stuff folks throw away as rubbish. That, to them is dead. But we take it, Wull and me, and bring it back to life! Our yard's full of life, lassie.' I hadn't a clue what she meant, but it made a lot of sense to her.

Folks were used to their coming and goings and never batted an eyelid, in fact many looked upon the pair as quite handy! If someone needed a piece of wood to finish building a shed, or a spare wheel for a pram, ten to a penny a visit round the backyard of the pair would prove useful (for a small fee, of course). Had they been active in this present day, my pair would have taken on the title of 'recyclers'.

Jenny and Wull stay firmly in my mind as two of the old Crieffites, who as I write have passed over to the other side. Well, to the lower right-hand side of the old scrapyard along Ford Road, to be precise. The peaceful graveyard.

Mammy never felt comfortable wasting a bonny frock on Sundays, she much preferred putting me out in dungarees. For there was nothing surer than that I would find my way down to rake among the midden rubbish with my two pals.

Now, believe this if you like, but I heard it said more than once, that Wull and Jenny were worth a fortune! Sad to say, though, my midden-raking only ever netted me a few pounds from whatever scrappy was the most generous. Nevertheless, it was immense fun!

§

Every Saturday afternoon found us queuing up alongside the local children at the door of the Ritz Cinema. This was just the best entertainment a wee bairn could ask for. To sit in front of the big screen and be part of the fantastic film acted out before our very eyes was, as the female half of the Krankies sings, fan-dabby-dozy!

Cowboys riding with the wind on palomino horses, either chasing after or fleeing from painted Red Indians. Tarzan swinging through the trees, adventure upon exciting adventure. I used to float from that matinee cinema all the way home, in a daze.

This brings me to my very first injury! Remember I mentioned toilets? Well, listen to what this silly wee youngster went and did.

'Mammy, Daddy, there was a big man in the pictures yesterday who flew!' I was referring to none other than the great Batman.

'Away, you don't say!' said Daddy, tossing another lump of butter followed by lashings of black pepper into the tatties, then plunging the masher through the fluffy contents of the big pot.

'Aye, Dad, he was dressed in black, every bit of him, only his eyes were showing. And he had a great spread of bat's wings on himself!' I was almost breathless with excitement.

'Did the gadgy hang upside down, Jessie, my wee lamb, like the bat?' smiled my mother, counting the plates for supper.

'No, Mammy, but you should have seen the way he ran up buildings and jumped off the roofs!'

'God bless us and save us the day, imagine that, eh,' laughed my father, stifling a peppery sneeze.

'Aye, Daddy, he spread out his shiny black wings and flew. Oh my, it was rare to watch.'

'Here lass, sit down and eat your food,' said Mammy, adding, 'It was only make-believe—people can't fly. Tell her, Charlie.'

'Jess, your mother's right. It's called tricks of the camera, he didn't really fly.'

I felt angry; my parents seemed to be mocking me. 'Yes he did, for I seen him with my own two eyes, nobody could make that up, the big bat gadgy flew!'

Mammy would hear no more about my fantasy and told me so, adding, 'Go and play, the floor needs a wash and I don't want you running in and out, so away with you!'

I went off towards the broom, where my cousin Anna and other travelling bairns were playing, but I couldn't get the thought out of my head. Did he fly or not?

I asked my clever cousin who always seemed to know more about the world than I did. 'Anna, that Batman we saw in the cinema, he was really flying, wasn't he?'

'Of course he was,' she said, then added, 'He fairly knew his stuff. See how he tied all the baddies up with his bat rope!'

'I never knew people flew, did you?' I asked her, 'The folks said it was tricks; camera ones.'

'Well, maybe someone sewed the bat wings onto his back,' she said, not wanting to go against adult knowledge.

'Or maybe he really did have wings like a bird,' I answered.

'Jessie, what if everybody could fly?' Thoughts of flying above the ground made Anna laugh. She continued, 'Instead of shooting the grouse you could stick yer hand out and grab it.'

I added my fantasies: 'Think on hazelnut time, all we'd need do is to flutter round about a tree and empty the whole thing.'

'Oh, there's no end to what a handy pair of wings could do for a body!' Anna's comment brought hilarious laughter from us both.

From then on we sat on a little patch of grass discussing the benefits of flying.

Suddenly a thought came into my head. I jumped up and declared, 'I'm going to try it.'

'Try what?' enquired Anna, rising to her feet.

'Flying, of course, dafty. What did you think I meant?'

'Don't talk rot, how the hell are you going to do it?'

I then disclosed my ingenious plan. 'See the lavvie roof, well it's just high enough to give me a start in the air,' I said, pointing over at the sloping toilet roof.

'I'm away to tell Mammy on you, Jessie,' shouted Mary, who'd joined us on our flattened grass patch. 'That's really high up you know.'

I threatened instant death if she told on me, and just managed to grab her saying, 'Come back here, Mary, if you dare tell I'll drown you in the Earn inch by inch. Look, come on and let's see if I can fly. I've got a belly-feeling if Batman can do it so can I. Now are you with me?'

By now other curious bairns had joined us. They looked at each other as if to say, 'Well, if this daft lassie is willing to give us all a show, why stop her?'

So off we went to see me attempt the death-defying jump of the century!

Gathering as many big stones as we could find, we then piled a heap big enough to reach the lowest part of the lavvie roof. Thankfully I managed to jump up with a push from a big laddie who'd joined our group and was soon staring down on my followers from the highest point.

I remember thinking, 'Gosh almighty, they don't half seem far away!' But if ever a day was meant for flying it was this one!

The sky was a clear blue; the sun filled every space. I was above the caravan site, above the river and the yellow broom. I was 'on top of the world, Ma', as Jimmy Cagney said.

Well, the lavvie roof, to be precise. But this was my first flight; next time I would go further.

With one last look down, I stepped out into mid-air, arms stretched, head up!

Now, isn't it annoying how even a maestro can be distracted. Below me, thinking himself in a private cubicle, a big fat lad, before relieving himself of the contents of his stappit-full bowel, let rip the biggest and loudest fart I'd ever heard. I felt my body teeter backwards, then forwards, then over I went. Down towards the stones we had so neatly piled minutes earlier.

Drifting in and out of consciousness, I heard bairns screaming. Someone carried me by one leg, somebody else by the other. Daddy was shouting, 'What happened?' Mammy was cuddling me, crying, 'My wee lassie, my wee lassie.' She tried reassuring me, but all I could feel was the searing pain shooting up my right leg.

'I can't do anything with that leg, you need a surgeon. Take the bairn to Bridge of Earn hospital, they have all the means there,' said the doctor that my father eventually found.

It was Sunday, and the local doctors were either away or having dinner with family and friends.

Daddy pleaded with the man, 'Please look at the state of my bairn, can you give her something?' The man closed his door behind him, saying, 'I can't do that in case an operation's needed, now hurry up, get her seen!'

As I lay stretched out on the hard floor of wee Fordy, I wished to a thousand gods I'd never gone to the picture house and seen yon big stupid Batman!

I still remember the awful pain as Daddy drove with the utmost haste to Bridge of Earn hospital, twenty-three miles away. Every bump in the road sent me into excruciating agony. The right leg (as a result of my attempt at flying) was broken in five places.

When the surgeon eventually finished working on my leg, Daddy put it to him, 'Are you telling me I've to go home and tell her mother her wee leg's in bits?'

'Yes, Mr Riley, that I am. She'll be here for the next six weeks at least.' He wasn't kidding neither! So for the next six weeks I became a permanent fixture in the orthopaedic children's ward of the Hospital over the Bridge, under which flows the Earn. The very same river I saw before falling from my flying future.

Daddy had some work to see to in the Black Isle, so they were forced to move on without me. Mammy tried to see me as often as she could, but it's a right far distance from where they were camped to the hospital. So nothing else for it than to ask relatives if they would keep an eye on me. As if I was going anywhere!

I wasn't short of visitors. Aunts, uncles and cousins came from all of Perthshire. I must mention one person, though, who came faithfully each week, D. O. Mclean, the headmaster of Crieff's Junior Secondary School. A lad from Crieff was there, like me nursing a broken leg, and D.O. came to visit him. The ward matron told him about my accident happening in his home town. So he popped into the girl's ward to see me also.

When the lad went home D.O. continued visiting me. Now, was that not a nice man! I have never forgotten his act of kindness, seldom shown to Traveller children outwith their own kind!

By the time Mammy came for me my leg was well and truly stiffened. Still in its stooky (plaster) I had to be carried into the ambulance. From Perth railway station we took the train to Inverness. We then went on the very choppy Kessock ferry. Then finally a taxi to the campsite on the Black Isle. The journey was repeated to have the plaster off! Thankfully a relative gave Daddy a loan of his big Humber Hawk, with lots of room in the back seat to stretch my injured leg.

I remember hopping onto the beach at Munlochy Bay and attempting to stand on my yellowed, hairy, skinny leg. It was more than very sore I can tell you!

Soon, though, my wee right leg was the same as the left one and I was running, climbing, swimming, midden-raking, doing everything youngsters enjoy, with one very definite exception—flying! Well, come on, how stupid did you think I was?

5

JOEY'S BRAINWORK

Because we had spent a few extra weeks on the Black Isle the 'Berries' were in full swing when we got back. The tale I'm about to share with you may bring to mind a similar experience of your own, because we all went through it, in our own way. This was my introduction to (red face coming on) anatomy! The male anatomy, that is.

Two things old Nell Macdonald could not abide: one was folks abusing the Sabbath, and the other was a woman drinking alcohol. She never hesitated to let you know if you were an offender. The 'you' on this bonny Sunday morning at Blairgowrie was my father's sister Maggie, an offender on both accounts!

The old woman glowered at Auntie Maggie hanging out her washing and said in her sternest voice, 'You'll bring the wrath of God on your head for that, my lass, washing clothes on the holy day.'

Maggie ignored the old woman and continued with her chore.

'I said,' Nell continued, leaning on her stick with one hand, moving the clay pipe between the last two teeth in her head with the other hand, 'no good at all, mark my words.'

Maggie was in her early thirties and had to give the old woman the respect her eighty years demanded, but could not resist saying something in her own defence. 'I've been that busy all week I just never had a minute to call my own.'

As quick as a flash Nell took the breath from my auntie by her replying: 'If you hadn't spent the whole of yesterday standing in the Well Meadow pub drinkin' beside the men, you'd have had time to do all the washing in the entire green!'

Maggie drew in her breath, bit her top lip and continued hanging out her washing. There was no way she would be drawn into an argument with old 'viper-tongue' Macdonald.

My mother, who was listening to the old woman's ranting, couldn't help but say something in Maggie's defence. 'Now, Nell, the lassie only went into the pub to get her man. She needed help with the messages. It's a steep hill and fine you know. Did she not have the two biggest boxes of the stuff to hump?'

The old woman went back to her tent to plait the hair of one of her many grand-daughters, muttering in a tongue known only to herself.

My cousin Joey, the eldest of Maggie's two sons, who was standing over by the old stone dyke that ran all the way from the farm steadings to the Alyth road, called across to me. 'Bell, are you coming down for a rout among the strawberries?' Joey called me Bell because he knew it annoyed me. And his favourite pastime was annoying me!

'Don't you dare call me that,' I warned him. 'Fine you know I was christened Jessie, not Jezebel, but if you want to give me my Sunday best then call me Jessica!'

'Oh, stop your moaning face, sure I'm only pulling your leg. Now are you going down the field, or not?'

'I'm not,' was my answer. 'I'm playing at brainwork.'

It was far too warm to go raking for strawberries, playing rounders, or climbing trees. The only enjoyable leisure pursuit on that hot day was swimming, and as none of the men were willing to pile us all into a van and take us to the Gothans, then brainwork it was.

Before I go on, let me explain that the Gothans was a place three miles outside Blairgowrie on the Perth road which was the campsite favoured by the traveller folks before the last war. The Lunan burn flowed past the site on its way to join the River Isla, and featured a perfect deep pool for dooking. As a matter of fact, ask most of the travellers in Perthshire where they learned to swim, and they'll tell you the Gothans.

'This brainwork,' asked Joey, 'can I do it?'

'Do you mean to tell me there isn't any wee beasties for you to torture?' I enquired.

Joey was the cruellest laddie in the whole of God's kingdom. Just that very morning I stopped him chopping a worm into a dozen bits by pulling his jersey over his head so he couldn't see where he was cutting. Joey was in his glory catching grasshoppers just so he could pull the legs off them. In the spring of the previous year, did he not leap the rocks across the Dochart Falls holding a bonny wee kitten by the back legs, with me in full pursuit screaming at him to give it to me? And not until I near pulled the two lugs off him did he let it go.

'No,' he answered, 'I was bit right hard on my finger by a wee mouse that refused to come out of the dyke over by Nickum's farm last night.'

'What, may I ask, were you doing there? It's near half a mile along the main road.'

'Well, auld Macdonald was hiding from Nell on account of him being blind drunk after beating all the men in the green at pontoon.'

'And how was he in that state winning a game of cards?' I asked.

'Now, Jess, do you think the old man could go home with all that money in his pocket without Nell wondering where it came from?'

'Of course, I forgot, she is just as much against gambling as she is Sabbath abuse,' I answered.

Joey continued: 'The auld man said he'd give me half a crown if I would bide and be looky-out for him, that being until he sobered up.'

'And how long did you bide?' I asked.

'Until the wee crabbit mouse bit me,' was his obvious reply.

'She didn't half plough into your Ma earlier for washing on the holy day,' I told Joey. 'Did you not hear her?'

'Aye, that I did, fair put Mother into a right mood, so I'd best keep on her good side until she comes round.' Joey would hang from a cliff face before aggravating his Mam. 'But never mind her, look at my finger,' he said, quickly changing the subject. 'That wee mouse gave it a right sore bite, here, look at that.' Joey shoved a red swollen pinkie into my face, and I felt a sense of victory for all mice as I examined the swelt finger.

'Did the old man sober up?' I asked him, ignoring the injured digit.

'No, I left him to sleep it off. He didn't give me the promised half crown though. Instead he gave me sixpence this morning for not letting old Nell know where he was. But I'm not doing it again, he's untrustworthy.'

'He's an angry old drunk,' I reminded him. 'No wonder his poor old wife is always crabbit!'

'Anyhow, what's this brainwork you're on about?' enquired my impish cousin.

'Well, have you ever wondered how aeroplanes can fly? In addition, why is it that ships don't sink?' I quizzed him with my seven-year-old intellect.

'Nope, I never give it a thought,' said Joey, with his hands on hips and head tossed back.

'Liar,' I said, 'Everybody wonders about those things.'

With those words said, my cousin, myself, and several other bairns who had joined us, spent most of the afternoon discussing the hows, whys and whats of life.

As we sat on the long grass which had escaped the ravages of tents, caravans and campfires, it didn't take long for the lads to revert to their usual antics: teasing the lassies. Soon our large gathering became smaller, as one by one the girls huffed off to do other things, leaving me alone with three lads and Cousin Joey.

'Bell,' he asked, again to my annoyance, 'I bet you can't guess what I've got down my trousers?'

I didn't answer him, because he knew calling me by that name fair peeved me, and secondly, knowing his cruelty towards wee beasties, I was certain he was about to sicken me with producing a wriggly or its like.

Joey turned his back on me and proudly showed the lads what he was concealing within his khaki shorts. It must have been something right comical because they all went into hysterics laughing.

What happened next was to be my introduction to anatomy! Quicker than the flick of a lamb's tail, Joey turned toward me and pulled what looked like a very short, pale-coloured slow-worm from the front of his trousers. Holding the helpless creature by the neck with one hand he squeezed it with the other. A spray of water came spurting from its mouth all over my Auntie Maggie's clean white sheet.

Red anger welled inside me, I had seen too much cruelty to

lesser living things. It was time to take a stand. Joey had gone too far this time. 'Give me that, you cruel bissum!' I screamed, as I lunged at Joey's trousers'-front, determined to save this helpless soul from certain death.

Imagine my utter horror as I grabbed its head and pulled, only to find it had attached itself to Joey's body. I screamed again and this time pulled even harder, but by now Joey was turning a very deep red and begging me to let go.

'Help, help me!', he squealed, hanging on to the other end of the slow-worm. It went limp and I thought we'd killed it.

'Give me it right now,' I ordered, 'or else I'll tell Auntie Maggie on you.'

Now, reader, I imagine you've got the picture, and I can hear you saying; 'No way!' But I swear that was the truth. I was one of eight girls, had never seen a lad before, so how was I to know? Come to think of it, I'd not seen many a slow-worm neither.

Auntie Maggie, Mammy and old Nell came rushing over to see what all the commotion was. 'Now,' said the old woman, 'did I not tell ye that no good would come of washing on the Sabbath day, look at the mess of your sheet with these weans playing dirty tricks.'

Auntie Maggie walloped both of us with a hazel switch as we took off in opposite directions, Joey with a swollen you-know-what, and me utterly stumped as to what I'd done wrong. 'Och, this is a strange world,' I thought. What in Rabbie's name had I done?

I had no intentions of putting my brain through that kind of work again, so a wee chat with my Mammy before I slept that night fair put my cousin Joey into an entirely different light, I can tell you!

6

MURDER IN CLOVER

There we were, then, trundling up the road towards Pitlochry, singing the roof off the old bus and the tar off the A9.

'Kindallachan.' shouts Daddy, 'We'll camp here for a week or two.' He manoeuvred the bus into a fine bit at the wood-end between several trees. Mammy wasn't long in getting a fine washing line tied up while he got the fire on the go, and before long the kettle-lid was dancing away happily.

Within a day or two several other traveller families arrived and soon we had a fine gathering of hantel (people). Daddy's sister Anna, her man Robert and their lassie Berta also arrived. Aberdeen was where they hailed from and they lived in a grand house on the banks of the river Don. At night, round the campfire, there was fine crack, merriment and singing, everybody knew each other and all got on well.

The menfolk tied a thick, long rope over a sturdy branch of an old oak tree for us bairns to swing on. Further into the wood we built ourselves a braw wee tree house where we promised to stay friends forever, exchanging trinkety keepsakes, the odd earring or ring sealing our friendships till time's end. Chances were when we parted it was unlikely we would meet again for a few years, and by that time would have forgotten who pledged what to who. Never matter, this was now, and now was all that counted to us bairns.

We were stopped on that campsite for a week or two, and as we played, we noticed after supper each evening a couple would come walking up the windy farm road. Nothing unusual about that, you might say, but this man and woman would clamber over the dyke and disappear into a field of clover. Strange way of doing for adults, wouldn't you think?

Any road, us bairns decided to have a meeting, because it became a question on everyone's lips—just what were they doing?

Wee Tommy 'One-Eye' Docherty (this didn't mean Tommy was missing an eye, it only meant he blinked constantly with his right eye when the nerves were on him) thought the couple had stashed a treasure in the field, and they were checking up on it in the gloaming. Our Mary thought they might be having a wee sleep.

'Do you know,' said 'Sooky Kate' (so called because she always sucked the edge of her cardigan) 'maybe they're catching mice to feed their cats. Country folks have piles of cats—my heilan granny telt me that and she never ever lied.'

'Na, na, cats catch their own mice,' said cousin Berta, in her thick Aberdonian accent, 'they're richt fussy craturs and they'll no just eat ony kind o' mice, you know.' Cousin Berta thought she knew everything, but she didn't really. If she did then why did she call sherbet bon-bons, jap-deserts? 'They folks are spies,' she informed us, 'Hitler's ones.'

'He's dead,' I told the group, 'don't listen to her.'

'He is nut,' she screamed at me.

Calmly I enlightened my cousin that the German heid yin was found feet up in a bucket!

'Bunker,' said wee Tommy, 'he was found dead in a bunker.'

'Well, is that no the German word for a bucket?' asked Sooky.

Both Tommy and I agreed we didn't know and left it at that.

Any road it was a mystery to us what this couple did, and we just had to solve it. After much consultation we decided to follow them and hide in some trees just over from the dyke. We'd crouch down behind the oakies and watch. Right reason or not, the mystery would be solved that very night.

Now, just as they had done each night, the couple appeared on time and they seemed oblivious to our folks cracking round the fire as they walked past arm in arm, gazing into each other's eyes. As usual, approaching the end of the road, they went over the dyke, into the clover, and down they went.

'Right, now are you lot with me?' I asked. My comrades nodded in unison. 'Then let's go.'

One by one, like sojers of the SAS, we stealthily slid our bodies over the dyke, one on top of the other in the thick green clover.

'Mind out, would you,' said wee Tommy, as Sooky's right foot landed him one in the face.

'Sorry, Tommy,' she apologised, then stuck her cardigan back in her mouth.

'Quiet, you two, or you'll give the game away,' said Cousin Berta.

Our Babs was sneezing with the pollen off the cloverheads, and I knew if she came any further into the field, the couple would hear us, so I ordered her to stay put!

'Jessie, would you take me back into the wood for me needing the lavvie?' said my wee sister, looking awfy desperate.

'You'll just have to be needing a whiley longer, because we're on a secret mission. Now sit down there and don't move until we get back.'

I went first, creeping on all fours, until I could hear moaning sounds. I turned, and said in a whisper to Cousin Berta whose nose was glued to my right buttock, 'Can you hear that?'

'Aye, what do you think is going on?' she whispered back. Then came another moan, louder this time, then a scream.

'God almighty! The wimmin's gitten murdert,' roared wee Tommy, with his right eye blinking out of control.

At this we all got to our feet to see the man lying on top of the poor woman, and her thrusting her legs up into the air, trying with all her might to breathe.

We turned and ran like mad through the field, over the dyke, grabbing wee Babs on route. Down the road we raced, to summon the help of the big folks. 'Mammy, Daddy, hurry, for the love of Moses, there's a poor cratur getting murdered over yonder in the clover,' I squealed at the top of my voice, and so did the rest of us. We were making such a din nobody could make out what we were saying.

'Wheesht, bairns,' said Katy's mother Helen, 'now, one at a time.'

Berta, as usual, managed to get her words out first. 'Do you know yon quine and loonie who stroll arm in arm up the old road every night, them that passed no more than several minities ago?' Helen folded her arms and nodded. 'Well, he's got the cratur flattened, every mouthful o' air is gettin squashed out o' her!'

Now, the strangest thing, all the women laughed. I thought they were thinking we were pulling at their legs.

'You better get up there before she turns into a corpse!' I blurted out, practically foaming at the mouth.

My mother came over, folded her arms and smiled. Then said, in response to this heinous crime, 'Now, weans, I'm sure there's nobody getting hurt. I think thon two are having a wee bit o' a private cuddle.'

'Na, na, Mammy, I know what I saw—thon woman was being strangled.'

By this time the men were getting to hear snippets, and I couldn't understand why they were all sniggering. So I pushed my comrades aside, jumped on a wooden stool and proclaimed to the whole gathering, 'You'll be sorry when the polis find her body, then you'll wish you'd listened tae us.' I was adamant a murder had taken place, so with certainty I added in my loudest voice, 'Well, he'll not get far, because I'll tell the polis his name.'

My father, who'd been reading a newspaper up till then, tried to keep a straight face as he said, 'His name Jess, and what was his name, pet?'

Positioning my two fists firmly on my hips I drew in the biggest breath and said, 'His name was Dinnie.'

'You mean Danny?' chipped in old Docherty, who'd been grooming one of his four lurcher dogs nearby.

'Or perhaps Donnie?' came a voice from a caravan over by the dyke.

'No, it was Dinnie,' I called out, totally exasperated. 'I clearly heard the woman saying, "Dinnie stop! Dinnie stop!"'

Well, the whole campsite went into a fit of laughter. Us bairns thought our folks were mad and should be locked up. Mammy, on the other hand, really was mad because our Babs had filled her knickers, and the contents by this time had caked hard onto her wee backside. Two guesses who got the job of taking her and the carbolic over to the burn to wash it off.

For the duration of our stay at Kindallachan we played on our rope swing and told ghostie stories in the wee tree house, but as for fields of clover, they were strictly out of bounds. Well, were they not filled with murdered women?

The couple—we never saw them again, so you never know.

The Dochertys took themselves off to somewhere in Fife. Auntie Anna, cousin Berta and Uncle Robert never said where they had planned to go, so there was a good chance we might run into them again.

The other good folks who we met later that summer at the Berries seemed to speak of nothing other than our murderous couple —strange, do you not think?

'Did the hornies [police] find Dinnie, Jess?' was the first thing they asked me!

Soon it was time for Daddy to sit behind the wheel of the bus and Mammy behind the wheel of the Fordy. 'Where to now?' 'Horse on, Macduff, we'll camp at dawn.' That was the type of conversation my parents had whenever we were ready to go. I can see them now as I sit here writing this down; my, they didn't half make us lassies laugh. They were a pair right enough.

That day, though, we went up to Pitlochry to visit with our two Grannies. Mammy's mother Granny Power who stayed at the Bobbin mill, on the other side of the railway station, and Daddy's mother Granny Riley who lived outside Moulin in a bonnie wee croft called 'Leattoch Beg'.

A pot of raspberry jam and two loaves later, we headed on up the A9 toward Inverness, but a stop-off at Blair Atholl found me in my Mammy's bad books. Listen now while I tell you what I did.

7

THE HUNTRESS

We stopped there at quiet Blair Atholl by the burnside, and this, folks, is a wee tale from the week I spent among the surrounding fields and hillsides.

Auntie Anna, Uncle Robert and ken-it-all Berta pulled on at our backs. Within an hour my cousin and me fell out about a rope-swing the local weans left on a nearby tree. I told her she was too heavy and would break it. 'Na, na, it'll take the weight of a dozen men,' she called, as she duly ran at the poor thing. I can still hear the crack of the branch splitting in two. Aye, she broke it! I had planned to play on that rope all day, hence the moody with our Berta, so instead I went into the village with Mammy and my wee sister Mary.

The plumpy lady who ran the village post office was more than pleased to crack with our mother that morning, on account of them knowing each other, while Mary and me had a blether with some scaldy laddies.

'What you doing?' I asked, watching them carrying a bucket and a ball of string up towards a clump of trees behind an old derelict house.

'We're catching birds,' answered one lad.

'What for?' Mary asked.

'Cat's fur, stupid,' answered a wee fat one (who looked more like a red and brown turnip than a boy), obviously offended by our unwelcome intrusion. Do you notice that short men, even at a young age, always have more to say for themselves than the rest?

'We're going to trap birds under this bucket, but we have no intentions of harming any,' said the tallest laddie. (See, I told you, only the wee chaps are lippy!)

'Come on with us,' he continued, 'you can watch how it's done.'

'Don't let them come, giggling women give the game away!' said the neep-on-legs.

'No we won't, we can be quieter than laddies,' I promised.

The neep stared into my face and then gave the real reason for excluding us. 'Well, if you lot come, then the smell of you tinky stinkies will send the birds shrieking to the moon!'

I looked at my sister, knowing full well what her response to this uncouth laddie was about to be.

'Say your prayers, you flea-ridden dung heap!' she roared as she lunged, sinking talons into the wee fat lad's two lugs. Rolling in among the grass and gravel she clung onto the lugs as if it were them that had offended us and not their owner.

'Mary, get up out of there, that's a disgusting way to behave. A' these lads can see the big tear in your knickers,' I said, worried that Mammy was about to come out of the shop and find her daughter wrestling in the dirt and gravel with a local laddie. Too late, she did, and was she not fury on fire!

'Get that stopped this instant, you're shaming me to death,' she shouted.

Mary drew back, but managed a fine kick into the right shin of her opponent, who I'm more than certain wished he'd kept his mouth shut that quiet afternoon. Mary was not a big bairn, but by God, she was a fiery one, and it wasn't the first time she flew at someone for calling her a tinker!

Mammy dragged the both of us along the river bank by the scruff and muttered away to herself at the same time, 'Lord, I can't turn my head for a shaking of a lamb's tail and look what you two are up to. The village is out of bounds to you both, now are you hearing me?'

I nodded, but Mary did a fool thing by saying, 'If you hadn't appeared when you did, Mam, that wee cack-pot was a dead duck.'

'She's for it now,' I thought. One thing we did NOT do, was answer Mammy back. Realising too late what she just said, Mary, in an attempt to make amends, blurted out, 'Sorry, Mam, I didn't mean that!'

Mammy was roused to the point of no return. Staring Mary in the eye, she told her, 'You're grounded!'

With Cousin Berta and me not speaking and our Mary kept in, I had nobody to play with. Our wee Renie was swingeing about a sore bellyache, so she was no use. And there was no way I would take Babsy to play, after her fouling her breeks back at Kindallachan, I didn't want a repeat of that.

I told Daddy about the bird-trapping the Blair Atholl lads were planning on doing, and which they were going to show us until our Mary put a stop to that.

'Och, we used to trap birds when I was a laddie,' he told me. 'Come, I'll show you how it's done.' He took a piece of twig, a bitty string and a saucer, then proceeded to skill me in the art of a 'Bird-Trapper' of the highest degree.

'Courie yourself flat on the ground,' he said. 'The first rule is don't be seen. No bird will fly within a mile if it can deek [see] you, so rule number one is hide. Number two, make sure the string is long enough so when it is tied round the twig it can be concealed in the grass from there to your hand. Three, when you have your bird under the saucer,' (this was only a guide, he reminded me, I'd need something a lot bigger than a saucer) 'yank at breakneck speed and walla, a pet bird!'

Auntie Anna who was listening to us said, 'You don't want to be lying in among the undergrowth for fear of the wee throat-ripper, lassie!'

'What was that, Auntie?' I asked, pulling my collar up under my chin!

She leaned over and whispered in my ear, 'He's a Dracula beastie, drinks rabbit blood, in fact any kind a blood at all, he's no' fussy. Folks say through the years over a hundred weans were sucked dry by the fiend, aye, right here in this very place. King o' the weasels he's known as, the Blair Atholl vampire!'

'Auntie, for God's sake, you don't say!' I burst out laughing, and so did my Daddy.

'There's a wee fat lad with two swelt lugs in the village, I doubt the bloodsucker must have missed him,' I told her, 'because you should have seen the blood Queen Mary (Mrs Dracula) removed from him!'

'Aye, you may well laugh, but there's many a tale about the cold-blooded beastie. Just make sure you and him dinna come face to face one of these days, bairn. Mark my words, it will stay the whole of your life with you!'

That evening I spent ages lying on my back watching the first of the swallows winging by on the first stage of their long journey to the other side of the world. I remember thinking, 'How in the name do these tottie wee craturs stay up in the sky? Surely the angels help them.' Whenever I didn't understand things, I always found the answers my young brain sought in the work of the angels, then changed the subject of my thoughts.

I walked up the sandy bank of the burnside, tiptoeing as rabbit upon rabbit scooted in and out their burrows, and I thought on the dreaded weasel, father's snares and, not least, the Gamey. What I didn't know then was that the dreaded mixi disease was lingering in the shadows to almost scour the poor beasties from the face of the earth.

They certainly had little going for them, the poor souls. But that was in their future and mine. That evening was so beautiful, so peaceful. The 'too-too-the-noo' of the wood pigeon and the water wriggling on its never-ending journey down the burn were the only sounds to be heard. Then another sound filled my ears: 'Jessie, Jessie, cocoa!'

'That will do for me,' I thought, 'I hope Mammy's made scones, I'm dying o' hunger.'

Next morning the sun hadn't made up his mind if he wanted to shine or not, but it was fairly warm.

'There's thunder in the air the day,' said Uncle Robert. Like his brother Wullie, he was never wrong with his weather predictions.

'Will it be worth my while hanging out a washing then, Robert?' asked Mammy.

'Well, to tell you the truth, Jeannie, I think you'll be a'right, it's heading over from the west south-west,' he added, sticking one finger in the air, wetting it on his tongue, then thrusting it back up again.

'Strange,' I thought. 'How would that tell him if my mother should do a washing or not?'

'It will reach us by the late afternoon,' he concluded.

That news had her hurrying out the washing tub, as Uncle put the thickest sticks on the fire.

Daddy had left before we stirred, to do a bit of moling round the local farms. I tried to break the ice between Cousin Berta and myself, but she huffed her eyes shut and turned her back. Honestly, she could be right throng, that lass, when she put her mind to it.

'You please yourself,' I told her, adding, before striding off, 'life's too short for that carry-on.'

Mary had positioned herself halfway up the tree that Mammy hung her washing-line from, and sat there, legs dangling over a branch, so that she could keep an eye on her.

So it looked like I was on my own to go bird-trapping.

The ball of string I took from the handy box kept in the bus boot seemed okay for the job. A broken stick flung down by Mary from her perch would be fine, but what was I going to use to trap the birds?

'Jessie,' called my suds-covered mother, 'before you go playing, pet, can you do me a big favour and wash the dishes?'

'Och! Mam, do I have to?'

'Would you look at the mountain of dirty clothes piled at my feet, lassie. Now, if you don't want to join the craw in the tree,' (meaning Mary) 'get washing the dishes!'

I looked up at Mary and thought she did resemble a crow. Rather than sit arguing with her all day, then the cursed dishes it was.

This, though, was a blessing in disguise, for with each porridge plate plonked into the water, a big smile spread over my face. I had found my 'trap'! Why, of course, the dish-basin, none other.

'Mam, can I use the basin?' I asked, approaching her gingerly.

'What for?' she asked, rubbing the soapsuds from her rolled-up sleeves.

'Something.' I answered, keeping my eyelids lowered.

'No!'

'Please Mammy, It's not for anything dirty, like keeping baggy minnows in.'

'Go and play. Dish-basins are for dishes, and nothing else!'

I remember a countrywoman we saw once washing her baby's nappies in her basin. Mammy called her a filthy, clattie manishie (woman) and refused a cup of tea from the kind wife. 'I'd rather die o' the drouth than take tea from a cup that'd been washed in the same basin as shitty hippins,' she said.

But the trapping was on me and I had to have the basin. Anyway, there was a big difference between a bum wrap and a bird trap.

'Mammy will kill me for sure,' were the thoughts racing through my head as I found the perfect spot, with basin securely held under my arm. I quickly set about propping it up with the string-tied twig. Lastly, a sprinkling of breadcrumbs finished the job. I stood back, and when I thought it looked right, took the loose end of the string and found a braw bit in the undergrowth to hide in from any suspicious birdy.

I may have lain in that spot for hours, for I soon lost all track of time, when a flutter of wings caught my attention. A blackbird was filling itself to its brim with my tasty crumbs. 'Jings, I'm not needing a bird of that size,' I thought. 'And if it bides under the basin it'll not leave any bread for wee-er birds. Away with you greedy blackie,' I called out, 'the free meal's not for you, go!' Instantly it flew off to pastures new.

Just when I thought my luck was out at this trapping carry-on, a wee curious bird settled itself at the mouth of the basin. It was, of all birds, my favourite: a wee cock-sparra. The hoppitty-hop curiosity of the tiny bird at the basin told me Blackie had left some crumbs, and yes, the little visitor was making his way under my trap.

I gently tightened my grip on the string and yanked as fast as I could. 'Got you!' I screamed. Jumping to my feet with excitement I ran over to check on my captive spug pet. Then a thought flashed to mind: 'How can I lift the basin up without him fleeing away? I'd best go and see if Mammy will help me make a cage for my new pet.'

Well, if ever a mistake was in the making that was it. I can still to this day mind the look on her face when I told her what I'd done.

'You've done what?' she roared. 'Do you mean to tell me you've got a wild bird trapped?'

'It won't be wild for long, Mam. Sure, if a flea can be trained, then surely a bird would be a doddle.' I went on, 'Can you not make a cage for him? He'd look grand sitting in the back windy.'

'Would you like to be stuffed in a cage sitting in the back window, my lass?'

'No, but...'

'Never mind but. Listen to me, now, Jess, this is a lesson! When the good Lord gave you two legs to run with, he also gave yon wee sparra wings to fly with. How would you feel if you hadn't the use of your legs?'

'Wheesht, Mammy, for God's sake, heaven forbid,' I squirmed at the question.

'Well then, the sparra's trapped and can't use his wings.'

My mother stared at me as if staring into my very soul. Only mothers can do that. Tears filled my eyes as I thought on what I'd done. She put her arm round my shoulder and continued: 'When travelling folks camp in the countryside they must leave it as they found it, nothing taken, or abused. You see, this would offend Mother Nature and she doesn't look too kindly on abusers of the land. Some, who have spoilt her pattern, find she won't let them back. They say such people have had all their belongings lost, either in floods or landslide, aye, and some found a living impossible to make. Now, lassie, away and set free yon wee sparra, that is if it's still alive.'

My mother's lesson fairly filled my head as I sped off to release my captive. I began to think that Mother Nature must be married to God, because Granny Power told me he was the one who made everything. 'One big painting, Poppy' she would say (she called every wean that), 'painted by the Master Himself. Birds singing, spring and autumn colours, winter's frock o' white. He does the paintings. She gives it life.' And here was I interfering in Their way of things.

'Oh dear, better pray the sparra hasn't died with fright!' I thought, running with the stretch of a pursued hind at rutting time.

I hurried back to my wee captive, and with trembling hands gently lifted up the basin. 'Are you dead, bird?' I whispered, peering underneath. The spug sat there with marbled, glazed eyes, not a single tweet or movement, just silence. Lifting my head towards the heavens, I prayed, 'I didn't mean it harm, God, only thought it would mak a fine pet. Please can you see a way to forgive a helpless wean?'

The sparra sat staring. I sat grovelling, even promised to wash every dish the family used indefinitely.

Unable to contain my fears at what the Almighty and his woman had planned for my future, I took hold of the dish-basin and threw it a mile in the air. The noise it made as it stotted against a tree trunk did the trick. Our wee sparra was only kidding on, one look at the dish-basin rolling in his direction sent him reaching for the sun, with the healthiest pair of wings I'd ever seen.

'You wee cheat, there was nothing wrong with you,' I screamed pointing at the heavens. 'It's a bating [spank] for you if we meet again, I can tell you, my lad.'

After teetering on the brink of God's wrath, I swore I'd leave all birds alone, and spend my time from now on playing bairns' games! But isn't it peculiar when we're young how we soon forget our wrongs, so within a minute the basin was propped up again and I was hidden in the undergrowth awaiting my next victim.

'Oh my, what a naughty girl!', I hear you say, but well, ha, ha, you're wrong!

I would leave the spugs alone and go for the big black hoodie. Mammy hated the clumsy creature, the witch's favourite. Many times she stretched her fist towards the sky and called out, 'You can't leave a crumb out to feed the wee birds when yon big ugly black things steal it!' I even heard old wives say the hoodie was a bird of the Devil.

So seeing as nobody liked ugly craws, I'd make it up with both mothers—nature's and my own—and catch one.

So there I was, concealed in my now familiar hidey-hole, string clasped firmly in my hand, awaiting the unsuspecting prey.

I waited, and waited, and better waited, but yon wee sparra must have spread the word that the big bird-trapper was operating in town.

As I lay there, only the odd thin-legged spider ventured without fear across my bum, up my back and down my arm, then trotted off to disappear under the basin. Apart from him, nothing, not even a wasp, ventured within a mile of my trap.

It might have been nearing suppertime, my belly was rumbling, but by golly it wasn't the only thing, for the thunder that my Uncle Robert had predicted was splitting the heavens.

I could hear away in the distance Mammy's beckoning whistle, calling her brood home. 'Home,' I thought, 'best get back.'

But, before I stood up, something caught my eye. A rabbit was making its curious approach to the basin mouth. 'Jeeps', I cringed, 'if Mother Nature takes a heavy at birds, she'd be a damn sight more peeved if I trap a rabbit.'

The next few minutes of my life in the undergrowth that late afternoon were for sure the most terrifying I've ever lived, so take heed as I relive the horror.

Directly behind the unsuspecting bunny I saw him. Standing on hind legs, swaying like a red cobra, was Auntie Anna's demon throat-ripper! He stood poised, ready to strike my unsuspecting wee ball of innocent fur. Like a snake he swayed from side to side as if hypnotising the poor wee rabbit. His prey went rigid and so did I. I could hear deep in my head a high pitched shrill, a sound I'd never heard before, like a scream from a dying fairy brownie.

Now, I don't know if it was the thunder and lightning, Mammy's whistle or Auntie Anna's tale of blood-sucking, but my whole body froze from top to toe. All I could manage to move were my fingers, which I pushed into the soft earth, filling my fingernails with peaty soil and rye grass.

It mattered not a jot if rabbit was on Dracula weasel's menu that day or not, as long as it wasn't me. I became terror-struck. Bit by bit, from teeth to feet, the fear of weasels spread across my rigid body, giving birth to a lifelong phobia.

As I lay in the undergrowth with my dirty nails and dry throat, I could not have cared less for the raging electric storm, my whistling Mammy, Mother Nature, God—aye, even the fate of the poor wee rabbit. No, my throat and its contents were all I cared for. So, with the last ounce of strength in my now useless body, I up and like the banshee herself, shrieked across the now rain-sodden grass.

Wallop! My mother's slap brought me spinning back to the world of the living.

'Where's my basin?' she shouted, 'and why did you ignore me, your supper's frozen cold?'

'Mammy, dear, ken I fine we've not to disobey you, but I'll take the worst of your hand before I go back there into the kingdom of King Weasel for a simple basin.' Those words said, I threw myself over her knee.

> Beware the wee weasel wha hides in the green,
> For he'll rip oot yer tonsils, an' gouge oot yer een.

8

OUR PRAYER

The remainder of our journey that summer in the bus took us to Kingussie, where we met a Minister's wife. I will tell you briefly how yon wife tried to do more for the cause than I'd imagine her man ever did. Let me take you with Mammy and me when we knocked at her door doing a bit of hawking.

'Good morning tae ye, wife,' said Mammy, 'would your sewing basket be the better of some of my threads, laces or buttons?' The lady of the manse, without a single peep into my mother's basket, grabbed us both by the arm and ushered us in. Inside the old church house, bookshelves lined the front hall and continued into each room. Even the kitchen was an array of reading material.

'My,' whispered Mammy, being respectful to the good woman's status, 'a long, cold winter's night would pass in no time with all these books to take yer pick from.'

'These books are all centred on the Path,' the wife explained. 'Now, sit down the pair of you and I'll say a prayer for the saving of your heathen souls.'

I could see my mother flinch at the woman's words, but she said nothing. Perhaps she was comforted by the idea that a benevolent minister's wife would not have us leave, so to speak, empty-handed. She held her tongue and played along. I just stared at the millions of books, and prayed the dishtowels drying on the Raeburn rail wouldn't catch fire and spread.

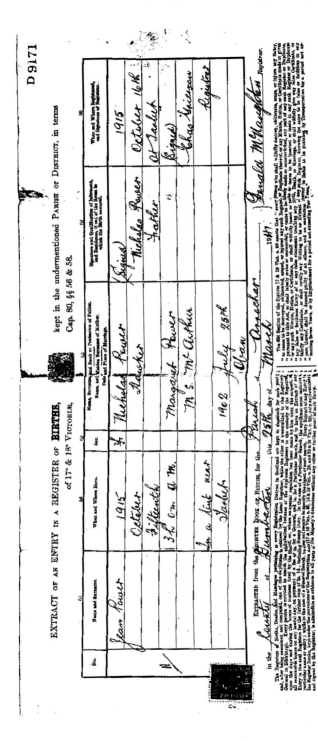

Jessie's mother's birth certificate, stating that she was born 'in a tent near Tarbet'

Four generations of the Power family, headed by Granny Power (seated)

Granny Riley

Granny Power

Granny Riley and Auntie Maggie
as a child

Jessie's father, Charles Riley
(right), aged 15

A gathering of relatives at 'The Berries'

Jessie's mother and father in 1940

Jessie's mother and Uncle Charlie   Jessie's father (right)

'How many family have you got?' she enquired of my mother.

'There is my man and me, and eight daughters,' answered Mammy.

'Well, if you all come to the church on Sunday I'll buy half the contents of your basket, and I'll even fill a bag of cast-off clothing. Oh, and a baked currant loaf will be added, now how does that sound?'

Mammy was obviously thinking the same as me. This was Monday and Daddy was planning to shift up to Inverness on the morrow. There was no way he'd hang around for nothing more than a few shillings and a bag of secondhand clothes smelling of moth-balls, currant loaf or not. She thanked the wife but refused her offer.

This brought floods of tears from the wife. 'You'll go to hell,' she screamed at us, 'hell, I say—the devil, I can see him now, rubbing his hands!'

My mother picked her basket from the stone floor, grabbed my hand and said to the woman, 'I have no fear of hell, only of my God, and it is out of respect to him that I hold my tongue in this house of misery. I'll give a wee bit advice, though—why not stick to baking your currant loaves, and leave the soul-saving to the man.'

'Stupid bitch,' she muttered to herself as we half-ran along the village street. 'I could have hawked all the countryside the time wasted meeting in with mad biddies like yon. I've a good mind to send every dealer I meet to her door.'

For the rest of the day I played with some traveller bairns who'd camped beside us. We pretended to be Highlanders and redcoats rampaging through Ruthven Barracks, it was great fun.

That night, as our old bus trundled its way on to Inverness, we laughed thinking on the holy wife who'd lost her way. Even though her house was filled with Christian books.

We only ever said one little prayer. This is it, and it sometimes brought on the odd giggle-fit:

> *Matthew, Mark, Luke and John*
> *Bless this bed that I lay on,*
> *If I should die before I wake,*
> *I give the Lord my soul to take.*

Lovely words for a child to say you *may* think, but children can be wee devils on their way through life, and we were no exception.

If the weather was warm it could get pretty unbearable trying to sleep four to a bed in the bus. The bus being mostly windows meant that, if it had been a hot sunny day, it was well into the night before it cooled. It was surprising that we didn't sprout like tattie shaws in the bus-cum-greenhouse we had to sleep in.

So there we were, the four of us younger lassies, saying our wee prayer while our proud mother stood over us, when Mary would, without warning, replace the words 'if I should die before I wake' with 'if I should bake before I wake, I give the Lord my soles to take.'

The giggles followed, and inevitably, so did the wallops! Sleep was hard to find after that, because the rest of us did our Burns bit to Mammy's wee prayer, and try as she might it wasn't long before she too was laughing. Then Daddy would chip in with his verse—

Matthew, Mark, Luke and John
Double in size this bed that I lay on,
Or I will fry before too long.

More laughter followed, louder this time because our parents were being disrespectful to the Almighty! I would be surprised, though, if He wasn't having a good laugh himself at our antics.

Mammy would then prepare us for sleep with a drink of milk and a tale from her never-ending store of bedtime stories. Then, one by one, we gave in to the heat of the night, which we were none the worse for in the early morning rising.

We spent a week at Inverness before making our way down country to settle a quiet winter at Stirling Green.

The following summer we more or less followed the same route as before. The next memory I will recall comes from Ballinluig, not far from Pitlochry. It gives a wee insight into how crowded bedtime could become when the older girls were with us.

9

BUS-BOOT BED

Daddy found his favourite spot in a wood near Ballinluig, and reversed the bus between the River Tummel and silver birch trees. Chrissie and Shirley, fed up kipping down in the wee Fordy, pestered the life out of Mammy to sleep in the bus boot!

'Girls, are you mad, just imagine the danger! Laying sleeping in a place where any wild man could steal you away in the dead of night.' Mammy wouldn't even entertain the idea.

The girls laughed, saying who in their right mind would want to do a mad thing like that?

'The boot doesn't lock,' she reminded them, annoyed at her lassies for harping on. 'Even if it did, what about you and your claustrophobia, Shirley?'

'We'll keep the boot open, Ma, and I'll sleep to the front just in case I feel chokit!' pleaded Shirley.

'There is no way you two are sleeping a night in there. Now go and do something useful like peel a pot of tatties or collect more sticks for the fire.'

Shirley had a pot of tatties peeled in no time, while Chrissie gathered up a pile of dried driftwood heaped on the riverbank after a recent flood. Shirley tried again, 'Can we sleep in it now, Mam, please?'

'Look,' said Mammy, 'let me talk this over with your father. I'll see what he says.'

This was right up Shirley's street, because if anybody could wrap Daddy round their little finger, it was her!

Dad's brothers, Joe and Wullie, had arrived for a wee visit, and these two lads didn't half rib the lassies whenever in their company. More so when they found the girls discussing a bus-boot bed.

'Do you know there's wolves in this wood, Shirley?' teased Joe.

'Aye, and they say at night a river monster, I think it's a cousin of Nessie, has been seen to rise from the Tummel and help itself to a cow or two,' added Wullie.

'Away and not talk rot, next you'll be telling me that giant puddocks leap onto the road and piss over the cars!' said Shirley.

'Mammy, Shirley's speaking dirty again and giving me a red face,' clyped Janey. She'd spent the day sitting on a bank by the railway, counting passengers in the trains. As well as horses, Janey loved trains. She would spend ages counting people's hats or how many men and women were in each compartment. Trains held a fascination for our Janey. But those comments might sway Mammy's decision about the boot. So Shirley did what she always did, grabbed Janey by the neck and pulled her onto the ground.

My two uncles laughed at both my sisters, as they rolled about the grass hissing and spitting for all the world like a pair of scraggy cats. Mammy, affronted at the state of her daughters, took a dishtowel and came hard across their backsides, putting an end to their catfight!

'You two men stop filling their heads with rubbish about monsters and the likes, or else those two won't sleep tonight.'

'Oh Mam, does that mean we're getting to sleep in the boot after all? Did Daddy agree then?' asked Shirley, as she brushed off bits of twigs sticking to Janey's backside from their wrestling match, apologising at the same time.

'Yes, he did, but one single peep out of either of you and it'll be under the bus you can sleep, now, do I make myself clear?'

'Clear as a baggy minnow pool, Mam, in a pearl burn,' said Chrissie, giving her a big hug.

As the day came to a close, Dad, who'd not seen his brothers for months, cracked round the fire well into the night. They discussed the Berries. Who was there, who'd died, who'd married, who was in the jail, and so forth.

Soon it was time for the last cup of tea. Mammy had made a fine batch of scones. These were served up with dollops of butter and tablespoonfuls of just-made raspberry jam. Well-fed and well-cracked, the two lads said their goodnights and went home, not without a parting word for the girls to watch out for monsters prowling round the bus while they were at the mercy of the night.

Daddy took the rolled-up mattress from wee Fordy and put it in the bus boot, while Mam added a pillow and the tartan rug from the driver's seat. In no time we were all bedded, including the lassies in the bus boot.

Whether it was the clamminess of that August night or Uncle Joe's parting comments, who knows, but Shirley found it hard to sleep.

'Chrissie,' she asked, prodding her sister in the ribs, 'are you thinking about what our uncles said?'

'No, I'm trying to sleep, that's what I'm thinking about,' answered Chrissie, pulling another few inches of the tartan rug that her sister had claimed for herself.

But Shirley continued: 'I heard a noise, and I think it came from over by that old twisted oak tree.'

'You do too much thinking, full stop. What kind of noise?'

'I don't know, a kind of rustling-in-the-bushes noise!'

Chrissie sat bolt upright in the bed, banging her head off the low roof. 'Ouch! you stupid fool, are you trying to put the fear in me? You're no better than the men,' she shouted.

This wakened Daddy and prompted a bang on the floor. 'Get to bloody sleep, you two, or you'll feel the back of my hand.' (I could never understand what that meant, for I am sure the front of his hand would have done a better job.)

Soon, though, after a fit of giggling, fear of the dark gave way to sleep, and peace ruled in the quiet night. Then, somewhere in the surrounding blackness, a deep, throaty growl was heard by the half-sleeping Shirley.

'Oh my God, what in Rabbie's name was that?' Shirley pushed her back into Chrissie's belly.

'You stupid bugger, you knocked the wind out from me!'

'Did you hear it, the growling, did you f---ing hear it?'

'Shirley, for the love of God, lassie, if the folks hear you cursing like that…'

'Never mind that. There's something in the night, out there in the pitch. Can you feel its presence?'

The two girls lay huddled close together, straining their ears and listening. They didn't have long to wait, when suddenly a blood-curdling growl shook the leaves on the whispering silver birch trees. Two hooting hoolits spread their wings and glided up and over the bus.

'Oh God, Shirley, you're right enough, it's a monster, let's run into the bus!'

'No, if we do, Daddy will say we're making it up!'

'I'm willing to take a leathering, rather than face whatever is lurking out there.'

As my two sisters sat almost glued together, staring into the darkness, a movement in the trees made Chrissie shoot like a bullet beneath the tartan rug while Shirley stiffened with fear. Now, readers, when she did this, a strange form of temper would come on her. Instead of running like the clappers, as any normal teenager would do, my big sister faced whatever or whoever was responsible for her terrified state. This is exactly what she did now.

She ripped off her long cotton gown and ran screaming, mother-naked, into the night towards the beast! Lunging, she grabbed its arm, and with the strength of a dozen big men flung the mesmerised creature straight into the River Tummel! 'Get back where you came from!' she screamed. 'Frighten me, would you, you bastard, I'll give you frightening wee lassies.'

That wasn't the end of it. Oh no, she decided to give it one more kick. So into the freezing river she went. 'Come out here right now and fight like a man!' By now her temper was totally out of control. Foam came from her mouth, her eyes rolled in their sockets and her body began to shake. The dripping monster was struggling for breath as it spat clumps of river reeds from its mouth. It crawled onto the bank coughing and spluttering. She let out a kick.

'Help, stop it, Shirley! It's me, Uncle Joe, I was only joking you!'

'Look at the state of you, lassie,' said Mammy, who along with the rest of us had been awakened by Shirley's screams. 'Get some clothes on yourself,' she added, wrapping a coat round her dripping daughter's shoulders. 'And as for you, Joe, you should have known better. Don't you remember what she did to big Macallum's nose?'

Well, reader, who could forget that poor big man! We were up visiting with Auntie Maggie in Aberfeldy, when the said man decided to tickle Shirley's feet sticking out the back door of wee Fordy. Oh yes, folks, that's right, you've guessed. As fear gripped her, she kicked out and duly broke the gadgie's (man's) nose! The moral is, don't play bogeyman on our Shirley!

One good thing came from that incident on the banks of the Tummel—the lassies never again asked to sleep in the bus-boot bed! Well, who knows, if another monster came a-creeping it might not have been a friendly uncle.

With another winter soon to be upon us we headed for Crieff, the Perthshire town surrounded by tattie fields, neep fields and farms, and where there was—yuk—a school.

10

THE MIXI RABBIT

Here we are, then, in a cosy wee bit at the foot of Tomaknock hill, surrounded by the fields of Dollerie. Tattie-lifting is in full swing, and I'm imprisoned in Crieff Junior Secondary School. This is what I remember from that winter.

My father came in, slumped down in his chair, shifted his bunnet to the back of his head and said, 'there's not a rabbit living without two swelt eyes. Every place I turn the craturs are blindly wandering all over, bumping into everything. Pain, they're in awful pain. It's a bad thing right enough. Six year in the war, never have I seen such awfulness.' He heaved a sigh that seemed to come from far in his soul.

I couldn't understand why a man who killed rabbits and fed his family on them should be bothered one way or the other, and told him so.

'I never thought the sight of a live rabbit would put you into such a state, seeing as you make a living from killing them,' I said.

'That's got nothing to do with it, Jess. I kill them quick.'

'Aye, but now the Mixi fly does it for you.' I never usually spoke back to my father.

Daddy picked his stare very carefully and said, 'Have you seen one yet?'

I shook my head.

'Well, my lass, knowing how you go mental with your cousin

Grant for cutting worms for fishing, I suggest you take a cycle ower the Braidhaugh, it's full of it there.'

Cousin Grant was a first-class fisherman. Even from the earliest age he knew all about where to fish and when. He was my Auntie Jenny's oldest son and lived in Muthill. Sometimes he'd come travelling with us. Mammy loved having him. Not only was he a perfect gent, but he was, what was sorely lacking in our home, a boy!

Daddy described how, as he'd done for years, he had approached the usual farmers to do the rabbiting with his snares and gun, only to be told they now had far better, and cheaper, ways than his.

'Aye, man,' said the farmer, beaming. 'I'm right pleased, a rare wee fly inserted deep inside the burrow, and before you know, it's spread a deadly disease through the whole lot of them. Isn't it great?'

The proud farmer then took my Dad up on the braeside to see for himself. The sight had him coming home grey-coloured, with no stomach for his supper.

'Yes, that's a terrible sight. Some unnatural body discovered that method of vermin control. He'll not be missed on judgement day, I can tell you, and I hope I'm there to see it.'

Next day, I decided to bike it over from Tomaknock and see for myself the dreaded myxomatosis that had perplexed my father so much.

The Braidhaugh lies to the west side of Crieff by the low Comrie road. Resting my bike against the end of the Earn bridge, I walked on up towards the sprawling fields of Alichmore, seeking out a mixi rabbit. I didn't have far to go before the nightmarish sight my father spoke of came blindly stumbling through my very legs. The rabbits were dragging pain-wracked bodies and desperately sniffing at runs for one that would lead back to a safe, dark burrow. Swollen red eyes looked so out of place on the usual bundles of grey fur. I wished I hadn't been so eager to see this sight. I cursed below my breath, for I was too young to do it aloud. But, by God, I was sorely tempted that moment to scream at the top of my voice, 'WHY?'

Behind me I heard the sound of feet crunching on grass. 'This is private ground, who gave you permission to be here?' I turned to see a big, bunneted man glowering at me, sleeves rolled up, crook in hand, collie dogs slithering round his legs like snakes with feet. The temper was on me, though. I had no fear of the stranger.

'Permission is it? No, I have none, but I see the Devil has his!'

I answered, pointing at the tortured rabbits, blood trickling from their eyes.

'Look, lassie, sure I'm as scunnered as yourself by the disease. I've no stomach for unnatural doings, but a shepherd is what I am, and a busy one at that, so if you can get away from here before the gamey comes, I would be grateful.'

'To fiery hell and back with the gamey! I hope he writhes there in agony with scabby eyes for eternity.' My voice rose higher.

If my parents had heard the way I addressed this older person I would have got the back of a hand for sure.

'It's the new way the farmer has of vermin control, and nothing to do with the gamey,' said my shepherd, before whistling in his collie dogs that had ventured too far from his legs. They obediently gathered at his feet as if they had done the unthinkable.

He removed his bunnet, scratched his head, then said, 'Look, lassie, I can see you're pained, so I'll make a promise. If you go now, then I'll put these craturs out of their misery. I can't say fairer than that, now can I?'

The gentle man replaced his tweed cap, reached down, picked up my sick rabbit by the hind legs, and with two chops into the back of its neck, its pain was no more. Then another one, and soon three more pain-free bunnies lay limp at the feet of his faithful sheep dogs.

'There now, lassie, forget the sickness for the time being. No doubt you'll see a lot more from now on, if it's a traveller lass you are.'

'I can never forget what is nothing short of a crime against Mother Nature,' I said, 'but mark my words, one day she'll have her revenge. You're a good man, shepherd. She'll look kindly on you. God bless you, may you live a long and healthy life.'

I skipped off down the hillside to find my old bike, feeling that at least a few rabbits had been spared the awful fate that awaited millions. One thing certain, I would never put rabbit in my mouth again, and I didn't!

Mammy rowed me for being lippy to the shepherd, but Daddy gave me a toffee penny dainty (out of sight of my mother, of course). 'You have a tongue in your head, Jessie,' he said, 'for such a little one, but mind and use it wisely, and don't have a go at every gamey you come across. Some do more than you think, looking after the countryside.'

I smiled at my father's words and said, 'If he gives out the mixi fly, then I'll not miss him whatever he may do!'

Daddy though, was a worried man: a chunk of his livelihood was gone, and he was finding it harder and tougher to make a shilling. The tattie money, fine though it was, kept us awhiles, but we were getting bigger, food was getting dearer, school clothes were wanted for us four youngest; it meant not nearly enough was coming in and he had to find other ways of making money.

The summer had no such problems: there was the berry picking and gathering the brock wool. Mammy was hawking and doing fortunes, and, always well maintained, we ate and laughed. But times were changing; the old ways were, like the rabbits, on the decline.

'Jeannie,' said Daddy, one morning, 'I'll have to be making a proper living, one that brings in enough money. All this dodging here and there without a guarantee is no use. I have to earn enough so that we can put by for that rainy day you're always speaking about.'

'Do you mean that you're thinking on a house, Charlie?'

'Well, I could be doing just the very thing, hen, though I've no intentions of putting my old bus on the market, he stays for the summers.'

Mammy couldn't have been any more excited if you'd given her all the lowy (money/fortune) in America!

'Here in Crieff, Charlie, is as good a place as any. Chrissie has the eye of a fine local lad, and the bairns like the school.'

A visit with his old pal, the very man who owned the ground we were presently living on, secured a piece of it to build Mammy her dream home. Papers were drawn up of plans and the likes, with the help of a friendly lawyer. With assistance from some of Daddy's brothers and cousins, drainage pipes and foundations were laid. It looked like we were going to winter-settle, like many other travelling folks.

I sulked, while around me the older lassies could hardly contain themselves. How could they wish to be anchored to one spot? Seeing the same things, day in, day out. What about the hills of Glen Coe, the west coast isles, midden-raking, beach-combing, bluebell woods, campfires? I could go on and never stop, because the list was endless. I tossed so much in bed I had the blankets on and off the floor, and my young sisters shrieking at Mammy to make me sleep somewhere else.

'What's wrong with you, Jessie?' asked my parents after supper one night.

'Well, I thought we were supposed to be travelling people. Gad-a-bouts, tinkers, gypsies, hawkers, whatevers?'

'Aye, that we are,' laughed Mammy. 'But, child of mine, we'll always be travelling folks. Just because I want to have a secure warm home, doesn't mean we're not what God made us to be.'

'We are what we are, Jessie,' added Daddy.

'Look,' I blurted out, 'surely there's nothing wrong with our old bus. Is it not warm and secure when the wee stove is roaring away up the lum on a cold winter's night?'

'It's not that, Jessie,' answered Daddy, taking my hand in his, 'but when we've an address, I can find a business. Maybe building or painting, something that will bring in a decent living—you'll have to understand.'

I had answered them back once; any more and I'd be getting the back of the hand, but my mouth would not be closed on this issue. After all, wasn't my future at stake too? 'I hate this world, so I do, it's a cruel, cruel place. Mixi rabbits and imprisoned wee lassies, it's a horrible place, I wish I was dead.'

The thought of leaving my bus to live in a big house, missing out on my travelling in among the west coast, Oban's sands, routing through Ruthven Barracks, and the many countless things I seen and done was tearing me apart. Och sure, we would travel in the summer, maybe now and again. But I had seen what happened to a lot of relatives who rooted down. So long as the security of a house was there, they got lazy, missed out April, May, maybe found time to put on the road in June.

That meant school. God bless and save us, imagine biding in school until then, I'd go pure moich, nothing surer!

But, as Rabbie Burns remarked, the best-laid plans of mice and men will sometimes gang astray.

This, however, wasn't a time for dwelling on the future. No, this was nearing April's end, lambs were coming and the frost was going. Building my mother's house just had to wait. Summertime, with all its bonny ways, sang out from the budding trees: 'Come on, you travelling folks, what are you waiting for? Get on the road again!'

66

I was just beaming when Mammy, holding me by the hand, went into school that Friday morning and knocked on the headmaster's door.

'Good morning, Mrs Riley, is it that time already?' asked D.O. Mclean, Head of Crieff Junior Secondary School. (Remember my visitor when I was in hospital with a broken leg?)

'Aye sir, time to be going,' she said, then sat down at his insistence.

'As I have said to you many times, these lassies o' yours, they are clever children, especially Jessie. If I were you, I certainly would think about putting her to Morrison's. We here at the school could help with funding.'

The man went on and on about 'proper education'. I bit my lip and prayed Mammy would get up and go before he could change her mind. There were plenty of friends and relatives who lived in and around the area. I knew for a fact they were more than willing to keep me while the rest of the family travelled. And, God almighty, he wanted me to go to Morrison's Academy, the snobs' school!

'You fair gladden my heart when you speak of my lassies like that. And to think that our Jessie is paying attention to her teacher means she is enjoying her lessons. But,' (and to me this was the biggest 'but' in the world) 'when she reaches the eleven-plus year, then I'll think seriously on what you say, Mr Maclean.'

'Please do, Mrs Riley, please do that. Here's the leaving certificate for you. Have a good summer now, will you?'

'Thanks again, sir, the same to yourself,' said my mother, before adding, 'Where are you holidaying this year?'

'I'm taking the family up the west coast,' he answered, rising from his leather chair to open the door for us.

'Well, if Charlie has a mind, we'll be round the coast ourselves. Might even run into you then?' Mammy had a lovely way with words, I always thought.

'I'll keep an eye out for the bus, then. Good day, and good health. Oh, talking about health, has the leg healed all right, pet?' he said, looking my left leg up and down, even although it was my right one that'd been injured.

'Yes sir, it's doing away fine,' I answered, thinking back on his visits to the hospital. That was then; now it was time to leave school for the whole summer, pure freedom!

Hello, yahoo and skip-to-ma-loo, she's got it! The certificate from the headmaster allowing us early leave from school clasped in her hand, Mammy and I walked up the High Street, purchased the day's messages, then got back home to finish packing.

When we arrived, Daddy met us, smiling from one ear to another. 'Jeannie, I took a run over to Perth, met two lads from down by the Borders. They told me most traveller lads are making their fortunes spray-painting.' He went on and on about all the money men in England were making. 'When we get back in the autumn, I'll give this spray-painting serious thought, could be the very thing, eh, Jeannie?'

Mammy was smiling as she nodded, then got on with the job, as me and my wee sisters bounced up and down on a big rubber tractor inner tube Daddy got from his pal, the farmer. Perhaps he felt guilty not hiring him to do the same vermin control as in the past. Daddy did do his moles for him, though. Thankfully, nobody has yet discovered a flea that can wipe out those wee underground funnel-nosed creatures—not yet, anyway.

WILLIAM 'KEITH' MACPHERSON, 1893–1973. Born at Chattan in Comrie, he was a very gifted poet. When he met you, sure as fate a poem would be penned in your honour. Keith was the proprietor of the Bridgend Garage, and took great delight in driving the school bus through the glens and villages. His poem 'The Auld Schule Car' is a classic. It was also a song. It is to his daughter, Maimie Carson, my dear friend, I owe many thanks for allowing me to accompany the above tale of the mixi rabbit with her father's poem.

TO A RABBIT

Wee hoppin' loupin' scurrin' beastie,
Whiles ham and veal, whiles chicken tasty,
I think they've been a wee bit hasty,
Plottin yer end.
Myxomatotis new and nasty,
My furry friend.

Tae me, ye've been a lad o' pairts,
A problem child in a' the airts,
They say ye broke some fairmers' he'rts,
That weel may be,
But catch a poacher, then, ma certs!
Yer value see.

Or see the trapper, cap in hand,
Go bargain for the rabbit land,
Tae me, it's hard tae understand,
Despite the hairm
Ye dae the fairmer, he'll demand
The rent o' fairm.

In Parliament they've used yer name,
Classed ye as vermin, just the same,
I think ye merit some sma' fame,
A slight ovation,
In war when things were tight at hame,
Ye fed a nation.

But mappie, dinna fret oor sair,
Ye'll weather this, o' that I'm shair,
And multiply, aye mair and mair
Roond ilka clachan;
Now what's that echo? I declare
The trapper's lauchin'.

11

LOCHGILPHEAD MONKEY

I'll take you over to Lochgilphead now on the west coast, and see if you believe this next tale. There are many who didn't.

My namesake Auntie Jessie, her man Wullie, and their kids Anna and Wullie, had arrived the day before. It was grand seeing the fire blazing away and a braw big pot of tea brewing on the fire. Have you got yours? Good, then I'll begin.

There are monkeys in Lochgilphead, you know, and not pet ones neither. I mean real wild ones in the wood. You don't believe me? Well, read on.

The sky was a deep grey as we pulled on to our favourite spot on the shore a mile from the Argyllshire village of Lochgilphead. The mist on the hills in the distance seemed to roll down to meet the ocean and cover it with fingers of grey. It rained a lot; well, at least it did when we were there. I didn't mind, though, because this part of the Scottish coastline had miles of shale beach, and that meant, for me at least, a good rake, or, to put it in general terms, beach-combing.

There was no swimming or sun-soaking while we were camped in this part of Bonnie Scotland—I had other things to do. For the purposes of my midden-raking, I kept a big jute sack (a tattie-bag) and in it I put all kinds of sellable metal. Brass, copper, lead—whatever the scrapman bought, if I found it, then into my bag it went.

I soon became quite an expert on scrap metal, and knew what

it was worth just by its weight. Daddy used jokingly to warn folks not to leave their jeely pans lying about, or else I'd be slipping them into my bag.

The filling of my sack would take most of the summer; then came the best bit of all, the selling of it. I found the scrappy enjoyed a good haggle with me before a price was agreed on. We'd go through the best of the green-coloured brass, he'd offer me this or that, and I'd hum and haw before I accepted his offer. Then, after the entire contents of my bag had been scrutinised, the tired man would pay me the princely sum of two pounds. It was a great feeling walking away from that scrapyard, sack folded neatly under my arm, eagerly awaiting the coming summer when it would be filled again. This, then, was my goal—the filling of my big jute bag.

Folks used to comment on the sad wee lassie with the hanging head, the ones who didn't know me, that is, for those who did, knew exactly what I was doing. I was scouring the ground for scrap. A right wee entrepreneur, if ever there was one. My ambition was one day to own a fleet of scrap lorries, and become the richest scrappy in the land. The lorries would be bright red with the Queen's emblem on the doors, 'By Appointment to Her Majesty'.

Sometimes I'd come across discarded cable-cuts, which meant the rubber casing had to be burned off, exposing the copper wire inside. Mammy avoided dressing me in frocks, because I didn't half get reekit black with the burning rubber.

By the time we got settled at the shore the mist was thinning, and through low cloud little glints of sunshine were throwing their welcome light onto the stony beach. The tide was out, and my eyes greedily scanned as far as they could for anything with a metal look to it. I set about gathering up the odd bit. By the feel and the weight I soon knew what was worth popping into my sack. I walked for hundreds of yards, with head down and hands soaked from ramming them eagerly into thick, browny-green seaweed.

In no time I was heading home. I had so little in my bag that I could carry it over one shoulder, as I made my way through the now incoming tide back to the bus. My wee sisters were busy lifting crabs from rock pools. I returned in time to prise one from wee Babsy's pinkie before she turned blue with crying. 'Dear me, that wee sister of mine has the most greeting face amongst all the bairns in Scotland,' I thought, examining the crab of half an inch in width. Mind you, I was bitten by a crab myself up past Berrydale, and my finger throbbed for near on a fortnight. It was a mite of a thing as well.

I didn't find muckle on the beach that day, but that didn't bother me because the sea constantly cleaned herself. Therefore, like the beaver I awaited the next day when I was sure I'd find a fortune.

Mammy whistled us in for supper. Uncle Wullie had also been collecting the sea's bounty and had a braw fire going with some of the driftwood that lay in endless piles as far along the beach as the eye could see. My uncle, to his credit, was a dab hand at fires. He was also one of the best storytellers I'd ever heard; his tales of 'Jake the Adventurer' were renowned among travelling folks. And after I finish this wee story, I'll tell you about him!

So, when day gave way to the night, we settled round the warm glowing fire, and while Cousin Wullie played his guitar, we sang along, then headed off to bed to dream.

Apart from dreams of being the richest scrappy in the world, my nod times would take me into bonny Mull, where I found buried treasure. Then I would marry the Duke, to become Her Highness, the Honourable Duchess o' Argyll. Being one so noble, I'd put campsites all over Scotland for travellers, but only for ones that kept the place clean. People would say, 'She's a right fussy Duchess, that Jess Riley!' Now, for a bairn of tinker stock, that wasn't bad going, don't you think?

Come morning, the mist had found its way into every part of land and sea. It was a 'pea souper', as Uncle Wullie called it, 'but it'll be gone by dinner time, it's only morning mist.'

Mammy went hawking, taking wee Babsy, who was crabbit—or should I say 'crab-bit'—and Renie with her. Mary and I were left with the bus to tidy and the dishes to wash. Daddy had to work on the bus engine, because it needed a bit of attention. I made Mary and me a braw big piece in butter and jam, making sure I kept the heel to myself, before setting out on my day's raking. I'd made up my mind, while licking the raspberry jam dripping from my jeely piece: this day I'd fill my bag, even if it took the best part of the day to do it.

Mary and cousin Anna disappeared away down the beach, leaving me to finish the breakfast dishes. Daddy looked over at me, and as he pushed his hand into his pocket I just knew what was coming next: 'Jessie, here's ten bob, away into the village and get me ten fags, and mind my change, for I'm hard up this week.'

'Why does it have to be me? I am the one who always has to do the messages, and I'm fair seek, so I am. Did God say, the day I came into the world, "Here is wee Jess, she's to get all the shopping and not gather any scrap!"'

'Get you down that road, I'm gasping for a fag, and if you go raking along that beach you'll feel the back of my hand!'

He wasn't a big man, my father, but by God he had hands like shovels, and if one landed on you, then you didn't half feel it.

So, with silent reluctance, I sheepishly put the folded ten-shilling note into my cardigan pocket and skipped off down the road towards the village. I was determined not to loiter, because the shore had a lumpy look about it, and I was certain today it was heaving with goodies. In no time at all I was making my way homewards, with Daddy's fags and change securely held in my hand.

I was halfway home when, in the wood to my right, something caught my eye: an animal of some kind was moving up and down between the trees.

'Na, na,' I said to myself, 'I'm imagining it, quite common to see things that are not there in the mist', which by this time was thicker than ever. 'I doubt Uncle Wullie's prediction is away off mark today,' I thought, because it was past dinnertime. This was unusual, though, because his weather forecasts were always spot on.

I had decided to forget what I thought I saw and press on home with the old man's fags when suddenly the beast leapt up, no more than thirty or so feet from me, and this time I knew what it was—it was a monkey!

I had seen one on a Tarzan film, and I never doubted that this beastie was the same as thon thing with arms to the ground, trailing its fingers along behind it, then flinging them up in the air and making a 'hoo-hoo' sound. Yes, no mistaking a monkey: but how, in heaven's name, was it running wild through a wood at Lochgilphead?

I had to see more of this, so putting the fags and change into my cardigan pocket, with the curiosity of a dozen cats I leapt the dyke and into the wood after it. He, my finger-trailing friend, seemed aware of the chase, and weaved in and out of the trees keeping a good distance between us.

Judging by the chimp in Johnny Weissmuller's film, these beasties were nobody's fool, and neither was this wee bugger. I just couldn't get a good enough look at him, but I was sure he would tire, because I certainly was!

It would be braw if I could catch him, then I'd take him back to Daddy. God in Heaven! I had forgotten about the old man's fags and he'd be gasping, nothing surer. This was more important than any stupid monkey.

I turned to make my way back towards the dyke, but try as I might, the way was lost. I had run too far into the wood. There was no way I could make up time, it was the back of my father's hand for me, nothing surer. Even worse, my jute bag would be denied its fill.

Hour upon hour seemed to go by like lightning as I weaved in and out the trees, cursing the wee monkey to the fires of hell, who, by the way, had vanished, and was probably sitting laughing at me from the safety of a sturdy branch.

Just as I was beginning to feel genuine fear, I saw a familiar sight above some trees further up on my left—a spiral of grey smoke told me an open fire was near. I made my way over and, thanks be, there in an opening in the wood I could see the road, and there at the other side was our dear old bus. 'Someone must have been looking after me', as the old folks used to say.

I clambered the dyke and ran breathlessly over to my fagless father.

'Daddy, you'll not believe me, but may my dear Granny spin in her grave if I lie, I've been chasing after a monkey, all through the wood!' The words came fleeing from my mouth, and I swear to you I was having difficulty believing them myself, they sounded so unreal.

'Listen!' shouted Daddy, shutting me up with the tone of his voice, 'for a start off, your Granny is alive and well, so what she's doing spinning in her grave beats me, so don't use those words again, my lady. Now we'll say no more if you give me the fags.'

I could see the want of a fag was taking its toll on him, so I put my hands into my pocket. Then, as I ran my fingers inside, a terrible realisation came over me: Lord leap the spurtle stick, the fags and change were gone. Drawing in my breath, in whispering tones I told my father that I must have lost them. 'What!' he roared, 'you've done what?'

'It wasn't me, it wis the monkey.' Why, in the name of sanity, did I say that, because if ever an excuse was insulting to the intelligence then that was it.

Daddy pointed to the bus and that meant only one thing—grounded!

'Please, Daddy,' I pleaded. 'What about my bag, I'll no' get it filled if you ground me?' God, if I could get my fingers round thon ape I'd strangle it myself; aye, and I bet the brute's sitting watching me getting my punishment and having a damn good laugh to itself.

I stared out the window at Daddy and knew by the lines on his brow: a thunderstorm was going on in his head. He'd most likely decided to wait until Mammy came home. Thankfully, he didn't give me the back of his hand!

Mammy arrived home right pleased with her day's hawking. She came into the bus, where by this time I was greeting my eyes out at the idea of not being able to rake the beach. The fact that my Daddy didn't believe me made matters worse.

'Here, lassie, take this,' she said, handing me a handkerchief. 'Now, did you lose Daddy's fags while down raking the beach?'

'No, Mammy, you should have seen it, the monkey! It was leaping up and down, and all I could think was, if I caught it, how excited everybody would be.'

'Jessie, lass, you'll bring the wrath of your father on yourself, now stop that.'

'Lord roast me, Mother, if I tell a lie, but there was, really and truthfully, a monkey.'

'You've got to understand, my lass, you can't go using the Lord's name in vain like that—another week for you, alright!' My mother sank me a look, accompanied by hard slap on the leg.

'Oh, please don't!' I knew no one was going to believe me, and blamed myself for going into the wood in the first place. So there I was, a stinging slap to the leg and grounded for two weeks. All because of the truth. I was resigned to the fact that my scrappy dreams were to be put on hold for the duration of our stay at Lochgilphead.

Next day I was peeking out the back window. The beach looked as if it was brimming with all kinds of goodies, and here was I stuck in for telling the truth. My sisters were giggling at my misfortune, and I wished the biggest crab in the ocean would come crawling out of the water and nip the heads off them.

Sinking I was, deeper into misery, when I heard the sound of strangers' voices coming from outside. Looking through the curtains I saw two well-dressed men in conversation with my folks. They had the appearance of doctors, or perhaps lawyers, I really couldn't say; one thing certain, I distinctly heard Mammy say my name.

'Jessie, come on out, pet.'

I gingerly stepped down from the bus, leaving one hand securely grasping the door.

'Is this the wee lass?' asked one of the men.

'Aye, this is our Jess,' was my father's reply. 'These gentlemen are from the "Big Hoose", hen, and they want to ask you something.'

Everyone knew about the Big Hoose, because whenever we did something stupid, the old folks would say, 'That yin's heading for the Big Hoose.' It simply meant lunatic asylum!

Here, then, was what my parents had decided was to be my fate: I was to be locked up with all the dafties!

Looking in absolute horror at the two men, then at my parents, I screamed 'Mammy! Daddy! I did, I really did see a monkey in the wood yesterday, please believe me! Don't send me to the moich kier [mad house].'

'Now, now, bairn, calm yourself, nobody's sending you any place,' said one of the men. 'We came down from the hospital to tell you that there's a patient of ours who pretends to be animals. Some days he thinks he is a lion, and can be heard roaring in the wood, then he likes to imitate a dog, and barks and whimpers. He is quite harmless, lass, he wouldn't hurt a fly.'

'So that was my monkey then, was it?'

'Yes, that is his favourite beastie,' said the other man.

'Well, I can think of another description than harmless. Do you know he's got me grounded for weeks?'

I could feel my mouth going quite dry, as I realised the wee monkey was really a man.

Daddy was looking at me, and I could see by his eyes he was sorry for not believing me. He took my hand, gave it a squeeze, and a soft smile spread across his face. My parents thanked the two men, saying their visit had made a wee lassie very happy, meaning I could get on with my rake.

When the men had gone we all looked at each other and burst out laughing. The very idea of a wee man-cum-monkey sitting happy on the dyke with a fag in its mouth, and the change of a ten bob note in its pocket, was a thought and a half, right enough.

Lochgilphead and I did not too bad with my rake, because I filled the jute sack to overflowing. We weren't near a scrappy, but the travelling man camped along the beach gave me a full three pounds for the sackful. One pound more than Queen's at Pitlochry, my usual scrap dealer, gave me. So, apart from the monkey man incident, the Lochgilphead visit proved economically fruitful, I'm glad to say.

§

May was coming to an end, but before we said our goodbyes to the relatives, there unfolded another wee tale with a tail, and this time my father was the one who had to do the explaining!

12

MOUDIE'S FATE

The whole of the countryside was spotted with moudiehills—molehills to those of you not accustomed to the term used by northern folks. 'I've promised the factor to do the moles up and over yonder by the Big Hoose. Do you want to come, Jess?' asked my father, trying to make amends for not believing my tale about wee monkey-man.

'No thanks, there's no way I am going anywhere near thon place, you never know what form the ape man will take today. No, I'll bide on the beach, if that's all right, Dad!'

Janey and Shirley laughed, but he soon wiped the smiles off their faces when he ordered them to come and help. Excuses were ignored —lump it or like it, they were going.

Truth was, on my part it wasn't just the monkey-man that stopped me going with my father. I had no stomach for mole extermination. The knowledge a death was taking place, every time my Dad poked the mound of earth and dropped in yon awfy Cymax stuff, made my flesh creep. That by itself was bad enough, but you'll never guess what was used to make it tasty to wee Moudie—worms were rolled in it. Now, I ask you, was that not an abomination? Innocent worms rolled in poison, then dropped into a mole's den, awful!

To me, as a youngster, a mole was no different from a dog, a cow, aye, or even a bairn itself. The poor wee moudies didn't stand a chance. Being honest, I'm certain Daddy took a scunner to killing them, but a living had to be made and we had to eat.

'The beastie dies quick,' he'd say. I was never certain if that remark was to convince him or the listener! To sway himself further he'd add, 'If you seen the damage they do after they tunnel through miles of arable land, then perhaps you'd be getting rid as well.'

Breakfast over with, beds made, bus tidied, Mammy in among the soap-suds taking advantage of a braw west coast wind (first thing on rising she always pulled back the curtain to check if the day's wind was strong enough to dry her washing), found me and my wee sisters beach-combing.

Moudie-man (Daddy) and his helpers headed off towards the fields surrounding the Big Hoose.

'Ouch! a midge bit me,' cried Janey, swatting her arm.

'Look, lassie, there's no midges until the may's out, and fine you know, ya bisom ya.' Daddy was certain the pair would not undermine his authority, so he reminded them that the buds of the hawthorn bush (may) hadn't even showed themselves, let alone flowered. 'It will be the end of May before you see yon bonnie flower. Then there's at least a week or two before the odd midge bites, so you're working me if you think I'll fall for that yin!'

'I felt a bite from something too, Daddy!' Shirley felt duty-bound to back up her sister.

'Look, you two, it's a windy day! No insects, all right! Now give me over the poison and shut your mouths.'

My reluctant sisters moaned and moaned, until poor Daddy, sick to the eyebrows, ushered them out of his sight. 'Away and content yourselves beneath yon laburnum tree,' he said, pointing at the hillside further on where the spreading tree drooped its branches. 'I'd get on better doing the bloody job myself!'

They had won, and in doing so put him in a cracker of a mood. Now, whenever Daddy went into one of his moods, he talked constantly to himself. I think it was his way of dampening his temper. 'Only women get me this roused,' he would say to folk.

The lassies laughed and giggled as they lay under the shade of the big yellow umbrella tree, looking over at Daddy getting more and more roused because Mother Nature had cursed him with useless women instead of hardy sons!

Well, maybe that thought was one for the minute, because he

was usually proud of his daughters, and told everybody so, but not on this day for sure. No, they were getting the lashings of his tongue for not partaking of the moudie-kill.

Now, reader, I want you, if you will, to put this picture in your head: a bunneted man with a tin and a stick. In the distance a shady laburnum tree. Now the man proceeds to poke the stick into a molehill, at the same time telling some wee wriggly worms inside the tin that they were necessary to entice Mr Mole. While he is pouring powdered worms from the tin into the molehill, every now and then he gives the tree dog's abuse!

Well, I ask you, if you happened to be a couple of nurses having a fly fag round the back of the Big Hoose, what would you think on seeing our bunneted hero, eh? Aye, that's right. That is exactly what they did! With my Daddy protesting all the way into the asylum!

My older sisters had a bit of explaining and convincing to do, before they eventually got the male nurses to believe them that their father wasn't an inmate-to-be.

You can imagine the laughter our Dad's wee bit bother caused when Mammy and the rest of us found out.

'If you were kept in, Daddy, just think on the fun you and yon monkey could have, lowping among the trees!' I joked.

'That's done it, no more moudie-hills for me,' protested Daddy, adding, 'did you see the width of yon nurses' forearms? They were like ham shanks. Mighty me, Jeannie, if the lassies weren't there I'd have had a devil of a job explaining my way out of that!'

'Aye, I suppose they're good for something then, Charlie, these useless women of yours.'

That night as we tried to sleep, the laughter from our parents' 'courie-doon' kept us awake into the early hours.

We left Lochgilphead the next day. I think the family had had enough episodes with yon place, the Big Hoose.

§

Talking about 'episodes', have you ever wondered where soap operas originated?

Well, remember I told you about Uncle Wullie Murison's tales of Jake the Adventurer? You don't? Well, let me enlighten you, friend.

When night came and time for bed, traveller bairns were no different from any other kind of wean. Fighting and pushing each other for the best bit at the burnside to wash off the day's grime, after a wrestling match for control of the 'Lifebuoy' soap, that is.

A drink of creamy milk, a handful of broken biscuits and the fun began. I used to envy the weans who summered in tents, because, weather permitting, they got to lay with their heads sticking out, enjoying the crack from the campfire. I, on the other hand, was shut inside the bus. So imagine my joy when Auntie Jessie would make room in beside my cousin Anna's tent for one more body.

Some nights we were all hyped up, and carried on so much we couldn't sleep—singing, telling jokes, whatever. This annoyed the big folks because we took over much of the evening, denying them their time for relaxation. This, then, was when the Master Storyteller took control. He was my favourite Uncle Wullie, with his tales of Jake the Adventurer! Gathering us into a circle round his feet, he proceeded to hold each of us spellbound.

'Hanging from a slippy, slimy, ledge, a thousand feet below him giant crocodiles snapped and cracked hungry jaws and waited to devour brave Jake. His strong hands slipped, fingers loosened one by one until he hung by only the wee pinkie of his left hand, then by his pinkie nail, then, with a last attempt with his free hand, he grabbed a hanging vine, which just happened to blow his way.'

We sat on our hands and pushed them into the earth, as if vainly willing the brave Jake to save himself, when our storyteller would say, 'Goodnight bairns!'

'Och! Uncle, tell us what happens next, please, please, please,' we screamed out, prompting our mothers to shuffle on their seats, obviously displeased that Wullie was having the opposite affect on us kids than they wanted.

'The morra, I'll tell you all tomorrow,' he said, rising to his feet and walking off into the dark.

Protest followed protest, but nothing doing, we had to wait until the following night. We were still protesting when he wandered back from relieving himself in the nearby wood. 'I told you, when I say tomorrow I mean it. It's big folks' time now.' Then he'd add, 'But remember, only if you behave yourselves. If I hear that any of you have been bad weans, then the lot of you will be put to bed "Jakeless"!'

Can you imagine what fate awaited the bairn who misbehaved, thus causing the rest of us to be denied the next thrilling episode?

The following night found angelic children sitting round Uncle Wullie, eagerly waiting the concluding episode.

'Where was I?' he asked us.

'Crocodiles! Snap-happy crocs!' I shouted.

'No, he was hanging from his left pinkie nail!' Anna cried out.

'No, you're all wrong, it was the vine, the blowing-in-the-wind vine!' said cousin Wullie, who then almost choked himself on a broken biscuit.

Uncle Wullie's eyes scanned each of us to see if we had paid attention from the night before, paused, then said, 'Yes, the vine, well done ma lad. He grabbed the vine and pulled himself up from the wet, slippy ledge. As he lay on the ground peching, a roar from the jungle like nothing on this Earth told him to get a move-on! The giant tiger, the one with a permanent toothache, was on the growl, and needed something to rip!

Jake knew if he ran to the right, he'd run into sore jaws, and if he went left the snake people were sure to catch him—those crawling, disgusting, green and yella snakey folk.

Well, weans, what direction did he go?'

'Left, left! Snake folk are no threat to our Jake!' Anna screamed.

'No, he could escape no probs from yon tiger, he went right!' said I.

Again Uncle Wullie paused, drawing in a big breath, and we all did the same, thinking Jake's fate was now to be decided. Then our rotten uncle would sicken us by pulling the plug, saying, 'Now, if you lot do as good the morra as you did today, then you'll find out, all right kids?'

There was only so much suspense us children could take to bed with us, so we began to chant, 'Tell us what happens, tell us please.' Our teller of tales rose slowly to his feet, obviously to visit the loo. When he got back we were still unbedded, in a circle, waiting to find out the fate of Jake, the intrepid man of steel. But no, we would have to go to bed and wait until the next night.

'Och! Uncle Wullie, that's not fair, come on, just a wee bit more please,' we pleaded.

He gazed round us and thankfully relented. 'Well now, let me think, I suppose another five minutes.'

'Yippee, great, yon tiger and snake folk little know what's about to happen to them, isn't that right?'

'Well, let's see, did he go yin or yan? Neither, because with the length of time spent hanging, the blood was all in his feet, so what happened when he stood up?'

We gazed at each other, bottom lips dropping by the instant, dumbed and numbed.

'Jake fell down and banged his brow. Wallop!'

'Oh no!' we cried in unison.

' "Where am I?" he thought, as he picked himself off the jungle floor. Too late, the snake folk caught him.' This brought us closer to Uncle Wullie's feet.

'Hanging upside down from a banana tree, tied tightly by another vine, he caught sight of something slithering through the elephant grass. Well, blow me, a bloody big snake was giving him the evil eye. It was the queen slime of the jungle.

Anaconda looked up at Jake with hungry jaws, and said "I've seventy-five babies to feed. You'll keep them quiet for an hour or so!" But before she devoured our hanging-upside-down adventurer, a great big striped tiger came bounding up the jungle path. It was sore-mouthed and growling mad. "You can forget him, Annie Conda! He's my supper!" '

'He's had it now!' I called out.

'He'll get free, nothing can get our Jake, isn't that so, Uncle?' asked a traveller bairn who'd joined our group, a stranger, yet already he looked upon our uncle as his own.

'Well, bairns, that's what the morra will tell us. Off with you to bed!'

This, then, was the Master Storyteller at work. The Jake tale went on and on, night after night, and when it became time to part, yes, Jake's fate hung in the balance, continued either in the following campsite, or the next year.

Did Jake get too old? No! Did he fall foul of his enemies? No! What did happen to our hero?

I'm sorry, folks, but I haven't a clue.

Truth be, Uncle Wullie made him up each night as he went along, with our help if we but knew it! Each time he asked us what happened the night before, he wasn't seeing if we'd remembered through paying attention. It was because he knew one of us would remind him.

When my own children were little I too found Jake a grand

help at bedtime, and just the other night I heard my son tell Jake's Adventures to his own wee lad. You never know, but maybe some bairn took our Uncle's tales and turned the idea into what we now call soaps.

13

THE PIPER

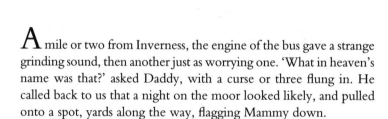

A mile or two from Inverness, the engine of the bus gave a strange grinding sound, then another just as worrying one. 'What in heaven's name was that?' asked Daddy, with a curse or three flung in. He called back to us that a night on the moor looked likely, and pulled onto a spot, yards along the way, flagging Mammy down.

'Wait to see her face when she finds out the bus is broken!' said Shirley.

The wait didn't take long; when she heard the news, like thunder it was!

'Charlie, if you think I'm biding on Culloden Moor think again. Drive further up to Inverness.'

'Well, lass, I would if the bus would, but for some reason it's not very happy today, so we'll bide the night here.'

She gave him one of her sour looks, tutted, then set about preparing a fire.

Culloden Moor and yon great but awful historical event that changed Scotland forever was the subject of many a traveller's campfire conversation, especially those from the Inverness area. There was always some hardy cratur who laid claim to being part of a line traced back to the battle itself.

'My Mother's great-great-granddad fought an' died for freedom's sword!' were words I heard myself, from an old Inverness man who camped beside us once.

The battle stories told to Mammy by her own folks when she was a child upset her. This was the reason she felt so edged whilst biding anywhere near the moor. There was of course another reason, that the strawberries were ripening down at Blairgowrie, and she never missed the early ones because they made the best jam!

Next day she and the older lassies went hawking, leaving Daddy to fix the engine—or else! Try as he might, though, the fault could not be found. Mammy arrived back muttering something like, 'The country hantel were not parting with much this fine day,' meaning she had had a bad morning round the doors. This, coupled with the broken-down bus, told me her mood wouldn't improve. That in mind, I took my wee sisters onto the moor for a play. After all, it meant nothing to children who Prince Charlie was or, to that matter, a Jacobite warrior neither! No, it was just another place for play, that's all.

We played hide and seek, wearied of that, then I-spy, but apart from sky, trees and purple heather, there wasn't that much to spy, not even a bird. You would think on a moor this size there would be plenty birds, but unusually birdless was Culloden. Apart from a screeching seagull flying high up in the clear blue, there was no other bird-sound. Strange that, do you not think?

So before long, boredom got hold and the wee ones began girning. Now, when I was a wean I could be a devil when boredom got the better of me, so in went the imagination and out went sense. Yes, you're right in what you're thinking, because that's what I did—I 'frightened and annoyed my wee sisters'.

'You know this, you two?' I said, gathering us into a circle, 'I heard two wizened wives cracking with Mammy one day, they said the moor is haunted by a giant Heilander who runs along a sheep track through the heather.'

'Is he wild and dangerous, Jessie?' asked Renie, glancing in every direction.

'Well, you know I never listen to words from the big folks' mouths, but one said, and I strained my lugs to hear this, that many a traveller who went onto the moor was never seen again!'

'Never?' asked Babsy.

'Not a single hair!' I said, fingering her thick pigtails. God, I wasn't half laying it on.

'Was it us kind of travellers?' said Renie, who by now was visibly shaking at the knees.

'Any kind, if they just happened tae be out when "Red Donald" was zigzagging along the sheep track.'

'Oh my, did you hear them say what he looked like, Jess?'

'Well, Renie, Mammy sank me a look and told me to go and play, but before I did I heard one wife say that the said lad had long bushy hair, spark-red it was. One staring green eye, on account of the other being scooped from its socket by a redcoat's sword. The wife said he stood seven feet tall, but not according to her pal, for she said he was nearer nine feet, and she swore by it!'

Wee Babsy was getting more and more frightened, as she darted her stare at the least noise. She clung on to my arm with her wee hands, trembling at the lip. I thought maybe I'd gone too far and had best tell them that I was only pretending, but I couldn't resist one last kiddy-on.

'He could well be eyeing us this very minute, lying on his belly watching to see if we're all alone. Oh, and another thing you best know just in case, he has a faithful hound who, during the Battle o' Culloden, ripped the throats from twenty hundred enemy sodgers! Now I ask you, what kind of a dog was that, eh?'

'He'd use us like raggity dolls then. We're away home—come on, Babsy!'

My, oh my, I'd gone too far. I might have known that these two feardies would go mental. 'Come back, I was only pulling your legs.'

Renie took off across the moor, dragging screaming Babsy by the hand and shouting back, 'You're a pig, wait till Mammy knows you've been scaring us. She's in a bad enough mood already. She'll kill you—I hope she does.' Then she added, 'You had better watch your back, for the devil loves a liar!'

'I've done it now,' I thought. 'Best stay away until things quieten down; I'll be well skelpit if I go back too soon.'

So off I wandered and played at rock skip (jumping from one rock to another without touching the earth between), but I slipped and walloped my bum on a right sharp stone, putting a stop to that. I looked for grouse feathers, but finding none made me think that perhaps the moor was haunted, and any decent hen flew across the place rather than rear a chick near there! I lay in a heather clearing staring up at the cloud-scattered sky. One fluffy cloud made me think of a castle with Lion Rampant flags flying from granite turrets. Two clouds were heading for each other like big fat wrestlers, emerging into an explosion of cotton wool! Little clouds chased each other across the sky like baby cherubs needing fed. I watched them until my eyes filled with water as they met the glare of the sun's rays. This brought me to my feet. Rubbing away the watery tears I caught sight of someone standing in front of me.

I rubbed my eyes again. The sight turned me to jelly, and brought a trickle of pee running down my leg.

For there was the very vision I had conjured up in my mind to frighten the life from my wee sisters. Red Donald himself! The devil loves a liar right enough. He'd sent me my lie in truth.

I slid onto my knees, numbed and speechless, I was at his mercy. The only part of me that moved was my eyes.

He stood tall, this ghost, in full Highland dress, Glengarry perched on the side of his head sporting a long feather and the white cockade of a great chieftain warrior. His plaidy hung over his shoulder, held at the chest by a large silvery crest.

I regained enough movement to clasp my hands together and murmur a prayer: 'Lord, pick me up an' run with me back to Daddy, for I am a dead duck when Red Donald whistles on his hound!'

The big man said nothing as he reached for something concealed in the heather.

Fear gave way to terror as I squealed, 'Please don't cut the head off me Donald, I am a good wean really!'

'What in blazes are you whelping about lassie?'

'Yon wild dog, is it hiding ready to rip my throat?'

With a bewildered stare he shook his head and continued about his business. 'I have no animal to speak of, I'm here to play my pipes as I do every year.'

'Are you not a ghost? Did you not fight alongside Bonnie Prince Charlie? My Dad's cried after him you know!'

'Ha, ha, a ghost indeed! I fought side by side with many a Charlie but none so Royal. Now you away home, your mother must wonder where you are. I take it there's a mother?'

'God,' I thought, 'a mother indeed, and she'll kill me, for sure it must be late, and no doubt the wee ones will have told her everything.' Still, this man fascinated me and I had to know more.

'So you're a real man? That's a relief, I can tell you, sir. Was I not saying to my sisters earlier a wild demon haunted this moor, and he was the spit of yourself.'

Once again the bewildered look spread across his face followed by a wide grin: 'Red Donald, ha!'

With the fear gone I was able to relax, and to wonder at why he came so far out of the way to play bagpipes.

He lifted his concealed pipes from the heather and placed them to his mouth. After two or three drones, he began to play the most beautiful music. I'd heard many a piper, but Lordy, this was the McCoy, I can tell you. He certainly knew his stuff, this look-a-like Jacobite ghost! On and on he played in the June heat, which must have been melting him for it was me, and me wearing only a vest and thin cotton shorts.

I listened to the man for ages before my empty belly told me it was way past time for making tracks back. I hoped Mammy's mood would be improved, and that she'd forgotten I'd frightened the wee ones. Maybe not! But if I took the piper back with me and said the poor cratur was dying with the thirst, perhaps I'd escape the wallops. I thought it worth a try.

'You must have an awfy drouth on yourself, piper. How does a grand cup o' tea and buttery scone sound to you?'

'It tells me a lassie shouldn't be so friendly with strange men, that's what I think. Don't your folks tell you it's wrong to speak with strangers? Get away home with you!'

'But surely you're thirsty?'

'That will keep till I get into Inverness. Now I'm losing my rag. I'll not tell you again, be off with you!'

I could see it was pointless trying to persuade him, so waving cheerio I shouted out, 'Well, here's hoping my Dad's got the bus engine fixed, I hate this creepy, dead place.'

'What did you say lassie?' he seemed to perk up at my mentioning the bus. 'Bus, did you say?'

So, after I'd told him all about our bus-home and engine being broke, the man said, 'I know a thing or two about buses, what kind is it?'

I knew everything about the bus and proudly answered, '1948 Bedford, with a long chassis, oh, and a Vauxhall engine!'

'Right then, wee lassie with the curly black hair, let's see this bus of yours.'

Arriving back I took one look at Mammy's face, and fine knew a wallop was coming with my supper. So, as quick as you like,

I got my bit in first: 'This is a piper who is dying of the drouth, Mam. I found him out on the moor, poor cratur asked me for a drap tea.'

Mammy looked at the heavily tartan-clad man and said, 'You're not to listen to my lassie. She'd do anything rather than take the licking that's due her.'

I thought the back o' the hand was heading my way, when, to my surprise, my 'ghost' said, 'Och, not at all, missus. This wee lass told me she had the best mother in all the world, but was a bit upset 'cause her Mam was missing the strawberries. She wondered if I might cheer you up with a blaw on the pipes.'

'Aye well, the difference between me and you, lad, is I know this wee madam and you don't. There's nothing she wouldn't do to escape a well-deserved leathering, but that will come later. Get you down and fill the kettle at the burn.' She ordered me in such a manner I knew I was for it.

Now, folks, if you could just see the size of this family heirloom and the colour of it—jet black with soot, from hundreds of years hanging over a blazing fire. A great muckle brute that took two hands to carry it, and blackened both legs into the bargain. But given the circumstances, who was I to protest? 'Will I fetch the milk you have cooling in the burn as well, Mammy?'

'Stop grovelling,' she said, 'Mary will get it.'

The piper, obviously more interested in my father's injured engine than my fate, walked over to Daddy who was elbow to thumb in sticky black oil, and within minutes the two were among the engine parts good style.

As I made my way back with the kettle, a sound I never thought I'd hear that day filled all our ears as the bus roared back to life. Mammy's face lit up like the North Star.

'Well done, piper,' Daddy thanked him, 'I never would have put it down to a wee bit bolt like that.'

Mammy hugged the life from the poor lad, as she forced him onto her cushioned stool and shoved a plate of hot buttered scones on his lap. 'You eat and drink your fill. If anybody deserves a bit menses, then it's you, my hardy piper.'

He didn't half enjoy those scones, downed with near on half the kettle of tea. I kept close to him, hoping Mammy would forget my leathering. After all, was it not due to me things had turned out so well that day? A little whisper in my ear from Dad, that she'd forgiven me, answered things.

Later, when everyone had eaten, I told my folks about how beautifully our guest played the pipes.

'Piper, would you start a ceilidh for us?' I asked him, touching his pipe box.

Mammy drew her Jew's harp from her skirt pocket and joined him. Daddy diddled Babsy on his knee as the rest of us sang and danced, while night drew in all round on sad Culloden Moor. I hoped the ghosts were enjoying our wee shindig. It would make a difference from the greeting and wailing that usually took place among the heather from followers of the battle.

Two hours later, the tired man folded his pipes away, saying it was time he was on his way. Mammy offered him a bed. He thanked her but refused, saying he'd things to be getting on with. Before saying his goodbyes, I just had to ask him why, in heaven's name, did he go onto the moor and play the pipes in the June heat? I felt humbled and a bit saddened by his answer.

'It's for all Scots lads who lost their lives in every battle since 1746. And where better than the wild Culloden Moor where so many fell defending and conserving the culture of this little country of ours!'

I felt guilty that, in my efforts to frighten my sisters, I had in my childish way used such sacred ground to gain a cheap laugh, but being a child, what did I know? From that day I never did such a thing again. My Jacobite ghost had taught me a solemn lesson.

'When you've done the dishes, lassies,' said Daddy, 'instead of going to bed we'll head on down to Blair.'

'Oh, I never asked the piper his name,' said Mammy.

'I think I heard him say Red Donald.' I said, smiling.

'Aye, would that be the same wild Heilander who runs along a sheep track swiping the heads off travellers?'

'Not at all, Mammy, where did you get such a ridiculous idea?'

'Where indeed, ye wee devil.'

That night while we slept Daddy trundled the long road to Blair, so that Mammy could pick her strawberries.

We were to run into my 'Red Donald' several times after that. Heading through the Pass of Glen Coe, we saw him blawing away to the tourists. Another time we glanced him high up on the Rest

And Be Thankful. And I'm certain the stirring pipes of the said lad were heard as we passed through Lochaber (Fort William) on our way to Spean Bridge.

I remember a wee old man about five feet tall who, like my piper, used to play in memory of the fallen of wars gone by. I met him at the point of the Devil's Elbow. I called him 'Arras'.

Arras was a town in France where many, many Scots lads made the final sacrifice defending the town in the Great War. He told me that two Scottish divisions, the 15th and the 51st, lost hundreds. His three brothers among them. He told me this little poem before we parted.

> *In the burgh toon o' Arras,*
> *When gloaming had come on,*
> *Fifty pipers played retreat*
> *As if they had been one,*
> *And the Grande Palace o' Arras*
> *Hummed with the Highland drone!*★

After playing he would bow his head and say, 'God bless ye lads, rest in peace at Arras.' And that's the reason I called him that.

Pipers are common amongst the travelling community. Most families made sure a set of pipes were at hand, just in case a lad or lassie took up the playing. My mother's great-grandfather was a gifted piper and he hailed from Kintyre. His name was Donald John Macarthur.

★I cannot say who wrote the above verse, because I do not know, but I thank whoever did.

14

GLEN COE

Wouldn't you know it, Daddy had forgotten he'd a bit of business to attend to, before heading for Blair.

'What, surely not!' Mammy was far from amused.

'I'm right sorry, Jeannie, I clean forgot about Runty's brock wool.'

Mammy stormed off and sat herself behind the steering wheel of Fordy, peeved to the eyeballs that she'd miss the first strawberries. I wasn't too happy myself, although my mother's necessity was to boil up the early strawberries for jam, and mine was only for the gorging of them!

Runty was a farmer from Tyndrum and every year Daddy collected up his brock wool. You know all those spare bits the sheep sheds from itself and leaves on fences, tree-trunks and the likes? Fine and warm in the winter is the woolly coat, but oh dearie, the creatures can see it far enough when the June sun all but bakes them. Have you seen a sheep rubbing itself on an old coarse tree, or a favourite fence-post? Have you also noticed how much loose wool lies around the fields? Well, that was another job the farmer needed traveller men to do for him, gathering the stuff in. There wasn't payment for this laborious job that came from selling the bagged wool on to the rag merchant, and given we're talking about pure wool, well, a few bob was made! Both parties benefited: farmers' fields were left clean, and the travellers fed the family for a month or two, depending on their prudence.

So then, to reach Runty's farm, we had the great pleasure of trundling through the mighty Glen Coe! I swear on my Granny's rest, no other place in the whole of Scotland can take precedence over this magnificent glen. We stopped at the roadside for dinner, and for a well-needed 'pee' behind a rock cluster.

'Well, bairns' said Mammy, 'if Daddy has the brock to do I want every one of you, sleeves up and all hands together, the quicker it's done the faster I'll get the strawberries.'

'Yuk! All that sheep's shit!' said my older sister, making a screwed-up face.

'Shirley, is it necessary for you to swear every time you open your mouth?' asked Daddy, washing his hands in one of the many small burns which tumbled down the mountains and flow into the river Coe.

'Och, no wonder, half the stuff is hanging from the sheep's bum,' she answered, joining him at the burn, rolling up her sleeves, then adding, 'Give us the soap please, auld yin.'

Daddy glowered at his whimsical lassie, draped the hand-towel over her head, then reminded my sister, 'God wasn't pleased the last time you came out with a mouthful like that, mind?'

Shirley cringed! Well she remembered the time a ploughman and she were arguing about her lifting heavier bags of tatties than he was. His chauvinistic attitude got her riled up! She was raring for an argument.

After giving him a volley of curses, she turned, stood on a pitch-fork handle and took a thumping great wallop to the face.

Shirley dried her hands, saying, 'Aye, all right, Dad, point taken!'

'Sure was, right on your two lips!' laughed our Janey.

Every one of us went into fits laughing, minding how for days poor Shirley had to suck sustenance through a straw.

'Now, now, that's enough, don't make fun of your sister like that,' said my mother. Mammy always calmed the waves before a storm.

Truth was, we were all looking forward to Blair, and none of us liked the brock-gathering. Shirley was right, some of the wool did smell and fingers inherited a green tinge, which took weeks of scrubbing with strong carbolic soap to remove. The only consolation was that the stuff did weigh double, a blessing indeed when time came for putting it on the scales.

Glen Coe wasn't half bonny, right enough: the mountains, each one different from the next, stretched their heads up into the clouds and beyond. I could picture God Himself, sitting up there, pleased at His creation. I bet He spent more time in Scotland than any other part of the world. I'm pretty sure He still does. How can anybody imagine this place as the setting for a massacre? For this is what historians teach about, 'the slaughter of the MacDonalds'. A horror story by any standards, that dreadful deed of murder carried out by the Campbells on the inhabitants of this beautiful, peaceful glen!

'While you're allowing the food settling-time in your bellies,' said my mother, 'I'll tell you a tale about your Granny, my own mother, and your Auntie Maggie when she was a bitty bairn. I hope it will leave you thinking about life's dangers to travellers in those days. At least it'll keep the lot of you quiet until we come to Runty's.'

This story happened at a time when Granny Power was camped a mile or two beyond the pass of Glen Coe, at the edge of Rannoch Moor. Now, there's a place that can bring the hairs to attention on the back of your neck. Ask any traveller if they know a tale or two about the place and sure enough it'll be a creepy one. Many a sleepless night I spent after a whiles round a campfire listening to ghost stories and Burker tales (stories of body-snatchers).

Was it the truth being told or not? Who can say, but it didn't half make me peer into the darkness, thinking, 'Was that a fox I heard in the undergrowth, or something creepily unnatural?'

Most stories were told by the older generation who lived in a time when there wasn't a forced law to register a birth or death. Travellers were easy prey for body-hungry scientists needing to know the ins and outs of the human form.

'Listen now, lassies, as I tell you this tale of terror, for never a truer tale was told!' said Mammy, slipping the last plate into a basin of soapy water.

'You tell the story, Jeannie, I'll wash these dishes.' Dad had heard the tale before. 'Then we'll be on our way.'

Finished eating, we gathered round our mother's feet, pushing and jostling for the best view at her face, so as not to miss a look, a gasp, or the usual closing of her eyes in apprehension that a fearful sight was coming to her mind!

'It happened before I was born,' she said. 'As my mother passed it to me, word for word I pass it to you. Take heed now, and one day you can give it to your own children.' I now share this tale, reader, with you, as my mother did all those years ago.

In the late summer of 1913, a year before the Great War, my granny and her third child, wee Maggie, were hawking in Glencoe village. Maggie was only three years old, too young to be left with sister Winnie and brother Mattie, the two oldest, at the campsite. Grandad was, as usual, sleeping off the night before's drink, and if the Devil himself brought him into hell's fire, he'd have slept through it. The night before's booze, as usual, resulted in Granny taking the brunt of his violent temper; the pain in her arm proved it. But the day's hawking had been fruitful. A bag of clothes from a kindly wife whose children had long since outgrown them, and an old lady who shared some meal and bread with her, meant that, for this day at least, they would eat.

Mattie, only six, was a braw wee fisherman. Though his hands were too small to hold large fish, he'd guddled the burn and caught several tiddlers. Left in the expert hands of eight-year-old Winnie, they were cleaned and ready for cooking whenever Granny returned.

As she sauntered home she looked upon the natural colours of the mountainside, saying to Maggie, 'Look how bonny the brown bracken mingles with the purple heather.'

She smiled at Maggie, asking if her wee feet were sore. Three miles was a long way for one so young. The bairn held her mother's hand, and nodded. 'If my arm wasn't so sore, I'd carry you awhiles, pet.'

As they came by the pass of Glen Coe the road narrowed through a gorge. At this point one leaves the mountains behind, and the vast expanse of Rannoch Moor stretches ahead.

Granny picked up an echo of a trotting horse and carriage far behind them. She'd no reason, but a sense of foreboding took hold as the sound made by the horse's hooves on the old road became louder and louder.

Turning a bend in the road Granny pushed her bairn and the pack between big rocks. 'Hide in there, my wee lamb, and not a sound, do you hear now!'

The bairn's eyes widened as she sensed her mother's apprehension.

'No matter what happens, don't show yourself—courie well down!'

Granny muttered a silent prayer that the coach and its passengers held no danger.

The coachman said nothing as he slowed his steed and passed her on the narrow road. Only a slight wave of the hand did he give. She kept her eyes fixed on his face for any sign of bad doings. No stranger could be trusted by a lone traveller woman in those days.

Before it trotted off, she saw one person, whom she took to be a man, inside the coach.

She knew a thing or two about horses: never, though, had she seen a bonnier stallion than that. All of sixteen hands at least, the mount of a gentleman; jet it was, as black as hell. The coach was adorned in brass livery, shining like a funeral carriage.

No, this fine gent would not interfere with a traveller woman and her wee one.

She felt much better and blamed the beating she received the previous night for her vulnerable feelings. Gathering up Maggie and her pack she set off on her way. 'Come on, Maggie, no need to concern ourselves. It's just a coach heading towards the hotel.'

At the spot where moor meets glen stands the King's House Hotel. Many a weary traveller has spent a night within its walls; cattlemen heading their beasts to market, some from as far away as Sutherland, gave thanks on seeing its light through a heavy snowstorm. That was two hundred years ago, and still the same warmth is given today to the tired mountaineer seeking a meal and to quench his drouth with a few beers.

As Granny and the wee lass turned the next bend in the road, a cold fear ran up her spine! Straddling her path, in the middle of the road, were the men with the black horse and coach. Her foreboding, well founded, returned!

Heart beating like a jungle drum in her chest, she knew then that they were after her!

She quickly scanned the moor for signs of help, perhaps a shepherd or even a wary poacher, but no! Only herself and Maggie shared the bleak Rannoch Moor with the fearful strangers.

'I'll hurry past, it could be they're waiting on somebody from the hotel.' That thought had little sense to it; were they not a mile from the place?

Dropping the much-needed pack she lifted Maggie, wincing at the sharp pain running up her injured arm, and hurried by. As she did so the coach door opened, a hand stretched out to grab Maggie, and their nightmare began.

They didn't want her! They wanted her little girl! Her precious child!

Ignoring the pained arm, she held her bairn tightly into her beating chest. 'Let her go, tinker, it's futile. Look round woman, there's nobody for miles!' roared the coachman, whip held ready to strike above poor Granny's head!

The coach passenger, a middle-aged man dressed in black, shouted almost level with her face, 'Give her to me, woman, we'll take her with or without your assistance!'

Big hands grabbed out at wee Maggie as she screamed in bewilderment, tiny fingers clinging to her mother with all their strength.

My Granny's arm felt like any minute it would be ripped apart! But there was no way she'd give up her child without a life-or-death struggle. 'You'll be murdering me first,' she screamed at the evil man. 'God grant a thousand curses on you for this!'

As the coachman cracked his leather whip above her head, she felt her grip on her wee lass weaken, and, for a horrifying second, it looked as if the strength of this attacker would win over her weakening grip.

Arm in agony, searing pain shooting through her body, she had to act quickly. If the wee lass were to be saved, then Granny had one last chance.

Standing close to the horse, so near she could see its eye whites and feel its hot breath against her face, she screamed at the man who would steal her child, 'Here, take the bairn if you need her so bad!'

Shoving Maggie out to the man in the coach, she added, 'Stop struggling with me, I give her to you. Do I not have a drunken bastard for a man, and two other bairns? What would one less mean to a poor woman like me?'

She knew to halt the horse the coachman would have to pull on the reins, and as he did so Granny retrieved her precious bundle and ran like the Banshee herself was after them, into the boggy ground of Rannoch Moor. She knew exactly where to go. For sure did she not have to shift herself onto the bog many times, escaping Grandad's constant beatings?

The pursuers, knowing their horse was unable to take men and coach onto the soft peaty ground, gave up the awful struggle.

Watching my fleeing grandmother skilfully dart away, they called out that they knew where she was camped and would come in the dead of night, then galloped off down the way they came, disappearing through the pass of Glen Coe!

Granny carried Maggie on her back, the injured arm hanging at her side. Arriving home, they swiftly ate the supper of fish Winnie and Mattie had prepared. She then bundled up what they could each carry, warning her vulnerable family the evil men would come in the night, and made a long weary journey to the far side of Loch Tulla. It was here her cousin Andrew and his family were camped, seven miles over the moor!

Just as the rising sun threw slivers of golden light upon the cairn of Ben Achaladair, Granny and her small flock arrived exhausted at their destination.

Grandad, on waking from his drunken sleep, did what he always did, found his usual spot (while camped on Rannoch Moor) at the bar of the hotel. Cousin Andrew took Granny to see a kindly doctor who was lodging at the Bridge o' Orchy hotel. He was in the area with a shooting party, and Andrew was beating for them.

'Your right arm is broken, wife,' he told her. 'Why did you not get it seen to earlier? It'll surely set crooked!'

'Why indeed, sir!' she answered, knowing, given her lot, this injury would not be the last! She never went back to camp on Rannoch Moor after that. Just in case a certain evil returned.

Granny and her drunkard of a husband reunited and had another seven children. Not one followed their father's wayward path!

§

'Come on Jeannie, best get moving before Runty thinks I'm not coming,' said Daddy, slipping into his usual position behind the bus steering-wheel. Mammy got into her seat behind the wheel of Fordy, our far-travelled wee van.

As we made our way along the windy road, which, since Granny's time, had now seen the covering of fine black tar, I shivered on thinking, 'what if those fiends had got Maggie, or killed my dear Granny in the process?'

I glanced over my shoulder at fingers of ghostly mist creeping in across the glen. By the silence from within the bus, it passed my mind that we were all thinking the same thing: the traveller's lot was indeed a fearful, dangerous one at times!

Three massive, heavy bags of brock wool, and many green, smelly fingers later, we headed for Blairgowrie, with another tale for you!

15

TINY

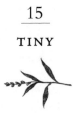

By the time we arrived at dear old Blair, every song worth singing had been given laldie, and for sure the whole lot of us were hoarse. Daddy cracked one of his droll sayings, 'Git on yer horse and gallop over to the well for water'. Mammy laughed at his attempt at imitating the great John Wayne and said, 'Tell him, lassies'.

In unison we all roared, 'Git off yer horse an' drink yer milk'. I haven't a clue if the big yankee cowboy man said that or not, but the world claimed he did, so it stuck.

'My, you're easy pleased, you lot,' said Daddy, manoeuvering the bus into its usual stance at the top end of Ponfads, the campsite on the outskirts of Rattray, on the Alyth road.

The following tale of that summer brought an addition to the family.

Tiny, a wee fox terrier, became our family pet. He was a family member when Mona left to start married life and was still around when Babsy, our youngest, did the same. I know you'll find this hard to believe, but when he passed away he had reached the age of twenty-one years. Aye, honest! When my parents stopped travelling and eventually settled into a house, he went with them. It was a sad day when the wee white dog with a black patch on one eye and brown stumpy tail died. Let me tell you how we came to be blessed with our Tiny.

When coming into the campsite, I noticed, as we drove past, a bowed camp at the far end of the green. A grand fire was blazing away, and, round an old woman nearby played three of the reddest-haired bairns I'd ever seen. No way would their mother misplace those bairns with hair like that.

After putting the tripod basin outside the bus door I skipped off to play. 'Don't you lot go too far, it'll be suppertime as soon as I get the stovies done,' Mammy reminded us as we took off in different directions to explore.

The thought of a nice big plate of steaming hot tatties, onions and corned beef made me call back, 'The hunger's on me, so don't worry, I'll be playing round the door.'

I was curious, though, and leaving my sisters playing in safe sight, I went to have a look at the bowed camp with the red-headed bairns.

This was the type of abode my folks lived in as youngsters, and it always held a fascination for me. The construction itself was an art handed down from father to son. With Scottish winters being so severe there was no room for error. If rain and draughts were allowed under those canvas structures then new-born babies and elderly parents would certainly suffer.

They were built like a skin around a ribcage. Animal skins were used originally, and later replaced by jute sacks, plastic sheeting or tarpaulin. Hazel sticks, which were formed into bows while the saplings were still young, became the skeleton for these nomadic homes. When the time came to move on, it was a simple matter of removing the cover and untying the sticks, which were all held together with a ridge pole, and piling them neatly onto the cart. Usually a small horse pulled the cart around the countryside. However, if there was no horse, the entire contents of the travellers' life were distributed onto their own sturdy backs. To add to the comfort of their tents, water was drained away by digging a shallow ditch at either side, allowing drainage water to run freely away from the floor. In winter heavy stones were used to stop strong winds blowing the cover off and away. Ropes were also used as extra security. Where two canvases joined, usually in the middle, a wee stove was secured to give heating and cooking. This was a lifesaver in the cold winters Scotland was at one time accustomed to. A long lum (chimney) was pushed through the roof to take away the smoke. Relatives told me of the ghost stories they heard as children during winter nights while huddled inside, with gales and blizzards swirling round their cosy homes of long ago.

'Hello,' I called (getting back to the tale in hand) over to the children sitting beside the old woman. They were shy wee things, and as I got nearer they couried their faces into the elderly woman's bosom.

'Hello to you', said a voice from inside the camp. At that a younger woman pushed her head out, and, deary me, she was another redhead!

'The weans are feart at strangers,' she told me.

'Och, I'm not going to hurt you,' I assured them.

'Where are you from, lassie?' asked the old woman, before adding, 'Was that you coming in on thon bus I saw a while back?'

'Yes, we travel all over in him, a grand home is the bus, and I'm a Riley from Aberfeldy.'

She took a stick from a neat pile at the side of the camp and tossed it on the fire. 'Never heard of you,' she said, turning her head towards the blaze, then added, 'B us is it? We always relied on wee Bonny. She was a grand palomino horse, but she died a week back. We have nothing now. To pull the cart, that is.'

I looked around. The horse must have brought them here, because horse tack lay across a tree adjacent to the camp. I asked who took the carcase away. She pulled her shawl over her head and went silent. I was thinking it strange that a man was absent from the group, and being a youngster I asked where the head of the family was?

'We're from Argyllshire. This is the first time we came to the Berries,' said the younger woman, brushing her long red hair as she stooped coming out of the camp. 'This is my Mam, Bella, and these wee bissoms are my chiels. Clara is the oldest, she's six, Rhorie here is a big four, aren't you my laddie, and Florrie, my baby, is three. The berry farmer kindly took our old Bonny away for us. She was over thirty, so, poor beast, was glad to go, I think. Mam loved her horse, though, and hates the thought of her not being here.' Then she freely told me that Ronald, her man, took with ill health and was no longer among us. A tear slid down her cheek. I felt guilty at my nosiness and instantly apologised, then quickly changed the subject.

'Oh, I love animals too, but we're not allowed any in case they ran under the bus and got squashed.' I turned to speak to the little ones. 'I bet you can't guess this, but I have seven sisters!' Ice broken, the bairns took to me straight away. I was fascinated by their hair colour. I wanted to take the little ones up to our pitch and show them to the folks and my sisters. 'Can I take them up to meet my wee sisters?' I asked.

'Na, na, lass,' said old Bella, 'it's nearing their bed-time. The morra's morning you're welcome back.' That said, she rose from the fireside and crawled into the tent.

'Aye, see you in the morning, pet,' said the children's mother, who told me her name was Isa. They waved me goodbye, as one by one they followed their granny into the camp for the night.

'Oh, Jessie,' called Bella, 'before you go would you like a peek at my wee dog's pups?'

Given my love of animals, nobody had to ask me that twice. The old woman gently held back the door to display a tender sight. Lying curled up beside their mother were four of the smallest pups I had ever seen.

'My, what wee they are,' was all I could say.

'The old dog is nearing her end,' whispered Isa. 'You know she's had a wayn of litters in her life, but I fear this last one will kill her.'

The poor old dog did look fairly peched, and didn't bat an eye-lid when I lifted up the nearest pup, a black and white ball of fluff. But this one didn't catch my attention. No, it was the smallest one. Snugly sucking away at its mother's milk, no bigger than my fist, a wee white cratur with a black patch covering the right eye, who looked at me.

All I could say was, 'My, you're tiny!' I gently laid the other wee mite beside his mother and looked round the camp. I told old Bella my folks lived their early years in the bowed camp. I was surprised to see how well constructed it was. Being that there was no man, these two women certainly knew their stuff.

Sitting round the blazing fire, tucking into my stovie supper, I told Mammy all about my new-found friends, and the pups of course.

'Don't you be bothering folk now, Jess. I saw thon old woman and she didn't look in the best of health—give her peace, and don't be running in and out the camp.'

As I washed for bed I promised my mother to do as she said. That night I filled my dreams with the bonnie tottie dog that slept beneath the canvas of the old bow camp, and further dreamt that he was mine.

For the next week the strawberry-picking was in full swing, and wherever I went the three red-headed weans came with me. The pups grew strong and I became more and more attached to Tiny. But when I mentioned him to Mammy she said 'No!'

'Keeping a dog in a house is fine enough, but it would be cruel in a bus,' she said, then added, 'I'd be forever tramping on the animal.'

Saturday morning after breakfast, I skipped off to take my new-found pals out for a play. Strange it was, when I arrived, to see the fire not lit. And why was the old woman not up and about? I stood at the closed camp doorway and quietly called to Isa.

'Wait there the now, Jess, I'll be out in a minute.' After a while she appeared and I noticed she'd been crying.

'Is there something up with one of the bairns?' I asked, concerned. She didn't answer, because a moan from within the camp had her dashing back inside. My concern had me intruding, as I gently leant down and pulled back the door. 'Can I help, what's wrong?' I asked again.

'Mam isn't the best this morning, lass. Do you think you could away and fetch your mother for me?' Isa looked frightened. I had seen that look before whenever folks were really poorly.

As fast as my legs could carry me, I ran home. Mammy was busy washing and was up to her elbows in soap-suds. 'Old Bella's not well this morning,' I told her, 'her lassie Isa needs help.' I was out of breath. Mammy could see something was wrong. She quietly stopped her chores, dried her hands and took off her wet apron.

'Now Jess,' she said softly, 'you dress the weans and light a fire, fill Isa's kettle and put it over the heat to boil.'

Without question I obeyed my mother. I then took the bewildered wee ones up to the bus, where I gave them each a plate of porridge. After I had wiped little Florrie's face we all went back to see how Bella was progressing.

'Come in, one at a time,' said my Mother.

I was puzzled, what was wrong? I had enough sense, though, to see this was big folks' ways of doing. So, without question, I ushered each wean in, then out, before asking if I could come in. Mammy took my hand, pulling me onto my knees as I went in. The old woman's colour was drained white. Isa was sobbing into a flannel cloth, at the same time holding her mother's hand to her face.

Bella turned slowly to look at me. With a faint gesture she pointed to her feet where the old dog and her sleeping pups lay. 'Take the yin with the black patch, bonny lass, it's yours,' she said in a whisper.

I looked at my mother and she nodded. I was confused. She was adamant about no dogs, yet here she was, giving approval for the very thing I had been denied.

She ushered me out, saying in a whisper: 'Take the wee ones away to play. At dinner time take them up and feed them at the bus with soup from the big pot.' Before I could question her as to why it was necessary to keep them away she added, 'Here's a bob, buy sweeties.'

All I could think was, this poor old woman is awfy sickly if I'm getting all this money for sweets. Little did I, or the weans, know just how sick Bella really was.

We played 'hide-and-seek' in the high berry drills, stopping every now and then to pop a juicy berry in our mouths, laughing at the way the red juice ran down our cheeks. Soon we forgot about the drama back in the bow camp as, like bairns the world over, we played.

Soon though, they tired of eating berries and playing in the high drills. So with the shilling Mammy gave me I knew the very thing that would bring smiles, a braw big tin of condensed milk. Off to the bothy shop with my shilling and my wee flock following behind, to devour the contents of heaven itself. But as we sat in a circle on a patch of clover it dawned on me we needed a tin-opener. I told my flock of hungry bairns we'd have to go back to the bus and get one.

'Not necessary,' said Clara, 'I have the very thing.' Pushing her thin fingers inside a concealed pocket in her shorts, she pulled out a rusty nail. Without a word she ran her hand across the ground and picked up a medium-sized stone

'Well done,' I said, as I hammered the dirty nail into the top of the tin.

In no time the thick, sweet, glue-like milk was spewing from the holes, and each of us in turn sucked and licked to our heart's content. Florrie, though, because of her age, just hadn't mastered the art of sooking. This resulted in half her ration disappearing up her nose. We were in fits of giggles watching her wee tongue try to lick the contents of her nose along with the sweet, creamy milk.

When time came to eat my mother's big pot of soup they had little appetite. Hardly surprising really.

By late afternoon they were all played out and wearied for their mother. I had no choice but to take them home. 'Perhaps the hours of peace from the bairns would have done her good, and she'd be a little better,' I thought.

'Poor Bella must still be poorly,' I said to myself when I noticed the fire was still out. 'Wait the now, bairns,' I told the children, 'I'll see if your granny is sleeping.'

Gently pulling back the door-cover, I whispered, 'Is it all right to come in?'

'Here Jess,' said my mother, handing me a cardboard box with the sleepy pups huddled together. I did as I was told and sat the puppy box down on the grass.

Isa came out, said nothing and reached for her bairns, holding them in to her breast. I looked over her head at a sight that comes vividly into my mind even now. Bella was covered over by a blanket. Unable to stop myself I pulled the cover from her face. 'She'll suffocate,' I shouted out. Mammy squeezed my hand and whispered in my ear that Bella had died, then lifted me away from the old woman's death-bed. I took one last look before dashing outside. She was grey-coloured. Her eyelids half shut, chin resting on her chest. So this was how dead folks looked!

My mother slipped her arm through mine and said, 'Come now, pet, let's leave this family to their grief.' She then added, picking up the pups, 'I'll have to get homes for these dogs.' I wondered why she didn't take the bitch as well, and asked her so.

'The strangest thing,' she said. 'The minute the old woman went, the bitch went with her. The old dog just gave a heavy sigh, stretched her legs and died! Now, my God, was that not a way of doing, Jess!' She shook her head, repeating, 'My God, a strange way indeed!'

Thinking on my mother's previous promise I peered in the box to see if Tiny was still there. 'You're not giving my wee one away, Mam, are you?' I asked, thinking she only had said I could have it to keep the dying woman content.

'No, don't fret, lassie, you should know me better. When I make a promise, I keep it.'

'Great, I've got a dog!' I said, forgetting for an instant the sadness back inside the bowed camp.

'No, Jessie, the pup belongs to the family, although I don't want it under my feet, mind!'

'Mammy, it's not the size of tuppence, you'll not even know it's there,' I said, as I squeezed my mother's arm with excitement.

'You don't know what size it'll grow to, lassie,' she answered, shaking her head.

'He'll be tiny, Mam, I have a feeling.'

'Never mind that just now,' she said. 'A doctor has to be brought in and relatives to be contacted. Isa asked me to go into Blair and get the polis to contact the minister at Appin church. He'll find her brother Wullie. His last known address was somewhere near the coastal village.'

My mother then fixed me with her 'this is important' stare and said, 'Now, lass, a death has taken place here this day, so away and tell as many bairns as you can to mind their wheest!'

Travelling folks have a mountain of respect for the dead, and as old Bella rested peacefully that Saturday at the Berries, a pin would have been heard dropping.

Next day I was up with the dew to look after Isa's sad weans, but when I went to where the camp was they were gone, and I ran back hoping my mother could tell me where they were.

'Mammy, the camp, old Bella's body, God rest her soul, and everybody have gone, where are they?'

'Well, lass, I expect the polis managed to get Isa's brother Wullie, because before day broke a lorry driven by a red-headed man arrived and took everything away. They've gone.' Mammy continued, 'the heart-broken woman came up to thank us, said if we were in Argyll we were to visit them.'

After breakfast I wandered down to the spot where the camp had been pitched. Only the flattened grass and the burned circle made by the fire were still to be seen. There was one other thing, though—a wee cross where they'd taken the time before leaving to bury Tiny's mother, the tired old bitch.

As promised, my mother found good homes for the three remaining pups. One went to a ploughman's daughter, a bonny lassie with a calipered leg. The other two found good homes with rat-catchers.

After that year's berry-picking was over, we trundled up to visit awhiles with a farmer friend at Balquhidder. Come with us, and I'll introduce you.

16

JAMIE'S REST

Being so young, Death and his ways seldom spent a whiles in my head, but as I thought on the old woman who I had come to know, albeit briefly, I wondered where she would rest. I had visited the odd graveyard with Mammy and watched her, with bowed head, say a soft prayer over the departed relative sleeping peacefully beneath the soil.

The little marble stone carved with their name made certain folks know where exactly the grave was. What, though, if no such marker existed? How would one know where to put the flowers or pay respects on birthdays or any special event? This nagging thought prompted me to ask Mammy if there were any places she knew that didn't have headstones. Like the olden days of the poorhouse, or battlefields: what happened to the bodies that lay about peckit by the craws?

No, she had no such knowledge, but she did know a tale of a 'Tinkers' Graveyard', and she said there was no place more honourable than yon holy ground. If it's comfortable ye are, then I'll begin.

§

In certain travelling families—or tinkers as some Highlanders called them—kept secret from all but their own was the last resting place, the ancestral burial ground. If death came prematurely, and the family were far away, then a long journey awaited the departed and the grievers back to the resting place. I cannot disclose the names of the folks in my tale; I hope you will understand, and respect my reasons for doing so.

Jamie was a proud tinker laddie who waved farewell to his parents as he set off to join his fellow Scots on the battlefields of France in the year of 1914, the time of the Great War. Tinkers were treated like vermin in those days, but they still fought alongside many, and fell alongside them as well. A soldier once wrote: 'generals', privates', dogs', and tinkers' blood mingles in the earth, an' nane can tell the difference.' Notice the tinker is listed below a dog. They lie in foreign lands, having given the final sacrifice for their country, and only the folks back home grieve with respect.

Jamie, though, was the exception, for he soon shone above others for his friendly mannerisms, strength, and bravery. All his comrades liked him, as he told jokes and helped the injured in those awful mud-filled trenches where so many young men died. He fought like a true Highlander and was the pride of his command, twice saving the lives of his comrades in the line of fire. While many brave lads were reduced to tears, young Jamie continued to shine. His final act of courage came when he carried a wounded soldier through enemy lines for over a mile. For this act of unselfish heroism he was awarded an honourable medal, which he kept in his tunic pocket.

Two months before the end of the war, Jamie took a sniper's bullet to his left leg. The injury wasn't serious but his officer sent him home with the wounded, telling him to see a doctor when he got back.

The young man thought nothing of his injury as he made his long journey home to his people in the Highlands. In due course he eventually found them pearl-fishing in Caithness. His folks were over the moon that their laddie was returned them, aye, and him with a medal. Sad to say, his leg-wound was far more serious than he thought; poison had found its way into his bone. In those days this was fatal, and within a month Jamie, the brave tinker laddie who gave so much on the fields of France, died in his father's arms.

Relatives came for miles to mourn the brave laddie. While the men wandered back and forth discussing Jamie's heroics, the women prepared his body for the long rest.

Little balls of flax were placed in his ears and nostrils; this stopped evil spirits from entering his body and stealing away his soul. A small piece of ancient plaid embroidered with his family name was placed across his heart, ensuring a heavenly home for all the family. Lastly there was a gentle kiss from his parents before his body was wrapped tightly in thin muslin cloth. Young Jamie's earthbound remains were mummified from head to toe for his spiritless rest.

Within three days, over a hundred relatives had gathered for the journey to the secret burial ground. This sacred piece of land lay deep in a Highland glen, towered over on either side by high mountains, as if guarding their secret from the outside world. At the head of the little glen remnants of a once great Caledonian pine forest scatter themselves, bent with age, ravaged by rook and osprey nests, refusing to fall as if their very existence was a mark of Scotland herself.

From where Jamie's funeral procession began to the hidden spot was thankfully only fifteen miles, a day's walk following the horse and cart. But that was before the old laird passed away himself. He had no problem with tinkers; in fact a mutual respect existed between them. This, though, was not the attitude of the new owner, who loathed tinkers with a vengeance.

The old laird never knew, or ever wanted to know, the whereabouts of the burial ground, but the new laird was not so tolerant. Folks say he was assaulted by a gypsy while serving with the 'Bubbly Jocks' (nickname for the 2nd Dragoons, The Scots Greys, from the Border country). The incident, so folks said, arose from cowardice on the laird's part, and left him twisted and angry with every nomadic person.

Imagine the reaction from the funeral party when, at the start of their road, a great iron gate barred the way. Wooden fences ran as far as the eye could see, while the factor, with estate workers sporting guns, menacingly shouted abuse at the grieving relatives of heroic Jamie.

That was a bad do, right enough. The parents of our dear deceased, heart-broken as they were, asked everyone to sit down and wait until they returned. They decided to approach the big house, home of the angry laird, and put to him the importance of their son being laid among his ancestors.

'I will under nae circumstances allow vermin tae be burret on ma land. Now afore I gie the order fur the hale gang o' ye tae be run through, I'll let an hour pass fur ye a' tae git aff ma grun!'

Without a single word the parents turned, heads hung down, and walked away.

The laird's men laughed and mocked as the mourners walked back down the way they had come. When out of sight, though, the travelling folks took on a totally different view of the situation, and sat behind a broad dyke concealing their hero laddie's body, planning a strategic battle with the brave lairdy and his henchmen. It mattered not to them how many the enemy were, or the amount of guns they held, Jamie *would* rest in his rightful place, and before that day ended. 'I made a promise tae ma boy,' said his father, 'an yon stuffed, port-supping, turkey o' a laird will not stop me frae keepin a promise tae ma Jamie.'

So, as dusk fell and the laird's men had all retreated home, the tinkers led the horse and cart with its precious cargo up the rhododendron driveway of the 'big hoose'. And as the women wailed and the piper played a lament the men dug a six-foot hole in a beautiful flowerbed, yards from the laird's front door, then gently lowered Jamie's body into the freshly dug grave.

Now imagine the red anger of himself when he witnessed the desecration taking place on his very own doorstep. 'Get that oot o' there or I'll blow the heeds aff ye. Dae as I say, I'm warning ye.'

But, as before, not a single word was uttered, apart from the women, who were still wailing, and the piper, who was still lamenting.

Now, folks, in the Highlands of Scotland it matters not if you're a duke, a tramp or a dog—no one on any account desecrates a grave!

The laird screamed at his house servants, his factor, in fact all his household who were lined up outside, to 'Dig up the vermin an' dump it or burn it,' but 'Na! Na! that was deevil's work', and more important than the laird's employment was the future of one's soul! 'What will ye tak tae get that aff ma doorstep?' he shouted to the grievers. Still keeping silent, the father pointed to the hills in the distance.

'My Lord, it would be a fool who stood in the way of the tinkers,' said the laird's old butler. 'Many is the curse which falls on the house of whoever stops the burial!'

The red face of the enraged man glowed, like the now-full moon shining brightly in the night sky, as he turned and marched up the steps of his stately home, leaving matters to those he hated, but knew he could not defeat.

So, as the women wailed and the piper played, our Jamie was duly dug up.

Two lads stayed on guard within the remnants of the ancient pines as the rest went on to the secret burial ground. 'Wait,' said Jamie's father, and before they lowered his boy to his rest he bent down and gently pinned a little silver medal on his chest.

So there you have it, in an unmarked grave somewhere in a Highland glen, a soldier sleeps peacefully, guarded over by two mighty giants. I will only give you a tiny clue: each of the giants goes by the name of 'Ben'!

§

It is with the kind permission of John Gilbert I now include my favourite poem. These beautiful words were written by his late grandfather of the same name. He came from Comrie in Perthshire, and was a very gifted poet. Thank you, John.

The Tinker's Grave

In the drowsie sound o' a murmurin burn
Far ben in the hert o' a boskie glen,
There they left the tinker sleepin,
But whaur? There's nane but the tinkers ken.

Was it close tae the silvery stream o' the Earn
Or set by the Ruchill's rocky bed?
The fairies that dance on the Leadnaig's banks
Do they lull his sleep wi' their airy tread?

His bed was lined wi' the saft green mosses
His shroud was the tent he had sleepit in.
His dirge was the tune o' that wimplin burnie,
Played on the sough o' the saft west wind.

Owre him they made the tinker ritual,
They merched roond the grave an they keepit time,
Chatterin aye wi' a mystic mutter
Some cryptic words in a queer auld rhyme.

The lovelorn merl there in the lerac,
Singin his mate tae sleep fur the nicht,
Soondit the last post owre the tinker,
Full and clear in the fadin licht.

Never a mound did they raise aboon him,
Nor chiseled a stane fur his grave tae mark
That unkent spot in the phantom country,
That lies merched in twixt the licht an the dark.

There in the land o' mellowin gloamin
Whaur the evenin shadows begin tae fa',
Whaur the nicht comes quietly creepin forrit,
An the day goes gently wastin awa.

In the drowsie soond o' that murmurin burnie,
Far ben in the hert o' that boskie glen,
There they left the tinker sleepin,
Whaur? There's nane but the tinkers ken.

17

BALQUHIDDER VISIT

I can't remember the journey to Strathyre; I was too busy sewing a lining into an old wicker basket for the wee dog. Daddy glanced over his shoulder and said, 'If that's where the pup's going to sleep make sure it can slip beneath the bed, I am not wanting it lying in the road of my feet, all right, Jess?'

'Och, Dad, he's a terrier for goodness sake! Did you see the size of the mother, no bigger than a Golden Wonder tattie.'

'No, I didn't see the bitch, but do you see thon tramp over yonder on the right hand side of the road?'

I stretched myself to see an elderly gent of the road sleeping peacefully beside a stumpy tree trunk, and nodded.

'Well, my lass, he'll be the proud owner of a wee dog if I get any more of your cheek.'

I changed the subject by pretending to prick my finger on the needle, then muttered something about driving too fast round a sharp bend on the road.

Janey lifted her eyes from above a book she was reading and said, 'You'd have a face on yourself if he got up in the dark for a pee and stood on the wee dog.'

I suppose that thought had never reached my head. 'Aye, Janey, I can hear the roar out of him if he did. And what if the dog, when fully grown, took a lump out of him?'

That brought hilarious laughter from the two of us.

A glower in the mirror was enough to tell us he had heard, so I continued sewing while Janey went back to her book.

Renie whinging that the floor was soaked soon broke our blissful peace. 'Daddy, the dog needs the lavvie, there's a puddle on the floor,' she said.

'Shut up, Renie, if he sees that he'll give Tiny away.' I whispered I'd shove her finger into a Devil's thimble (foxglove flower). She had got it into her head that if one's finger was inserted the Devil kept it. I don't know who told her that. No, it wasn't me!

Thankfully Dad was listening to the gearbox as it crunched its way from top to bottom while tackling a very steep hill, and wouldn't have heard her anyway.

Janey threw an old towel on the floor covering the dog's pee, and mopped her foot across the wetness, pointing a finger at me as if to say, 'You're owing me!'

Tiny's basket slid under the bed without any bother, so he didn't get stood on. Mind you, my father took to him so much the wee dog was given the best bed in the place, under the feather-filled quilt on my parents' bed.

Before long the little village of Strathyre, which my parents held so dear, came into view. Daddy pulled on to a stretch of grass behind an old ruin. The reason they had such a special affection for this picturesque village was because in the nearby church they were wed as teenagers, before setting off on a year's honeymoon hitch-hiking round Scotland, the only time they shared together before we came along.

My mother loved this area for other reasons also—she had folks who looked for her coming to do their fortunes. Bags of clothes, shoes and the likes that their bairns outgrew were laid aside for her visit, and many a grand rake among the bags did we have. Once I got a braw pair of navy blue shorts. I think they were Girl Guide ones. They were never off me, even when my bum grew to such a size that the cheeks stuck out beneath them, I still squeezed myself inside. You find that, don't you? There are clothes that hang in a wardrobe never worn, and some that never see the inside of one because you can't take them off.

Next day Mammy and the older lassies went hawking in Strathyre, while us young ones went to visit Daddy's mate, Geordie Mackay.

Geordie and his wife Faimie farmed a smallholding at the far end of Kirkton Glen, on the Braes o' Balquhidder. He and Daddy were boyhood friends. Whenever my father's family wintered in the area of Glenlyon, both lads went to the same school. The things they got up to when lads do not bear repeating. But I'll tell you one wee incident just so you can imagine their shenanigans. It goes like this. After giving the teacher a wayn of trouble over several weeks, they were duly brought before the headmaster.

'You two lads are old enough to know better,' he warned them. 'I am setting an example to the rest of the school. At nine on Monday in front of everybody you will be birched!'

Now Geordie had a big round backside, whereas Daddy, poor thing, had a skleff bum, hardly any flesh to take the wallop of a birch.

The two rascals decided they were not deserving of such a severe punishment, so set about a plan to prevent Monday's martyrdom of their hindquarters. A sloped roof covered the headmaster's office. A boulder of massive size was rolled by the two lads on to the said roof, with the sole intention of killing the head of the school.

'It was him or us,' agreed my Dad.

'Aye, an' he had tae go,' said his mate.

Frozen hands and four hours later they released the deadly weapon. The big round stone careered down the sloped roof and missed by miles the head's baldy napper! So with the duo dragged to their execution screaming in agony even before a hand was laid on them, the punishment went ahead.

Geordie stopped whingeing and took it like a man. Daddy went to his fate, fainted and wakened up with as big a bum as his pal, except that his took longer to heal than his mate's.

This, then, was the bond that tied these two friends. And never would my father come this way without a visit to his old pal. Of course the dastardly deed would be relived, and each time the storytellers added another wee bit. If I told you all that was said we would be here all day. Even the school changed venues in the telling.

Geordie and Faimie had only themselves on the wee holding. As they had never been blessed with bairns it meant we got a double helping of being spoiled. The back and front doors of the house on the brae were never closed. Dogs, cats and hens wandered in and out. Sometimes, if Faimie took an afternoon snooze, she would wake to find an old fat hen roosting on her knee. Mammy told me that once Faimie woke up to find two brown eggs deposited on her lap.

And if the sun got too hot, Jack and Jean, the pet goats, came in to share the house as well. They, because of age, had pride of place in the kitchen to eat and rest to their hearts' content. Aye, never have I seen such royal goats. The length of the beards dangling from their chins told me they might have been a hundred years old and more!

Faimie shooed out the dogs and hens as she welcomed us in. 'You're in time for some dinner,' she said, patting me several times on the head, then added, 'My, Jessie, what big you've grown since last I saw you.'

'Mammy said it was the amount of scones I ate last time we visited you, Mrs Mackay.'

'Och, and I suppose you'll be wanting a bigger dod of butter this time.' she said.

'You know me and my buttery scones, Mrs Mackay.'

'If I didn't know how much all you lassies meant to your folks I'd ask to keep you for myself.' She smiled at me with all the love and longing in her face for her own child, and it was at that time I wished there were two of me, so I could leave my double with this kindly lady in the glen. I gave her a cuddle; she wasn't used to such a show of affection and, blushing, she quickly ushered me out to fetch the men.

I ran round to the barn with an old cock-a-doodle snapping at my heels, and shouted to the two pals that their food was on the table. The men, who were into the guts of an old tractor like two surgeons discussing the innards of a patient, hardly gave me a second glance.

'Come on, before your food gets cold and this wild bird eats a hole in my gillie's heel,' I called, as I failed to keep the cockerel from pecking my feet.

'It's Achilles' heel, you silly lassie,' said Daddy, glancing briefly at my red-and-brown-feathered attacker.

'What's killing you, Daddy?' I called back.

'You'll get it right one of these days,' laughed Geordie, as he kicked out at the crabbit cockerel, deliberately missing it. 'That's what you do to him, Jessie lass, show him who's boss.'

'The problem with my family, Geordie,' joked my Dad, 'is that they're all women, with not an ounce of common sense.'

'Aye, I think my head would be scrambled with eight daughters. It's a medal waiting on you. Nothing short of a recommendation for you, Charlie, when you arrive at the pearly gates.'

I was far too young to understand the misplaced wisdom of their words, and continued to remind them it was dinner time. While waiting, I observed my father's friend and a thought came into mind—how much he resembled Santa Claus. Two red-appled cheeks nestling in a fluffy beard, albeit a black one. Yes, Father Christmas in tweeds and a floppy bunnet.

My mother and sisters arrived in time for dinner, filling the wee house to capacity.

'Why don't you come back in the spring, Charlie, then I'd get all these extra hands to do the planting and ploughing?' asked Geordie.

'Aye, Geordie,' answered my father, shoving a slice of bread into one of the goats' mouths that had pushed its way in through the half-open door. 'I don't know about the rest of them, but if the school rules changed, oor Jess would be up here in a shot.'

'Oh, she'd be a grand help to me right enough,' he said.

'Aye, but I telt her the real reason why you'd need her help.'

Everybody laughed.

You see, folks, the year before when it was ploughing time, my father said if we were in the glen, Geordie would have me standing on the back of his Davie Broon tractor for one purpose, to be lookie-out for birds' nests. Daddy told me that Geordie would have me point any golden plovers circling above the area of the tractor. Then he would have me jump off the back, and search among the peaty ground. If a nest was in the path of the plough, he'd stop, push his big hands into the earth and lift the precious bundle out of harm's way. As long as the eggs were not handled, the mother wouldn't desert them and would soon be settling on her nest. Geordie said he'd do everything possible not to upset nesting birds, and that's why I knew I'd feel like a chariot queen, standing on the back of the tractor, one hand on the farmer's shoulder, the other to my brow, eyes scouring the countryside all around.

This, though, was the coming of autumn, and all the young birds were flown, nests were deserted. I felt robbed in some way that I hadn't been able to visit with our friends in the spring. Geordie noticed my disappointment and tried to compensate. 'Why don't you come and help me tomorrow, Jessie. I'm cutting and stacking. I could do with a hand, that is if it's all right with mum.'

'Can I, Mammy, please?' I asked breathlessly.

'Well, all right, but mind now and don't go wandering away, and do as Mr Mackay tells you.'

I could hardly sleep with excitement, and was up before the owl finished his evening meal. Daddy dropped me off at the crossroads, saying he'd be back at teatime.

Davie Broon the tractor was ticking over when I arrived after a very early breakfast. The old male hen was too busy crowing away good style on the slate roof of the outside cludgie (toilet) to waste time nipping my what-do-you-call-it-heel.

'Here's a jeely piece, Jess,' said Faimie, draping a woolly scarf round my neck and muttering something about 'an early winter brought on a North wind'. She pushed a bag of sandwiches under my arm, saying I'd get hungry, being a growing bairn.

I thanked her, saying I'd had enough breakfast to keep me going.

'That's hard work stooking on the braeside, lassie, you'll need a lot more.'

I took the jam piece, catching with my tongue juicy rasps dropping from between the slices of bread. 'Thanks, Mrs Mackay. My, you haven't spared the raspberry jam. Did you empty the jar between the bread?'

'Away now, lass, I hear Geordie whistling in the barn, he'll be waiting on you.'

Before heading off on my day's harvesting, I just had to give Faimie a cuddle, saying, 'You're my favourite farm wifie in a' the whole world.'

'Och! I am right important am I not, being as you know that many farmer wives?'

'Och, I know every one between John o' Groats and Tushielaw,' I joked.

She laughed out loud and once again patted my hair flat.

'Cheerio, Mrs Mackay. Leave the dishes, I'll do them when I get finished.'

'Well, I'll be a fine wife if I leave dishes to such a hard-working lassie, cheerio you.'

To reach the field where Geordie's harvest work awaited, a short journey on the old tractor made up for missing out on springtime. I steadied myself with one hand on the farmer's shoulder and pointed to a flock of sand martins. Round and round they flew as if each one was chasing the other's tail.

'They are getting ready for the long flight ahead of them,' said Geordie.

'Where are they going?' I asked, 'I know it's at the far end of the world, but where is that?'

'I think it's a place where the sun is a lot hotter than here,' he told me, 'Africa, aye, that's the place.'

'That's a few mile away, Mr Mackay, for teeny birds like that, eh!'

'Hardy wee craturs for sure, Jessie.' Geordie went on to say that one day man would copy these streamlined birds and build planes that flew just like them. If he only knew how right he was.

As we bobbed over the stony road, I told him about another bit thing, our family's new-got pet, Tiny. 'He's over young to go out, but when we come back next year I'll have him up to meet with you and the good wife.'

'I'll give him a spin among the rats,' he said. 'If a terrier is in him, then he'll catch no bother. That will please Faimie, she never fails to shack them out of the hay.'

I spent most of the day helping Geordie, him slicing through the hay with a scythe bigger than himself, me stacking it up. When we trundled back towards the house, the erratic martins had gone, leaving the sky empty of summer birds. I wondered how many would make the journeys, there and back. I blew a kiss towards the sky, silently followed by a prayer to the angels, to 'please keep them safe from harm's way'.

Waving cheerio to Geordie and Faimie, I skipped off down the road towards the crossroads where Daddy would pick me up, avoiding one last attempt by the crabbit old cockerel to snip my heel.

As I passed the graveyard I noticed a woman reading an inscription on a tombstone.

'Hello, have you a friend lies among the dead folk in there?' I called out to her.

The woman laughed at my question, then came over to where I was and said: 'No, I was passing by and came in to see the resting place of the famous Rob Roy Macgregor.'

'Oh, you have, have you. I didn't know him, but some folks say he was a bad man and others say he was a hero from these parts,' I said.

'Are you from travelling hantel?' she asked.

'Aye, that I am, from Perthshire travellers.' I went on to tell her my family surnames. She said she'd certainly heard of us, but so far I was the first Riley she'd met.

'Have you a half hour to spare, lassie?' she asked. 'Like yourself I'm a traveller, and this tale I have I'll only pass it on to my own kind.'

I looked down to the spot where my father said he'd collect me. There was no sign of him, so I sat at the kirkyard wall with the stranger and listened to a tale of magic and wonder. I now have pleasure in sharing it with you today.

18

THE BABYSITTER

Bridget O'Connell, an only child of Irish immigrants, was brought into the world in a bow-camp at a wood beneath the Drum of Clashmore, in the Trossachs. She was a solitary lass, who spent most of her youth wandering among the trees of oak and birch dreaming of a world where fairies lived, and some say she could be heard talking to the wind as it rustled through the autumn leaves of golden brown.

One night, while filled with fever, she dreamt a strange dream. Rob Roy, the legendary hero from the pen of Walter Scott, came to Bridget. He told her in a strange cryptic verse '*A seventh son o' a seventh son would come from her seed and save his soul.*' She fretted over the dream and found sleep hard to come by for many a night after it. What could she have to do with such a thing? For sure, she was only a virgin lass of sixteen-years-old, who so far had neither the eye nor a wink from any lad.

This, though, was a change in the making, because Duncan (Pirie) Williamson, a handsome young Highlander who was fee-ed at a nearby farm, fell head over heels for the whimsical lass, and within the year they were wed.

They lived a healthy life and gave the world eight sons and three daughters, who all lived in and around the Trossachs, even after most married and had bairns of their own. Farmers in the area had plenty work and were more than glad to see the hardy clan of Duncan and Bridget when tatties needed lifting, and harvesting time came.

Bridget's family were raised on tales of fairies and little folk, and they were more than used to their mother ranting on about Rob Roy. But out of respect to her status, they never openly mocked or made fun of her fanciful tales of the wee folks, whom she maintained looked after them all.

She would say to them, 'Now mind and keep the place clean and not be upsetting the fairies,' then add, 'They'll watch out for you if you are mindful of them'.

Although fairies never age, folks do, and one night Duncan kissed his lass's cheek for the last time and slipped over to the other side. Bridget put on mourning clothes and gave her time to watching the wee ones, whilst the family worked hard on the nearby farms.

The old woman (for now she was the age of seventy-five) had plenty grandbairns to keep her eye on, and she loved them all, especially wee Robbie, her second youngest son's bairn.

'Have you ever seen such a pair of bonnie blue eyes on any other bairn?' she would ask visitors, cupping his little face lovingly with her hands, then adding, 'And look at this head of yellow curls.' This would be followed by, 'But deary me, he's into everything. I need eyes in the back of my head to watch this bit bairn, and him not three yet.'

Rob Roy and the fairies were put to the back of her mind as her role became more demanding. Still, every so often, she would glance into the rustling trees as if a whisper from within the silence met her ears. Little did she imagine that with each passing day fate was laying a path, a way that she had no control over, a path she had to follow!

One peaceful night, while her family slept soundly in their tents, the stranger who haunted her dreams all those years ago came back and this time he told her:

> *On the moss-carpeted ground*
> *In the wood at loch Ard,*
> *A man o' the cloth lies deed!*
> *Plunged a dirk tae his heart,*
> *By my very own hand,*
> *For no more than twa bawbees.*
> *Auld Nick waits tae tak ma soul*
> *Held in a secret place,*
> *By the fairies o' the Deil's waterfall,*

And only the son o' the seventh son
Can tak awa this disgrace.

On waking the next morning, she ran breathlessly round each of her children, telling them of her dream. The family told her she had to stop all this Rob Roy nonsense, or else she'd go moich.

'Anyway, he didn't hail from these parts,' said her eldest son, 'he came from over Balquhidder way, and some say Dochart saw his likes, but never here among the Trossachs, so stop this, Mother, and do it now!'

'Och, you're wrong,' she said in her defence. 'I mind the day I met a tramp who come from the west, a learned gentlemaun he was. He told me Rob went all over the place, and was seen as far away as Ayrshire. He also told me that Rob had even been chased by Redcoats out of Sutherland, not that far from where your dear father was born!'

She then proudly added that the learned tramp laughed at her when she asked if he'd been here in the Trossachs. 'Why, wife, this is Rob Roy country, just down the road a bit is the auld "Clachan of Aberfoyle" with Jean Macalpine's Inn. They say Rob Roy frequented the place oftentimes.'

Bridget reminded the tramp that she was a tinker woman, and took little to do with folks round about. 'I never went to school neither,' she added.

'So there you have it, family, I knew fine Rob Roy was as real as the Menteith Hills!'

'Och aye, Mother, you believe that if it makes you happy, but we think it's the Irish in you, all those stories told by your folks about Leprechauns.'

This brought a hearty burst of laughter amongst her brood. She sat down at the fire and wrapped her old shawl round thin shoulders. Taking a clay pipe from her apron and lighting it, she said, 'You can think what you want, but I know last night's dream was so life-like I could have wiped the sweat from Rob's brow if I'd a mind. Now away and start your day's work, I've the fire to stoke.'

'Will stovies do your tea?' she asked, pulling the big family pot from under its cover near the tent.

Because they were by now convinced she was failing in the head, they took most of the wee ones with them, leaving only little Robbie and his week-old sister, Bell. The children's mother Maggie, told Bridget she'd be home at midday to put wee Bell on the breast, and gave her a cuddle, saying stovies would be grand after a hard day. 'You must understand, it's because you're so precious, mother dear, we worry for your well-being. Now, will you be all right?' Young Maggie took the frail old woman in her arms, kissing her lined face.

Bridget returned her daughter-in-law's affection with a kiss, then watched the sprightly lassie run off down the road and disappear round the bend. She then set about cleaning the tents and shaking the crumpled bed covers before folding them neatly.

She and wee Robbie spent the rest of the morning gathering sticks. Later she peeled a multitude of tatties and onions for the family's promised stovie supper.

A rare heat was radiating from the fire when Maggie came home to feed her baby, who hadn't stirred an ounce since she left. 'The farmer's wife sent some scones up for you, Mammy. She sends her best an' hopes you'll visit her with a crack soon, when the tatties are finished,' said Maggie.

'Thank her for the good words. Aye, that would be fine. I haven't seen many folk this whiley back, not since my Duncan went. God, I can't even mind when I was last at the graveside. Perhaps I'll go this coming Sabbath and take wee Robbie.'

For the second time that day Bridget watched her daughter-in-law hurry off down the road, thinking it wasn't that long ago she'd the same spring in her step. She pulled the coarse, grey shawl up under her chin, thinking the frost wasn't far off, and put another clump of wood on the fire.

Much to her dread, little Robbie copied his granny by doing the same with a half-burned stick.

'God almighty, boy, don't you be standing so near the fire. Get back out of there!' she screamed at him, and the poor wee mite, startled by his granny's remark, began crying, rubbed a blackened fist across his chubby face and looked at her with pools of watery eyes. Her heart sank. 'Come to Granny, my bonnie wee cherub, sure I'm forgetting you're only an infant. But do you know how precious fingers are? Oh dear, if you burnt those wee fingers, my, oh my.' She picked him up into her bosom and cuddled him tight. Handing Robbie a wool ball to play with she went in-by her tent to check baby Bell, who was sleeping soundly, belly full of thick, healthy breast milk.

Refilling her clay pipe, she sat down beside the tent flap and stole a few minutes to herself. The October sun was low in the sky, minding her the stovies should be cooking. Before hanging the big black pot on the iron chitties straddling the fire, she turned to check on Robbie, but seeing no sign of him, her heart missed a beat. 'Where in the blazes is he? Rob, answer me now, bairn, Granny's needing you. Stop hiding from me, come out!'

Bridget peered into every tent, behind trees, in about the legs of the tethered ponies, squinted her eyes into slits and scanned as much of the wood as she could possibly see, but the lad had disappeared! 'This is the last time I take care of this bairn,' she thought. 'Sure he's far over precious to be left with an old woman, a stupid old one at that.' In apprehension she screwed the edge of her apron into a tight knot between her fists and called out, 'Robbie, Robbie!' Silence followed her cry, as if the very birds of the forest became anxious for the wee lad.

A soft murmur came from baby Bell, and Bridget's burden doubled. Her family would be home in an hour, they'd find him for sure, but she cried into herself, 'My God, a lot could happen in an hour!' At this thought a shiver ran through her body, more chilling than the coming winter's snows.

However, years of experience bringing up her family replaced the fearful thoughts, and gave her an inner strength. Wrapping wee Bell securely in the old shawl, she set off into the depths of the wood in search of her wandering grandson, telling herself he was just round the corner.

But every corner taken made her heart sound like a beating drum in her chest, as no sign of her charge appeared. Tears of fear rolled down her weather-beaten face, and a lifetime dreaming of Rob Roy Macgregor and the fairies was fading like vapor. Here was real life, her baby lamb lost in the dense forests of the Trossachs, at the mercy of God alone knows what. Not a dream or whispering trees, but a small vulnerable child wholly dependent on her care. Her family was right, she was a mad old woman!

Bridget sat down among some stones to relieve the strain in her back from carrying Bell, and thought how useless she'd become with age, wishing she was cold dead, lying beside her Duncan. A faint cry way over by the waterfall at the other side of the wood stirred her from out of the despair rapidly taking over her being.

'That's not a wood sound,' she thought, rising to her feet, and with one hand securing the now-stirring infant, made over to where the sound came from.

The waterfall was always out of bounds to her as a lass, aye, and to her own brood as well. It was a deep crevice in the ground, more akin to a hole than anything else, and very dangerous. 'God, not that awful hole!' She froze on thinking of the place. Oh, if that sound was her Robbie, Lord, please keep him safe from the Devil's Pot, she prayed.

Lifting her long black skirt she made towards the frightening slit in the forest floor. Thankfully the heavy rains which usually came at that time of the year had not yet appeared, making the waterfall a trickle rather than its usual cascading torrent.

There was no sign of the wee lad, though. Only a dead tree lay across the falls with branches stretching in many directions. Bridget peered into the hole and thought, thankfully, he hadn't come this way. 'No, I can't see him,' she sighed with relief; but then, 'Wait the now, what's that?' Staring deep down the long narrow gorge and squinting her old her eyes into narrow slits, she saw a different green. Not the decaying colour of the old tree but a khaki green, the very same as Robbie's breeches, the very ones she made for him out of Duncan's old trousers!

'Rob, Robbie!' She held her breath and waited on an answer. That is, if one was forthcoming.

Then, after a long pause, a heaven-sent voice whispered back to her, 'Stuck, Ganny, me stuck.'

Aye, for sure he was. Praise be, he'd been snared by one of the branches, but for how long? The wee bisum was well down into the gorge, how in heaven's name did he manage that? Bridget had to get down into the crevice, for there wasn't a minute to lose. She removed her skirt and rolled it into a warm nest. Within a clump of thick fern she put Bell snugly inside the skirt nest, then taking the old wool shawl she'd worn as long as her skin, she cut it to strips with a sharp stone. Hurriedly she tied the strips together to make a longish rope, and all the while she was calling out to Robbie she was coming, and not to struggle.

'Dinna move, now, bairn, Granny will have you tucking into a plate of stovies in no time.'

She peered in at the green slimy walls, which seemed to take the water into the depths of hell and the very door of old Nick himself! She prayed to God, the Fairies and anybody who had a hand in the impossible, before sliding her legs down towards the helpless lad, shawl rope tightly round her waist, the other end anchored on the dead tree's root. For the umpteenth time she prayed.

One wrong move, and she and the bairn would be victims of Mother Nature's uncaring moods.

Her feet dangled in mid-air as she tried and tried to get a foothold in the never-ending wet moss, but it seemed an unattainable task, for she was too old. Her legs hadn't dross of strength; her hands were gnarled with a lifetime working the soil. And worst of all, she was more than aware of it!

Wee Robbie shivered and sobbed on his life-saving branch while Bell, now awake, screamed. Her squeals were adding to Bridget's growing distress, which was about to take on a serious turn.

'Oh my God!' she cried, as the shawl's grip began to loosen from her waist and she stiffened with fear. She knew in her falling that Robbie and his tree would go with her. She closed her eyes and asked that wee Bell's screams would soon be heard, and she at least would be saved.

Then, as the old woman began to drop her legs and let go, something, very, very, strange happened. Strong yet tender hands lifted her gently from her impending doom, and laid her soaked body on the ground beside the skirt nest and baby Bell.

Taking the tail of her sodden grey flannel underskirt, she rubbed a little of the peat-water from her eyes. She looked round to thank her rescuer, but he was nowhere to be seen. Then a sight filled her vision that was so unbelievable she thought for a moment that Death had indeed claimed her and she was in a dream state.

Before her very eyes Robbie's wee shivering body came floating, yes, floating, from the edge of the waterfall! There wasn't a solitary soul to be seen as he was gently handed into her care.

'This,' she thought, 'is surely the work of the fairies.'

Bridget sat on the earth clutching her little grandson tightly to her bosom, when Bell let out another hungry squeal, bringing the old woman back to reality. She called out to the silence,

'That was you come back to save your soul through my wee lad, was it not Rob Roy Macgregor? I was right all along. I just knew you and I would cross paths. Go home, lad, you're free now. God grant we'll meet on the other side one day. Thank you kindly for choosing myself, a tinker of simple stock. I remember your words: *On the moss-carpeted ground*. You see, lad, I never forgot: *a seventh son o' a seventh son would save yer soul*. My wee Robbie is a seventh son, it was him. Are the fairies and yourself listening, do you hear me?' She cried out at the nothingness all around, but only a faint echo of her own voice carried itself from the gorge that seconds before beckoned her life's breath.

It was a wet but grateful old woman, holding a hungry baby in her arms, that followed on behind wee Robbie, the seventh son of her seventh son, as he ran to meet the workers.

She never told them what really happened; only that Robbie got stuck near the Deil's Pot. That was enough to tell them their mother was no longer capable of looking after the little ones. So they decided Maggie should stay behind in future and see to the campsite. Bridget was silently grateful for that; she'd done her bit. Although she never told her family what happened that day, she felt it only right that wee Bell should know. After all, was she not part of Rob Roy Macgregor's 'miracle'?

The passing years saw the family leave the Trossachs, scattering themselves throughout Scotland. Bridget however, refused to leave her campsite in the wood at the far end of Loch Ard. In fact only her tent remained, and there she stayed, until the fairies came in the silence of a quiet summer's night for her own soul.

Thankfully my father was late coming for me, allowing my storyteller enough time to finish her tale.

'Man, that was grand,' I thanked the woman. But before she left I asked her name.

'Bell,' was the reply, 'Bell Williamson,' she said, adding, 'Now, lassie, remember this unwritten tale, keep it fresh in your memory and tell it to travellers every chance you get.'

I now, with your help, reader, have told Bell's fairy story—the traveller's version of Rob Roy Macgregor—to you.

19

THE LIVING NIGHTMARE

That was a braw summer's jaunt in the old bus. Why the others were hankering after a house beats me. Back at Crieff, though, this is all the family spoke about, apart from Chrissie. The lad she left in the spring has returned with a yearning look in his eye, and Mammy thinks her second eldest is falling in love.

Daddy, as he'd planned earlier in the year, set about finding out the ways of spray-painting. The events this set in motion unfolded themselves into a living nightmare, though it began so well. He busied himself during the summer months offering his services to paint farm sheds, barns and the farmer's house if so desired (one eccentric wife had her farmhouse painted a bright pink, but that's another story). Soon he'd lined up several good jobs, but without the right equipment to take on such a task he was neither here nor there. So, unable to buy new, he bought second-hand.

Did he know that the compressor, spraying guns and pipes were stolen?

'I never knew,' was what he swore on the good book that cold morning standing in Perth Court accused of reset! The judge didn't believe him.

Now, this travelling-people hater of a judge decided, on that misty Monday morning in October, that an example should be made: '*Six months for reset.*'

'God in Heaven, that's richt steep for a first offence,' said Daddy's brother Wullie, who along with Cousin John went to the court with him.

Before my father was led away to serve his sentence, he glanced across the River Tay from the courthouse window, and leaning over at his brother he said, 'If I'm still in the stardy come next summer, take the lassies on the river for a wee bit pearl-fishing and make sure Jeannie knows how sorry I am for putting us in this pitiful state. Tell her I'm sorry about her house. I'll make it up to her when I get home!'

Mammy's anxious wait for the verdict was soon over. When she saw Cousin John drive the Fordy home she knew that she and her Charlie had hard times facing them, but how to keep us weans from learning the truth about him being in jail was more important.

'When he gets back we'll all pile in to build your house, Jeannie. Six months will fly by, don't you fret.' Cousin John was always a faithful friend to my folks. He took a sip of tea, then added, 'That is, if he minds his tongue and doesn't get extra time for his trouble.'

My mother wrung her hands tight and reminded John, 'He's an ex-soldier, he can take orders, aye, and give them too. He'll keep his mouth shut, for that's a place not even a dog would want to linger in. As for this house of mine, well, it's a pipe dream, all in my head. My Charlie could never be happy trapped between four walls. No, the road is to be our way of life. Most important is that the wee ones don't find out where their Daddy is.'

'They'll not find out from me,' John assured her. 'Why don't you tell them he's working far away quarrying or something. That'll satisfy their curiosity.'

'I'll tell the older lassies, because Lord knows I'll be needing their support. But it is going to be damn hard for sure, though, John.'

'You're a tough lass, Jeannie. Remember the six years you and the four weans lived in a hut beside the midden at the Bobbin Mill in Pitlochry, while Charlie was fighting. I bet there was many a night you lay in bed listening to the bombers going over, thinking you'd never see him again.'

'I'm not thinking of myself, John, it's my Charlie. God help him locked up in a wee cell for six months. How is he going to live like that, it'll kill him.'

'Now, don't you be getting ideas like that in your head—sure, he's a rugger is my cousin, a hardy chiel, with a lot to live for, and, as for the time, well, it'll flee by.'

I remember getting home from school that Monday; a freezing fog which settled around the Dollerie fields was making me shiver. I couldn't wait to get home and warm myself at wee Reekie.

I opened the door for my wee sisters, noticed the stove hadn't been lit and asked Mammy why, on such a cold day, the fire was out. Her face was unusually pale, the red from her cheeks had moved to her eyes and her appearance scared me a mite.

'Where's my Dad? I seen the Fordy outside, is he up the way cracking to old Suttie the farmer?' I asked her. This said gent owned Tomaknock, the ground on which we lived, and he and Daddy were good friends.

Mammy heaved a sigh, and looked blankly out the window before answering, 'He's away working for a few months, so there'll just be us lassies.'

Picking up each of my wee sisters' blazers from the floor and folding them neatly, I quizzed her, 'Has he got work painting, Mammy? That's good. You'll get your house built, and if he makes plenty money then maybe he'll buy us another bus when this one pegs out.'

She turned on me, which just wasn't like her at all. Grabbing the blazers from me she shouted, 'Shut up, will you, Jessie! I'm sick of you going on about this stupid bus, do you ever think of anything else?'

Her raised voice and angry reaction to my enquiry was completely out of character.

We all ran and cuddled her. She was obviously missing Daddy, and him only a morning away. Little did we know what burden our poor mother was shouldering that moment in time.

'Have you a sore head, Mammy?' asked Renie, running a little hand round her neck.

Mary muttered something about homework, then asked, 'Can I get a piece in jam? I'm starving to death, haven't had a thing to eat since my porridge,' then added, 'The food was yuck at the diney, wasn't it Jessie?'

'Aye, it was that,' I answered, 'The school dinner was rank the day all right, whoever cooked the mince did it blindfold, or blind drunk. I left most of mine too.'

Renie said with big watery eyes, 'Mammy, what a shame, a wean in my class peed her breeks. She was greeting 'cause horrible house bairns laughed and called her dirty names.' Renie always felt sorry for the hard-done-bys of the world.

Mary, on the other hand, wasn't so soft. 'She didn't just pee, she filled her knickers into the bargain as well.'

'Never did, that's a lie, I gave her a cuddle and would have smelt it,' protested Renie. 'She's horrible, Mammy. Have you a sore head? Looks as if you have one.'

'Bairns, wheest, wheest, stop all yapping at the same time.'

Mammy assured Renie that no, she didn't have a headache, and yes, 'Mary, you can have a piece, only don't eat all the jam,' adding that it must have been a shame for the child who never made it to the lavvie. She further told us that those bairns who made fun of the unfortunate would be visited upon by a similar experience, further adding, 'God's slow, but sure!'

I helped my sisters change into their playing clothes, all the time watching my mother. Something didn't feel right. I knew her red eyes had to do with Daddy's absence, but why shout at me? No, I was convinced there was more to it than that.

After the wee ones went out to play, I voiced my concerns. 'If Daddy's away working, then why leave the Fordy?'

Little did I know I was forcing my Mother to lie for the second time that day. It was bad enough saying he was working away from home, but now she had to invent a second person with a fictitious car, she was torn in pieces. Rather than face me, she took her crochet bag, removed a half-knitted glove, sat down and said, 'You're a nosey wee thing, Jess, but if you must know, it was an old friend of Daddy, a war buddy. They went in his car.'

'Oh, it wasn't Johnny, was it? Him who palled through the Black Forest with Dad? Did they go in his car? Was it, Mam? Daddy told me he gave a skinny man bully beef in a prison camp, so hungry was the poor soul that he tried to rip the can open with his teeth. You remember that story Dad told us, don't you Mam. Was it him? Was it Johnny Slay?'

Without a word she pulled me into her breast, and kissing the top of my head she said, 'My wee Jessie, Dad's right when he tells folk you've a tongue in your head. Listen to me now—he's working far away, in a quarry. Not with that friend but someone else, and he'll be home in six months' time.'

'Och, that's fine then, you're not needing to be crying, are you Ma?' I felt relieved.

'No, pet, but I'm used to him being here. Like you I'll miss the old bisom. Now, away and see the wee ones are safe playing outside. I'll get the fire lit, your big sisters will soon be home and they'll be scranning.'

I was retrieving my ball from the burn at the bottom of the field when the lassies came in from work, and, as far away as I was, I could hear the shouts from them. It was Daddy this, and Daddy that, and Oh My God, how could life ever be the same again!

'Dearie me!' I thought, that's no way to carry on. Surely him making a living wouldn't bring them to react in such an angry way. This put the dreaded thought in my head that perhaps Daddy wasn't working. Surely my Mother wasn't lying? He's not away is he, not left us? The more I thought on this, the more certain I became.

He's left home. Aye, I'm sure now, my dearest Daddy has left us, deserted us all! Wild thoughts raced around in my brain. I tried to think on his last angry words. The night before, when Auntie Maggie and Uncle Joe were in, he certainly was giving it laldy about the crowded bus and the way the big ones constantly bickered. Did I not hear him telling Uncle Joe, 'I can't move an inch, these lassies leave clothes lying all over the place. If I find another stiletto heel on my pillow I'll go moich!' When he found the lipstick on his clean white vest just the other day, Lord, the blood vessels in his neck, never have I seen a near-explosion like that. No wonder none of the lassies owned up.

If he really was gone, then why should Mammy tell me he'd be back in six months? Did she think it would take that time for me to get him out of my head?

Then I thought he might be ill, in a sanatorium. Maybe his bronchitis was worse than he let on. Oh, this is bad, I just know it. Where is my Dad?

Do you know, in all my anxiousness, I never once gave prison a thought, not one! Daddy was my 'War Hero', who'd spent six years defending the nation; he had the medals to prove it. He cared desperately for parentless bairns, sick animals, old people without relatives to care for them; a lonely hitcher on a wet Highland road was the better for his driving up and opening a welcome door. No, I never gave a prison cell one single inkling of a thought!

I made up my mind which was the real reason for his absence— desertion! And we were the cause of his unhappiness. We must have chased him away, poor Dad! So, for weeks, my nightly prayers were for his happiness, and that whoever took care of him saw that he ate plenty good, thick barley broth. Oh, and not forgetting his eggs, boiled for three minutes (he only ate watery yolks). 'Thank you, God, Amen.'

Every Saturday Mammy went to Perth, supposedly to visit Auntie Winnie, her oldest sister, who, so they said, was poorly. Truth was, she was visiting Daddy.

October moved on, November followed, tattie-lifting was finished. Shirley and Chrissie continued working on local farms, doing the same as burly ploughmen, including driving tractors and shifting heavy hay-bales for winter-feeding the cows.

Our bonny Janey, on the contrary, stepped up in the world; she got a job as lingerie assistant at Scrimgeour's, Crieff's equivalent of Harrods, and loved it. This magnificent store sprawled at the end of the High Street and round onto Comrie Road. It sold everything one could possibly need, from ball-gowns to ball-pens. In the early seventies, this regal monument was reduced to ashes by the fiercest fire Crieff had ever witnessed, and was replaced by a block of retirement flats.

Chrissie's boyfriend had become a permanent feature in the evenings round the fire. Indeed we were all becoming right fond of the shy, blonde, curly-headed lad. Nothing of him was traveller-like, but if our sister had asked it, he'd have moved on to the road in a flash, for that's how devoted he was to her!

Mona came and went that winter, flitting between grannies and relatives, only coming home for Christmas.

Not a day went by that I didn't yearn deeply after my Dad. The longer the wait, the worse I became. I'd stand looking down the road, peering behind the fat, warty, ancient oak across the way from the bus, hoping to be the first of us to see him come whistling, bunnet perched on the side of his head, up the old road. But the cold frost wrapped around the tree's bark would find me deserting my post to seek the warmth of wee Reekie, where I'd close my eyes and picture him in my head, still whistling, laughing and waving his bunnet, a sure sign to tell Mammy, 'get the kettle on'. I pained so much for the want of my father, and no one knew it. But for Mammy's sake I pretended not to miss him.

Although none of my sisters said, I knew they too in their own ways dealt with Daddy's absence as best they could. The Christmas of '53, when our mother was at death's door in a surgical ward of Manchester General Hospital, we called 'Mammyless'. This, then, was the 'Daddyless' Christmas. No carol singing, no Santa, no turkey, just another day needing to be over.

The tenth of March, my birthday, found me in bed with tonsillitis, a Monday it was. Mammy went as usual to Perth, Cousin John went with her. I wondered if poor Auntie Winnie had kicked the bucket? No, she was fine, said our Mona, who came home that weekend from Granny Riley's.

I had counted the six months on my fingers. If my mother was telling the truth, then our Dad would be coming home any day now—if she told the truth.

The thick, yellow medicine Dr Mitchell prescribed made me drowsy, and soon I was sound asleep. The bus door opened and a familiar voice awakened me.

'You got swelt tonsils again?' the voice said quietly. 'Hello, you skipping school?' asked the same voice, raised this time.

I thought for a second that I heard my father. How many times had I imagined his voice calling me? Sitting up I rubbed the sleep from my eyes. Was I dreaming? For standing there, right there in front of me, a sight I'd resigned myself never to see again, my Daddy!

I wasn't dreaming. It was him, a couple of feet from me, smiling, arms outstretched.

'I said, sleepy head, your throat bothering you again?'

I was speechless. He wasn't out of my life but here right in the bus, back home beside us, after all this time.

'Thank you God!' I whispered deep within myself, 'very, very much!' All my prayers were answered. I sat straight up, ignoring the pain in my neck, and leapt into his arms. 'Daddy! Daddy! My own precious Daddy!' was all I could croak.

I put myself between him and the door, fearing he might leave again, blurting out at the same time, 'Did you get plenty broth? Was your eggs boilt all right?'

Mammy was crying, so was Mona. Cousin John filled the kettle, saying 'I've a wild drouth. Is a man not for a drappy tea in this place?'

'You'll not leave us again, will you Daddy? Make me a soul promise. Anyroad, who could drive the bus as good as you?' I was by this time in floods of tears.

'No, bairn, I'll not leave you again. Now, who do you know can drive the old bus better than myself?' Those words rooted in my heart, I wound my arms round his waist and cuddled the father I thought never to see again. I never asked him where he had been, if working or otherwise; truth is, I didn't care, just to see him sitting in his own chair was all that mattered. The wee ones were all over him when they came home from school. Janey, back from Scrimgeour's, went on and on about the fancy shop, and the fact she had, that very day, been chosen as the year's 'Scrimgeour's Queen'—beaming she was, just beaming.

Daddy didn't look well. He'd lost weight, his bunnet was too big, and the moustache he'd grown made him look older than his years. Thin hands, white fingernails; strange for a quarry worker. This didn't suit his image one bit. I wondered if he had eaten at all, never mind three-minute eggs and barley broth. Main thing was, though, he was back; Mammy's clootie dumplins, some skirlie, and thick tattie and leek broth would have him his old self in no time.

Next day Janey took the wee ones to school, then went to work with her big head, knowing she was the bonniest lass in Crieff. It was official! Shirley and Chrissie left first thing, while Mammy and Mona went into Crieff for messages, leaving me (still throaty) with my Daddy. We played snakes and ladders, then noughts and crosses, followed by I-Spy.

But there was something I needed to know, so I asked him, 'Daddy, are you building Mammy her house this year, or will we be putting on the road?'

'Well, pet, your Mother and me, we've decided to forget the house, at least for the time being. Maybe when the years hinder us we'll settle.'

I was over the shiny moon. 'Great, that'll do me fine. But what about the older lassies, you know how much they want a house.'

'We, your mother and I, will have a blether with them and see. Now get back into bed, I see Dr Mitchell's car pulling in.'

'Hello there,' he said, 'My, here's a changed bairn from the one I saw last week.' He was a big man, was the Doctor, and had to stoop when coming in. 'Oh! I see Dad's home, this must be the reason for the miracle cure.'

The pair cracked away for a minute. I paid little heed to the conversation until I heard the doctor say, 'I meant to visit you last

week, Charlie, there was a patient of mine in Friarton Prison who—.'
Did he say 'prison'? Surely not?

Dr Mitchell left with instructions to mind and drink plenty fluids.

Daddy turned his back on my gaze and said, 'Don't ask me, lassie, not now. I'll tell you when you're older, old enough to understand.'

At the age of fifteen he thought me old enough, and these are his own words:

'Like the sick mixi rabbit, I looked with slit eyes, through narrow bars that were supposed to be windows. Travellers were, and still are, looked upon as vermin. I was a travelling man who suffered regular beatings, both by fellow prisoners and guards alike. I was given the vilest chores to do. The tiny cell I shared with a mindless thug made me suffer constant attacks of breathlessness. Worst of all was knowing that, come morning, the open spaces of the countryside, with its clean air, was denied me! Our kind, unable to feel the ground beneath our feet, are better beneath the earth, and this thought plagued me day in and miserable day out. I'm not religious by any manner of means, but all that I had in that horrible place was silent prayer, night after sickening night.

I thought on my bonny Jeannie, your mother, and eight growing lassies in the bus. Thought I'd never see any of you again. A nightmare it was, lass, a living hell. Once or twice it became almost too much, I prayed for a quick end. "Forgive a helpless man, Lord, and take my breath away, I'm better dead!"

Just like your wee sick rabbit Jess, I'd have been grateful if some good shepherd had chopped the back of my neck.'

This was the true reason for Mammy not getting her 'bonnie house'. He longed to be free, to move if the mood came on him—a Travelling Man!

Chrissie found it impossible to leave her curly-headed laddie, so that spring we lost the first of the family. Mammy's heart chipped a tiny bit when her second oldest stayed in Crieff. Mona, Shirley, Janey (who had fallen out with the manager of the shop for ordering her to get her hair cut, and told him where to put his lingerie job) and the rest of us left Crieff that spring to head on up the road.

'Horse on, Macduff,' said Mammy, as she slipped her arms round Daddy's neck. 'Brigadoon, here we come!' he shouted, running his hand over her hair, then lovingly round her waist.

As we drove away from Tomaknock I glanced out the back

window to see all that remained of my mother's dream: a foundation of bricks, deep-dug drains and a forgotten washing line loosely hanging between two old oak trees. Crieff gave us many happy memories. We would go back, but never to that peaceful spot across the way from the sprawling fields of Dollerie.

20

NEEP HEID

Daddy knew the minute he rose from his bed that morning his body had gained the flu. He was also aware that the car park attendant would shortly be knocking on the door and telling us to move on. The man had been more than generous, letting us stay over the weekend, but his boss usually checked on him come Monday. No doubt then he'd be in trouble with the discovery that a busload of travellers had stayed in the car park in Perth's Inch behind the old transport café.

Daddy thanked him for his kindness, then lowered his pain-wracked body behind the wheel and took to the road. Within minutes he had pulled onto a lay-by a wee bit from the village of Methven, on the back road, and coughed his lungs sore.

As he peered through watery eyes, his attempts at driving soon became hazardous to all, and Mammy insisted he find a woodend. There was no way she would drive behind the bus while he was so ill. Poor Daddy, I must admit his colour was near skull-grey.

Soon a long narrow wood came into view. 'This will do, at least until I'm feeling a wee bit better,' he said, then added, 'Jess, go you and open the gate.'

'Daddy, what if the farmer or whoever owns this place isn't one for travellers?' I asked.

'I'll worry about that problem if and when it is one.' He peered around him to see if there were signs of life, before saying, 'No, I can't see camping here for a day or two will upset anyone.' Within no time we were parked up between a thick oak and a boulder dyke. He managed to light the fire before crawling under the feather quilt, exhausted. Mammy put the basin and tripod outside with the soap and flannel. Mary, Renie, wee Babsy and I went into the wood and gathered as many sticks for the fire as we could carry. Mammy set up the chitties and hung the kettle on the hook.

'Poor Daddy, he didn't even want a cuppy,' said Mary.

'Well,' whispered Mammy, 'just let him be. If he gets a bit of peace I'm sure it won't be long before he's himself again.' This comment always made me smile; how could someone be someone else when they were ill?

Our mother busied herself washing a few things, then hung them over a discarded fence-wire loosely suspended from a half-rotted wooden post, forgotten by whoever erected the newer one running from beyond the tree and disappearing over the horizon.

With Daddy being ill it was down to our mother to put the food on the table. She decided, after carefully removing stones from a nearby riverbed and arranging the stone hearth round the fire, to go up the road a length to see if there were houses she could hawk. The stones were taken to provide a natural cooking area and put back into the river when it was time to go. This practice amongst travelling people was normal—well, in Perthshire it was. Further up-country, Highlanders used peat squares cut from the moors. They re-used them for fuel. Usually these hardy northerners were totally dependent on peat, given the clearly visible scarcity of forests.

Leaving some water and a sandwich for Daddy, then taking us wee ones with her, she set off round the farmhouses. Folks were kind and glad to see her with the filled basket of useful bits and bobs. Some folks bought needles, others took darning wool and so forth.

I recall a couthie wee woman with long grey plaited hair who seemed pleased to see us. By her torn skirt and cardigan frayed at the elbows you could see she didn't have much, but she still managed to give Mammy a few pennies and a wee bag of scones, 'for the bairns', she said. In return, Mammy told the woman a thing or two regarding her future. I wasn't listening, because a man running up the side of a ploughed field caught my eye. 'Here you,' he shouted, 'tinker woman, get tae hell away from there, we don't need your sorts round here. I saw that blue bus in my wood. Now get back to it and be away.'

Mammy ignored him; after all, what was one more angry farmer. Did she not have enough on her plate with a sick husband and small children to see to?

'You would do well to pay heed to him, lass,' warned the farm woman, half-closing her cottage door.

'Who is he?' asked my mother.

'He's the owner of the land for miles, and all who live and work on it', she answered, before slamming her door in our faces. For reasons known only to herself she opened the door and whispered something through the slit to my mother. I didn't hear what she said except, 'So please move as far from here as you can'. That said, the door was bolted and the curtains swiftly closed. The woman's words sent a bone-shiver through my mother as she picked her basket from the cottage step and ordered us away. Within seconds the roars from the farmer were close behind us as he rapidly closed the distance. We each grabbed an inch of Mammy's coat hem. 'You,' he shouted louder this time, 'Do as I say, stop! I want you lot off my land first thing in the morning!' Mammy didn't respond. Instead, she quietly turned, and we, like baby chicks, followed at her heel. I glanced back at the man, his face bright red with temper, spit trickling down one side of his mouth. He looked like a rabid dog. I'd never seen one, but if I did I'm sure that was how it would look.

Thankfully, 'red face' changed his direction and didn't come after us. We got back to the bus safely, and Mammy set about taking the washing from the fence. She then went into the bus to see how Daddy was.

'Tell him about him with the roaring face,' I said. 'That mad, slavering-mouthed farmer. Go on, Mam, tell him.'

'No, we won't worry him today. If he thought a farmer was angry with us then poor Dad would have to move. Now, we don't want that, do we, kids?' We all agreed, then skipped off to play nearby. Mammy would have been a lot happier if the older girls were there, but with them being on a visit to Aberfeldy we were quite alone, and she hoped red-face would stay away.

The flu had got the better of Daddy, and he was out like a light. She kept us outside for a while, not wanting to wake him, and prayed that red-face would give us peace for the night. After supper, Mammy put a little water on the fire and carefully poked the heart out of it so that it wouldn't start up in the night. With being so near to a wood it was always the practice to make open fires safe before going to bed.

We hardly slept a wink because Daddy was fevered quite badly. Mammy was up and down filling a wee water bowl to sponge his fevered brow, and constantly pulling open the curtain peering at the darkness, obviously concerned at our vulnerable position.

She was up with the crows in the morning and came with each of us to toilet in the trees. Usually we did it ourselves, but this farmer had put the fear in our mother right enough. She kept darting her stare from us to the farm road, as if expecting a battalion of ploughmen to converge on us in Champion tanks and machine-guns.

Daddy was no better, in fact if anything he was worse. She decided to speak with the angry owner to try to persuade him to let us stay a few days until Daddy was back on his feet.

However, the gent in question was at our door before we'd even finished breakfast. I remember thinking 'My Goodness!' when I got a right look at him, because he had a big head with a nose that took up half of his face, and two eyes that met in the middle! He seemed to be looking at his nose when he spoke.

Three thumps on the door almost loosened its handle-bolts. He ordered my father to come out. 'I told this woman of yours yesterday. Now, are you gonna move this thing or do I get my ploughmen to pull it off for you!' Poor Daddy, this was the last thing he needed. I watched my mother's cheeks turn red, then redder, eyes round and staring. If at one time she was afraid, then her fear was rapidly replaced by anger. We had met an irate farmer who instantly disliked us and was out to cause us worry and humiliation.

Mammy checked her tongue for our sake and tried to reason with him. 'We are not troublemakers, mister, in fact we're quite helpful round a farm.' She added, 'Is there anything you need doing?'

'Where's the men?' he shouted at her, 'I canna see any men. The only work I have is for big strapping lads.' Mammy informed him that although there weren't any laddies, her lassies who would join us in a day or two were just as strong and had done many a day's work on a farm. The man laughed, which made his head look even uglier. 'Lassies are as common as rabbits,' he laughed again, 'and just as much of a pest!'

That was the straw that broke the camel's back, for nobody miscalled her lassies. I still remember the look on his face when she let him have it. 'Oh! Now is that so!' By this time she was staring him clean in the face. 'Well, I'll tell you something here that's not as common as rabbits, and that's the big red neep heid with the two cockitt eyes that's perched above your neck, lad!' She wasn't one for making fun of people's looks, but had been pushed so far that day.

'But lad, I am neither bothered by the face on you or anything else. No, there is a matter far more serious. One that you and I know of, don't we, my gun-toting friend?' We looked at our mother in total amazement. Did she not meet our unfriendly guest only yesterday?

The farmer went deathly pale and leaned back against the dyke to support his unsteady body. Mammy, seeing his reaction, went over to him, stared him in the eyes and said: 'Last night a strange spirit came to my bed. An old road tramp he was, with a great hole in his chest. "Are you a gypsy woman?" he asked me, as he appeared out of nothing in the grey black night. "The gift, do you possess it?"'

We watched the farmer turn paler still at my mother's words, before he fell into the cold stones of the dyke to steady himself from sliding onto the ground.

Mammy pulled her cardigan from her shoulders and draped it over her head. 'I told my visitor from the other side,' she whispered, 'that yes, I have the gift. "Well, woman, I canna move on until I'm revenged," he cried, as he hovered above my head. "Oh!"' went on our mother, in a whimpering voice, '"What will you have me do?" He continued, "A bad man broke my life chain, he took the breath from me: but if I tell you I'm a 'Brangat', will you understand?"'

Our mother, now with her face almost touching Neep Heid's, said, 'I tell you this, farmer: as sure as the moon's cold light falls on a lonely grave, no one interferes with a Brangat's journey, no one at all!'

Our farmer was by now slumped against the cold stone of the old dyke, eyes staring in terror from their sockets, his appearance of menace long gone. His lips quivered as he asked my mother if the ghost told her anything.

She stood back, threw her hands up towards the heavens and said, 'He told me everything!'

'Oh Lord, I'm a doomed man, what can I do, gypsy?' He leapt to his feet and grabbed my mother's hand.

She thought for a moment, before answering: 'Why should you

have worry with my ghostly friend. What manner of crime would one with such wealth and property do, sir? Did you not stand up in court and swear on a bible that it was an accident?'

The man, whose reddened face had changed to grey, confessed on both knees. 'One winter's night a hen-run up at the farm was broken in, and my prize layer stole. I'd seen him, the tramp, loitering in the area, but I only meant to frighten the pest. It was pitch dark, you see, I didn't know he was so close. It was my hand that killed him. Oh my God, what manner of revenge will he take?'

'The spirit said you would have done better to tell the judge about a certain fox who you knew for sure had been also seen near the hen-run,' said Mammy, pointing a finger at the collapsed figure now sitting on the ground with head on knees against the old dyke.

She sat down on the bus step opposite the farmer, and said, 'He told me, the spirit did, that on the twelfth night of the month he comes back to begin his revenge!'

'This is the seventh! Do you mean to say he comes in only five days time? Can you contact the fiend and speak with him? Please, woman, I'm begging.'

'Sir, this is a very hard task for me, for once a Brangat comes there is no stopping him, except if a Cattling is done.'

'What is it? I'll do it, just tell me!'

'You must visit every farmer between Sutherland and Perth, and remove a scraping from one cow's horn. Then all the scrapes of bone must be brought back. Remember where you killed the Brangat, because this is the most important of all. At this spot you must make a circle with the bone shavings, and position yourself inside. Now, please listen to what will happen if you don't do exactly what I say. He will come back each year on the same night and take a piece of your flesh until you are stone dead!'

'I'll tell all my men to get started right away,' he called, hardly taking time to breathe. With those as his parting words he was off in his rattly truck, and didn't even look back once.

What a laugh we had. Daddy had been listening and knew Mammy was making it up as she went along. But one thing puzzled us all: how did she know about the dastardly deed?

'Well, remember the wife who gave us scones?' Yes, we did.

'When she opened her door a sliver, she whispered to me that he had shot a tramp!'

'You sly thing, Jeannie,' said Daddy. 'You gave him five days, enough time for this bloody flu to be gone from me.'

So we had perfect peace while waiting on our father gaining strength. Within four days we had moved away to Aberfeldy to collect the older girls. They had such a laugh when we told them, and wished to go back that way one day to see the 'Neep-Heid' farmer.

'Mammy, how long do you think he'd sit in the circle of bone-scrapings?' I asked her.

'Until a brisk wind blew them away,' she laughed, then added, 'If I hadn't smelt strong drink on his breath that morning I wouldn't have said to the man all the things I did. You see, pet, a spirit was already in the fool, all I did was add another one.'

'And do you think he paid heed to you about the cattling thing?'

'Well, lass, who can say? But if, when he sobered up, he realised a tinker woman had pulled the wool over his eyes, the shame of it made him stay clear of us. On the other hand, what a busy man he would have been, tracking the country and scraping cows' horns. Just think what his fellow farmers were thinking. Perhaps the cratur is settling his self in a secure "Cuckoo's Nest" somewhere.'

I was curious, though. 'The Brangat spirit, on his journey, is there such a thing?'

A shiver went up my spine at her answer. 'Yes, my lass, but that's another tale!'

21

A FALLEN MAN

I think Daddy was still a wee bit under the weather and didn't feel much like work, so he decided to spend a quiet time recuperating in gentle Glen Etive before heading to Oban.

This incident that happened at that time has a special place in my heart because I am a Munro walker, and have many times since then gone back to wander through this beautiful glen, to sit on the rocks and remember.

§

Daddy should have been given some kind of award for manoeuvring the bus into its position opposite big Ben Starav. The one-track road was bad enough, but even worse was meeting a bearded, grumpy ploughman driving a Fergy and bogey filled with steamy, stinky dung. A packet of Capstan Full Strength and an hour of blue air followed before the bearded one unhitched the bogey, leaving it plonked in the ditch, and allowed my father space to drive past. Not the best start for a recuperation week.

Mammy and I had lots in common, but more than anything else it was our love of walking. I think it was from her I forged my life-time bond with the track roads and high hills. Daddy, on the other hand, had no liking for such a pastime. He used to say that tramping during his young life behind the horse and cart did that to him. 'On a wet day,' he would remind me, 'a brown trail of gutters hardened all the way from my nose to my toes as the cart wheels and horses' hooves threw up a constant stream of muck.' No, not one to put a foot in front of the other was my Dad. So how Mammy managed to persuade him to come out for a walk on that warmer than usual May Day, beats me. Perhaps cuddling each other the previous night had something to do with it, who knows but he was in a lovely mood. So here we were then, me and the folks strolling along an old hill road, towering mountains on either side.

Mammy and I were discussing our May Day wash in the dawn dew while Daddy was lighting up his fourth fag. About a mile had been walked when Daddy stopped to sit yet again on a rock cluster. 'We'll never see a drop tea this morning, Charlie, if you don't put a feather in it.'

'Shhh, Jeannie. I thought I heard a stirring down there in the heather,' he said pointing down a steep slope strewn with large loose boulders. We both joined him and stared over the ledge.

'Help, is there somebody there?' called a voice from among the rocks and heather.

'God help and save us, it's a poor man fell down the side of the hill,' exclaimed Mammy. 'Are you hurt bad, chavie?' she called to him.

'It's my leg, I think it's a goner!' was the call from deep within the rocky terrain.

Daddy went quite pale. He reminded us he'd witnessed severed limbs during the war, and knew that if the lad didn't get help soon he'd die with blood loss. 'No telling how long he's been there already. We had best get help,' he told us, adding, 'Jeannie, you go down. Do what you can for the poor soul, but careful as you go, lassie. Jessie, we'll fetch the help.'

Mammy cannily lowered herself over the precarious edge, calling reassuringly to the man, not knowing what manner of injuries he'd incurred. We waited until she called back that she'd reached him before we set off. 'Come on, pet, there's not a moment to lose,' said Dad, removing his woolly jersey and tying it round his waist. He did well running at my pace, but the recent flu and years of smoking began to slow him down. I tried to coax him on: 'Daddy, think what Mam will do if the stranger conks on her. Please try a bitty harder, surely we'll come upon a cotter house soon,' I said.

I knew, though, by the skull-grey jowls on my father, that he'd run clean out of lung air. 'God curse thon stupid man for falling into the crevice in the first place, what fool thing is that to do?'

I asked him to stay where he was and let me go on ahead to get help.

'No, I'm all right. Let's go,' was his surprised answer.

So away we went running, walking fast and stopping every so often for a breather.

It seemed like ages, and still no sign of a house, cotter or otherwise, before at long last a figure could be seen on the horizon. We both shouted—well, I did, Dad had no air to make a sound, but I never had a problem being heard (important, when living among eight females). We ran on to meet the person coming towards us on the old hill road. It was the bearded one with the smelly bogey. He took us further down to his little cottage, where we clambered onto his Fergy tractor and rumbled back to the scene of the accident. Mammy shouted up that she had things under control, and not to worry, he wasn't as bad as first thought.

Lowering ourselves down, the beardy man and I joined the pair. Daddy, unable to find the energy, stayed at the top.

Now, it's a good thing he did, because when I went back up and told him we needed a screwdriver, he found that the air came back to his lungs alright. 'What! I'll kill the stupid idiot!'

Now, why a screwdriver? And had my father not run himself to near collapse to save the man's life? Well, let me enlighten you, dear reader.

If you remember, the victim called out that he feared his leg was lost. Indeed it was! It had unscrewed from its leather socket and became stuck between two boulders while he was bird-watching. A futile attempt to retrieve his wooden leg led to his predicament. I ran back to the cottage for a screwdriver while my mother and the beardy man helped Woody onto terra firma.

Of course, Daddy didn't kick the leg from the poor lad. In fact he screwed it back in for him, after giving him a good old talking-to about hill dangers. My mother, though, because of the amount of time they had spent together, had found a friend. He came home with us and shared our supper. His name was Fred Plumley, a Yorkshire man. I wonder if he continued as a 'twitcher' in the mountains after his incident in Glen Etive? If time has been kind to you and you're still out there, then know this, Freddie boy: you almost killed my father!

We stayed in the Glen not for a week but a month. June was fast approaching when at last Daddy drove the forty miles to beautiful, idyllic Oban.

§

So there we were, then, heading on towards Oban, singing and giggling. Weather absolutely roasting. Every window of the bus wound down. A chorus of 'Bonnie Dundee' had the tartan-and- shortbread tourists picnicking by the roadside shaking heads, obviously thinking we were a busload of cuckoos out for the day.

I'm brought to smiles when I think on our loud rendition of 'Haste ye back we lo'e ye dearly' as we stretched our torsos half out the windows. This removed any doubt in their minds that their first thoughts were probably right. We fell back into our seats in fits of giggles.

'You lot will be needing me to pull off the road shortly—all that carrying on will be hastening the emptying o' bladders.' Daddy reminded us of the last time he had to pull over while the older girls followed the call of nature. It was a sight to turn faces red, no doubt! Will I tell you? Oh, all right then.

Now it's one thing young women singing in a moving bus, but peeing in a rock cluster is something uncouth, I can tell you. It was unfortunate that no one saw the lorry load of soldiers cruising round the bend in the old Glen Affrick road. The driver slowed to a snail's pace so the lads had full view of my extremely embarrassed sisters.

'Hello, lassies, needing a hand?' was the call from the khaki-clad laddies, followed by wolf-whistles and the usual ape sounds. This turned my sisters a brighter red as they fumbled with belts and buttons. Not Shirley, though. She just stood up, slowly peeled on the tightest blue jeans one could wear and said with the toss of the head: 'Get to f---, morons, can you not see we're on relief duty?'

Daddy heard her, but said nothing at his daughter's cursing, except that she was lucky there were no elderly folks in the vicinity. A girl swearing like that in those days was not proper at all!

The incident put the girls into a sombre mood, until a certain hitch-hiker brought them smiling again. Six gorgeous feet of open-necked shirt, gleaming white teeth, shiny slicked back hair and Elvis eyes.

'Look at the bronzed biceps on him,' whispered Mona.

'He's mine,' said Shirley, slithering up to Daddy, begging him

The Devil's Elbow, Glenshee

Jessie's mother with older sisters: Mona, Chrissy and Shirley

The bus that served as the Rileys' home and the 'wee Fordy van'

Jessie's mother and father with three of her older sisters, Mona, Chrissy and Shirley

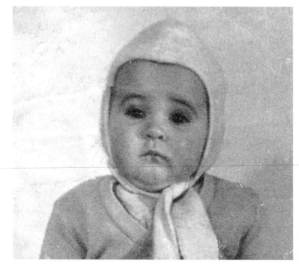

Jessie, eight months old

Jessie's mother, Jeannie (left). Uncle Wullie (Jake the Adenturer) is behind the car

Mona, Chrissy,
Shirley and Janey

Jess in her school uniform

Jess (aged 14) with her mother, Jeannie

Jess (aged 14) with her father, Charlie

to stop and give the lad a lift. Daddy never drove past a hitcher, and soon Elvis the second was surrounded by drooling females. 'Hi,' he said, in the hunkiest American drawl. A chorus of 'his' followed. Daddy asked him where he was going. He said he'd be happy to get to wherever. So for the remainder of our journey that day the girls were in heaven.

During his conversation we soon found out that although he had everything in the handsome department, the grey matter could have done with a wee bit help.

This was a conversation he had with Daddy.

'I asked this guy at the Mackinlay Distillery when the haggis-shooting begins,' said the hunk.

'Oh, now you did, and what did he tell you?' asked our father, biting his lip as he stifled a laugh.

'Sometimes this month,' was the innocent reply.

'Aye, and did he further tell you where the shoots took place?'

'As a matter of fact he said the nearest one was in the Nae Glen.'

'Och aye, that's up by thon Bonny Braes!' Daddy was near splitting his sides trying not to laugh. The girls were trying hard to stifle the same.

'Now, lad, that distillery hand was pulling your leg, because the haggis-shooting doesn't begin until late September, after the clootie shoots.' By now the girls had knuckles bitten trying not to give the game away, while the young hunk was seriously taking in every word Daddy said.

'That's a pity, because I'm heading home after August and will miss the clootie shooting.'

'Well, as it happens,' said our terrible liar of a father, 'my wife, Jeannie, just happens to have a cooked clootie in a tin ready for tonight's tea. Will you stay and share some with us?' The hunk was more than pleased, and that night sat as our guest by our campfire and ate the wee brown clootie, saying, when he had his fill, 'Is there a wish bone?' Yes, you've guessed it, we all burst sides laughing. The poor laddie thought us a happy bunch—though I've a sneaking suspicion he likened us to what they call in America, 'hillbillies'.

That night, as my sisters waved farewell to the big handsome hunk, they were less than pleased that he chose to give Mammy a big smacker of a kiss. Well, she was the one who cooked the delicious clootie, now wasn't she?

22

A NATURAL LOVE

Early June in Oban was a favourite time and place for travellers; we loved it there. No surprise, then, to find us camped not far from her lovely beaches. Mammy's brother Charlie had, as a laddie, arrived in Oban, fallen in love with the place and never left. He married Isabel, a local lass, and had three of a family.

Mammy would visit her brother and his family and keep them in touch with events and share a laugh and a crack. We bairns had other reasons to like the place: the beach had the bonniest pale sand, and, weather being on our side, we spent all day playing on it. We would catch the incoming tide in newly dug pools to bob in, and dig ditches to trap the outgoing tide. Sandcastles became villages, and we swam in the green water of the Atlantic until we looked more like prunes than bairns. The older lassies did nothing but listen to the wireless, as Elvis and Gene Vincent crooned across the ocean. They sunbathed until turning the colour of chocolate, so that the laddies would be chasing them at Blair, our next stop. This, then, was how we all spent early June at beautiful Oban.

In this particular summer our Janey had found a treasure. In a field near where we had camped was a beautiful big stallion. Jet-black he was, the bonniest creature Janey had seen in all her sixteen years.

She loved horses. Daddy knew if there were horses about nearby then that's where she would be. Our Janey had a way with them.

She would whisper in their ears, and although we never knew what she said the horses seemed to understand her. After a day she had to find out who owned the horse. 'Dad,' she enquired, 'who owns the big black beauty of a stallion?' Daddy looked at his daughter before answering, 'Janey, lass, I knew you'd be needing to know, so I asked the factor of the estate over thonder, and he told me the horse belongs to the landowner. Seems he has a daughter at university in England, and the horse is a surprise birthday present for her.' He added, 'Now, lass, don't you be going into the field beside him for he's not yet been broke.' Daddy raised his finger as a warning to his horse-loving daughter and left it at that.

'Aye, alright Dad.' She lowered her eyelids as she promised him she would stay away from the horse.

The night was clammy and Janey found it hard to fall asleep.

'Are you sleeping, Jess?' she whispered to me.

'Aye. Leave me alone, of course I'm sleeping!' I whispered back.

'You wee liar, you are not,' was her reply. 'I can ride the horse, Jess, I was on its back the day.' She could hardly contain herself as she shared her secret with me.

'God, Janey,' I answered, 'is there something missing in your head? If Daddy finds out he'll go mad moich.'

'Och, I was only sitting on him, I was hardly any distance.'

'Sister, dear, the horse might be bonny, but he's neither broke nor cut, and that's a dangerous mix; he could have killed you, lassie. Whatever were you thinking, you mad bisom?' I scolded her angrily.

'Shut your big mouth or the folks will wake up,' she said, clasping her hand over my mouth.

Next morning, Janey and I took ourselves off to see the landowner in the hope he'd let her ride the horse. Regardless of what was said, she was certain the beast was fairly tame.

The man was very nice, and he knew a lot about horses, but told Janey the horse needed lots of handling before a young lassie could go near him. Instead of telling her off, though, he showed her round his stables and happily left us to browse among his horses. We spent most of the morning wandering round the dung heaps and nose bags. My sister seemed to know instinctively what to say and do with these gentle beasts. It was difficult to think she'd hardly been near them in her life. Before we left she'd managed to brush three of them until their coats were gleaming.

The sun was exceptionally hot as we arrived home. I helped Mammy with the dishes as Janey rabbited on about the landowner's stables. I wriggled into my red cossie, still damp and sandy from the day before, and chased after the big breakers rolling onto the beach. My older sisters were still sunbathing on their towels and had turned the chocolate colour they had aimed for, as Elvis and Gene Vincent's voices still crooned over the sea. My parents went into Oban to visit Uncle Charlie and Aunt Isabel. Janey was, as usual, whispering in the stallion's lug, and that's how things were as the day headed for its end.

At supper that evening Daddy said, 'Well, lassies, in the morning we head for Blair, so check the place and make sure there's nothing left lying about. We don't want a mess left on the beach.' It was important to leave a place as one found it. A good name follows travellers who leave a camp tidy and clean. Local folks would soon remember clarty visitors on their doorsteps.

Mammy bade us all goodnight before she turned in. Daddy doused the fire before he too headed for his kip.

All was peaceful and in its place, when suddenly wee Babs noticed one of us was missing! 'Janey's not in her bed, Mammy,' she cried, sitting up and pulling the covers off the rest of us.

'I knew it, I just knew it, that bloody big stallion. She'll be half way to Kingdom Come by now!' said Mammy, rising hurriedly from her bed. Daddy quietened her down as he pulled on his trousers, then went outside to see where his horsey lassie was.

'She'll be for it now,' I thought.

Our father came back inside and said, 'Quick, bairns, come and see this.' We all rushed outside half-expecting to see Janey riding her horse, but not to see her tearing along the beach at full gallop. That was the most spectacular sight we'd ever seen. Horse and rider were one as they emerged into a blaze of black and orange, silhouetted against the red horizon. Janey knew on the morrow she and her horse would be parted forever, so she stole her only chance. She knew the animal was not a danger, and he knew, without any human handling, that she could be trusted. They had a bond that went beyond any understanding.

No one said a word as we waited anxiously for her safe return. She came back, leading her companion into its field; one last whisper, and she and horse parted. Our parents said nothing as they looked at this radiant, rosy-cheeked lassie of theirs; just a gentle arm from Mammy around Janey's shoulder, then, for the second time that night, we all took our weary bodies to bed. Janey put her hand on my arm, it was soaked with sweat. I knew, then, here was someone who would always have horses in her life.

§

If you're ever over by Brechin way, there's locals who might tell you about the middle-aged woman who rides her horses along the banks of the Esk. Janey keeps horses by her home there, never any fewer than four of them at a time, and there's always a bonny black one to remind her of her stallion. A Natural Love indeed!

23

GUNFIGHT AT 'OK YER A' DEID NOO!'

If my memory serves me right, we left Oban and went to the Berries. Here is an incident from that summer.

§

It was a Saturday afternoon. Womenfolk had shopped in the weekend's messages, bairns were quietly playing at skipping and other games that amused them, while the menfolk were either picking about with their motor engines or just cracking amongst themselves. Older children were in the nearby wood gathering sticks for campfires, whilst teenagers were sprawled lazily on the grass listening to their wee trannies, straining lugs to hear the latest top tens. An air of peaceful co-existence had settled over the campsite, and all was in its place.

I had had a grand week at the picking. Long, sunshine-enhanced days allowed me to earn a whole three pounds. Mammy was rare pleased with me, and after putting aside money for my school uniform there was two pounds for the family press. Because of my effort she said I deserved extra pocket money.

'I'm giving you half a crown, Jess, to buy whatever you want. But go easy with sweeties, all right?' She always added those words when giving me money because, 'Sugar rots teeth, so best avoid the things that are full of it, or else you'll be a gummy mouth.'

But do you know of any bairn that wasn't addicted to sookies, toffees and the likes? Therefore, with this vast amount of dosh I bought a scribbling pad, two charcoal pencils, and pocketfuls of gum-rotting sweeties.

There were many travellers on the green that year, in fact the place was near bursting at the seams. Some folks I knew quite well, others I'd never seen before. On the whole, traveller families get on fairly well together, I suppose a mutual respect for their own kind is how I'd describe it. The story I'm about to share with you, though, relates to two families who had no such respect for one another.

In the past they had argued over wintering boundaries, which each claimed as their own. This was a stretch of ground between Montrose and Arbroath, their extremely important winter home. In the early days before the families swelled to their present numbers there was plenty of room. With each new addition to the family the ground became too small. Where once it took the two families it could now only take one. Tempers flared as privacy was invaded, and children who had once played, bickered and fought.

So one cold winter's night the two heads of the said families, raged with drink, had a fight that ended in splitting them. The winner stayed put, the loser moved three miles up the road. The latter maintained his opponent cheated, the winner swore the fight was fair, and so a feud was born.

Old Geordie sucked on the clay pipe between his yellow teeth, then, spitting at the campfire with precision, leaned back in his outside armchair, pushed his bunnet forward until it covered his face, and succumbed to the hazy summer heat of that significant Saturday afternoon. His sworn enemy, old Frankie, camped at the opposite end of the green, was in the same blissful state as himself.

I was sitting under a branch of a sycamore tree sketching two wee laddies playing at marbles, when I heard Frankie shouting up to Geordie about a water-container. It seems one of the grandbairns from Geordie's lot had stolen it and Frankie's wife saw it happen. After a few choice words it wasn't long before the two old cadgers were out of their blissful existence shouting abuse at one another.

Before I continue, allow me to acquaint you with the families of the old lads. Geordie and his wife Pushkie had produced five big strapping sons. Frankie and his manshie Sally had three just as big laddies, and two lassies. Much to the horror of the elderly adversaries, Annie, the younger daughter, had that very winter secretly married Geordie's youngest son, Andra. The union was kept secret from both sides until that very summer. The newly-weds, having pitched their own wee tent between the two families, were so wrapped up in each other they could not have cared a tuppenny toss about the feuding fathers.

Now, where was I? Oh yes, as I was saying the shouting got louder as the old men continued to foul-mouth each other. At first the other members of each family left them to it, but blood flows thicker than water. Therefore when Frankie's wife, Sally, called Pushkie a 'foreigner', the two tribes went to war!

All the lads and lassies joined in. Chins were rammed forward, knuckles were clenched and broad shoulders met halfway. Fists were flying, legs kicking, handfuls of hair and skint shins were everywhere. There was roaring, screaming, blood-spattered noses, snotters, sleavers—michty, what a right old carry-on. In all my travelling, never had I witnessed such a sight. Every mother on the green quickly gathered in the weans, for fear they might get hurt if this wild melée spilled out beyond these fighting folk.

Andra and wee Annie tried their endeavours to stay neutral, but then she squealed out that her family didn't have as many laddies as her man's, and that wasn't fair. So, taking the wee tin berry luggy hanging from the guy rope of her bow tent, she walloped poor Andra on the side of his head. The love of her life stotted a mile in the air and landed with one ear a hundred times bigger than the other. 'Whit did ye cry that wife, a freendly cuddle?' he asked, clasping a hand over his swollen ear.

'Oh, now, I'm a richt fine wimin if I let yur entire breed kick ma femily up an doon the green, am I now!' she screamed at her moments-before loved one.

Suddenly the situation took on a far more drastic turn, when, from the mouth o' his tent, old Geordie gave an almighty roar: 'Yer a' deid noo!' As everybody turned to see what he meant they froze solid, because the old bisom had, of all things, the biggest shotgun that was ever seen in the hand of anybody that picked a berry!

I have to laugh to myself (though I didn't at the time), when I remember how the whole bunch of brawlers scattered into the safety of their tents. It was like shining a torch into an old barn shed in the dead of night, and watching mice and pullets flee in every direction, trampling over each other to avoid the wrath of a wife-nagged ploughman.

Frankie didn't run, though, no, not him. As cool as you like he turned his back on his gun-toting adversary, threw open the flap of the master tent, stooped inside and walked back out with as grand a firearm as Geordie's, saying 'and wha's deid noo, mash-mooth?'

This fine description was used for persons who, rather than purchase 'the water of life' from a Perthshire hidden-still man, begged it from the back door of a distillery, and drank the foul mash, rather than bothering to climb a hill and pay for the real Mackay.

By this time, every eye was staring out at the two old men from the safety of tent, tree or any place which offered relative cover from the guns. I was tempted to find a healthier spot myself, but the scene being enacted before my eyes seemed more important to my curiosity than my safety. My marble plonkers were up and gone, all abandoning their coloured glass balls to a playful puppy.

Wee Annie, full of remorse at scudding her Andra, was sobbing her two eyes out. 'Andra, ma maun, I'm no half sorry fur hittin out at ye, Lord roast me if I ever dae sic a thing again.'

'Wheest wimin,' said her bleeding spouse, 'yer faither's aboot tae blaw the heed aff ma auld Da, and a' ye kin think aboot is if I speak tae ye again.'

The stand-off continued as the two old godfathers exchanged insult for insult against relatives living and others long dead. At the same time, with each venomous mouthful, they both would take two steps forward, then two back, jumping up red with the anger, and each wondering who was going to make the fateful move. The name-calling continued, going as far back as kin that knew Rabbie the Bruce, but still the guns stayed silent. Apart from the gun-slingers, the only other sound to be heard on the green that day was the crackling of green sticks burning on now-deserted campfires.

Then it happened—old Geordie leapt a mite too high in the air, slipped and fell backwards, tripping over his own guy-rope and cracking his head on a big wooden tent peg.

Frankie, as fast as his tired bandy legs could go, was at his enemy's side. I covered my eyes with the scribbling-pad I had on my knee and thought that next the head was coming off Geordie. But, much to my and everyone else on the green's surprise, Frankie threw away the gun, and knelt down beside the slightly injured Geordie. He gently rested his one-time good friend's bruised head on a comforting arm. 'Come noo, auld freend, wit are ye dain lying there amongst the widden tent pegs? Give me yer haun, fur fine ye ken that's waur ye land when yer on the drams.'

'Well, wid ye credit that,' said wee Annie, who was expecting the stardy (police) to appear any minute and fling everybody head-first into a Black Maria van.

Hands were shaken as Geordie, nursing a roasted lump on the side of his head, said, 'Frankie, ma maun, hae ye ever seen sic a swellin on an auld maun's heid?'

Frankie laughed out loud and said, 'I swear by the Jore stane o' St Fillan himself, Geordie, better that than a hole through ma chast with yon wild gun o' yours.'

Geordie slapped his thigh and stretched his hands to the sky saying, 'Ha, wild gun indeed—my, there wisnae a firing pin in it!'

At those words Frankie went into fits of laughter, slapped his own rickety thigh and disclosed that his gun never had one either.

The feud was well and truly over; that night the two families buried the hatchets that had been wielded for many a year. When the blood stopped flowing, the beer and whisky poured in abundance. The two heads of the families spat out their anger into the burning embers of the fire, shook hands as is tradition, then vowed to remain friends until death.

'That's all well and good,' came the quiet voice of wee Annie, 'but in a' the carry-on, me and Andra's wee tent got flattened, so when ye've a mind tae it, wid ye baith git us another ane.'

As for their wintering ground, well, as each member of the family married and left home, it went back to its original size. The old friends continued to coexist until Pushkie was left a house by an old professor whom she cared for while he was bed-ridden. And it was here that she and Geordie lived out their last days.

On a more serious note, it is a known fact among travelling people that in the not so distant past, feuds between families have resulted in death. This strengthens my belief that after the Highland clearances many clan remnants, outlawed by church and government, joined with gypsies, tinkers to trade and wandering minstrels to survive. I do not have the proof needed to enter this into history books, but if you were to join a travellers' campfire sing-song and compare the experience with a Highland ceilidh you would be surprised by the similarities. It's such a pity historians have ignored the travellers' history in Scotland, given that so many have opted out of the old ways to settle in towns and cities, living a lie about their rich cultural past. Who could fail to understand their reasons, however, when harassment of travelling people begins with the breast milk.

24

THE SHEPHERDESS AND HER WEE DUG

As wee Tiny has been part of the family for some time now, I would like to share this little moment of canine joy with you. On leaving the Berries, Mammy often had a hankering to while away a few days in the area of her birth. This was one of those times.

§

Foxies can be, so I've heard, a mite crabbit in nature, but not our wee lad. He loved to sit in a doll's pram, dressed in a baby cardigan and woolly shorts, while all the bairns in the green took turns pushing him around. He must have felt like a wee king with a baby bunnet propped on his head. Everybody laughed, and the more they did so the more he seemed to enjoy himself.

He had another side to his nature though, because when Daddy went rabbiting and moling, the wee dog was set loose in barns to thin out rats, and this was where he revealed his true nature, and it certainly wasn't bonny!

He could be just as content on the road hawking with Mammy, being petted by folks as she went from door to door. Yes, Tiny was a family pet if ever there was one, and we loved him to bits.

The bus was mechanically sound and we were all fit, so Dad asked Mammy were she wanted to go. 'Is it to Brigadoon, wife?' he asked her jokingly.

'Hell, no, Macduff,' (her fun name for him) 'how about a trip to

Inveraray, it's a while since we were there, and given that the bracken cutting will be in full swing, we're sure to see a lot of other travellers.'

'Okay, wife of mine, the bonny wee white village it is.'

Mammy was drawn to Inveraray because, just a bit down the road, was the tiny picturesque town of Tarbet on the shores of Loch Fyne. It was here that my grandmother, many years ago, lay down exhausted and gave birth to my mother. Granny Power was on her way to visit her sick sister in Strachur when she went into labour with Mammy. It was late at night, and she'd been on the road for days. Unable to go any further she took a branch from a birch tree, inserting it into the sleeve of her coat. In pain she crawled under her makeshift shelter, then, without help from a single soul, brought the baby into the world. After cleansing the precious bundle in the loch, she fed her gift from God before resting and continuing on her journey. My mother's birth certificate states she was born in a tent, near Tarbet, Loch Fyne, 15 October 1915. No silver spoon there, just a pot of pure gold, because to me that is what she was. When she saw the wording on the document, she later told me it was untrue. 'I wasn't born in a tent, I came into this world under my mother's good tweed coat!'

The sea loch at Inveraray was, or so I thought anyway, much bluer than the rest of the ocean inlets, and warmer. The little town looked as if it had stayed the same for hundreds of years. Rows of wee boats bobbed in the harbour, while the main street of painted white houses shared their reflection in the crystal water with the little boats.

Do not be fooled, though, by Inveraray's beauty, because a couple of centuries ago, the mere mention of the place sent fear into the bravest heart the length and breadth of Scotland. The visitor rarely tarried here, because this was where the infamous courthouse and jail stood side by side. People were tortured for the pettiest of crimes. Little children were imprisoned alongside lunatics, and pregnant women locked up for not informing their spouse of their condition. Some poor souls, when the jail was overcrowded, never saw the inside of a cell. Instead, the bottom of the loch was their place of confinement, especially the vagabond or tramp who just happened to fall foul of Judge Death and Thumbscrews.

Recent work on both the courthouse and the jail has restored the once-derelict building to its former glory (if that is the proper word), and I assure you a visit to the place is well worth it.

Fortunately, my crime, which I will shortly tell about, took place in the twentieth century, and I thank my good God for that.

I'd walked up and down the beach for ages that first morning, looking for scrap metal for my scrappy bag. Finding small bits of green-coloured copper and the merest trickle of solidified molten lead and little else was enough to send me off to pastures new. My young sisters were content to play by the sea and her shoreline, but I had a hankering to explore the forest on the opposite side of the campsite. 'Mammy, can I go into the wood and play?' I asked my mother, as she filled the metal bath with hot water from the big black kettle on the open fire. She had the biggest pile of washing heaped beside the bath, so there was no doubting what she had planned to do with her day.

'Of course you can, my bonny wee lamb, but only if you take the dog with you,' she answered.

'Do I have to?' I protested, 'He'll frighten the baby bears, and you know what will happen if he gets his mouth round a squirrel's neck!'

She laughed at my ridiculous excuse. 'Bears here in Inverary, well, that's a new one on me! And as for yon wee squirrel, there's not a dog in the whole world can shift itself up a tree at yon speed.'

I could see that, if I wanted to explore the woods, then the dog was to be my companion, on that day at least. Making myself the biggest piece of jam my fingers could hold, I set off into the woods to play.

'Jessie, have you forgot someone?' shouted my Mother, pointing at wee Tiny, whose tail was about to propel him into the air with excitement as he wagged it so fast.

'Come on, wee monkey, but mind now and leave the beasties of the trees alone, all right!'

The forest was thick with giant fir trees. Leaving the open space and going into this place was like entering another world. Tiny was into every wee hole, nose glued to the ground and sniffing at tree roots in the hope he would prove my mother wrong by catching a speedy squirrel. Thank God, she was a hundred percent on this one.

Now and then a movement in the trees behind us had me swiftly glancing back to see what it was, but only the keenest eyes would catch a glimpse of the shy red deer staring back at them.

My companion and I explored what seemed like miles of dense trees, but apart from one squirrel sighted at the top of a very tall tree and a noisy jaybird, the forest was a wee bit of a disappointment. Soon we'd left the denseness of the woods behind us, and found ourselves staring out at a vast expanse of hillside, half covered in purple heather, and half in thick bracken.

Tiny was more at home in this terrain as he chased cocky rabbits in and out of the bracken, pushing his wee head out now and then to let me know he was still there. I did not mention that the year before we almost lost the daft dug when he got stuck in a rabbit warren and Daddy had to borrow a farmer's plough to dig up half a field to reach him. He was pretty near his end when he was found, because he slept for a week afterwards. He'd learned his lesson, though, and always stopped at the mouth of the burrow, not going one step past it! That incident cost my father dear. In payment for the use of the plough, he had to do the farmer's moles—five acres of them.

That morning, Tiny and I had explored quite a large chunk of Inveraray's countryside. I imagined that this must have been how David Livingstone felt, going through the jungles and plains of Central Africa. Of course this was no such place: here on Scotland's rugged west coastline was the land of the Duke of Argyll, and there were plenty people looking after it.

As my companion and I reached yet another purple hilltop, we stopped and sat down to watch a shepherd way down in the glen rounding up his sheep. He had four collie dogs. Each one followed the commanding whistle their master gave them, going in different directions until all the sheep were huddled together. I stared down at my wee mongrel dug crouching beside me and wished for a second that he was an obedient collie instead of a wee ratter! Tiny sat up, licked my face, then gave a sad whine as if to say, 'It's not my fault I'm a terrier.' When he stared at me with those big brown eyes I felt so guilty.

'Och, yon collie dogs would make useless pets; nothing like you, my wee pal,' I whispered in his perked ear, giving a reassuring hug at the same time.

We watched the shepherd and his dogs until every sheep was safely in the pen. Securely closing the heavy iron gate, he gave a final whistle and the four obedient animals were at his heel. Resting his crook against the gate, he took a pipe from his jacket, filled it with baccy and lit up. Adjusting the bunnet on his head he retrieved his stick, gave his flock one last look, then set off down the road, probably for his dinner. I thought about mine, and the dog looked a mite hungry as well, but before I headed for home I couldn't resist a wee look at the shepherd's sheep. Ignoring my empty belly I skipped down to where they were safely penned in. Tiny stayed at the hill's brow, refusing to join me. He well remembered the time Daddy used a stick on him for chasing sheep at Furry Murdoch's farm. There's many a traveller lost dogs to a bullet for being too near sheep.

As I walked round the crowded pen, I imagined myself in the proud role of 'Shepherdess to the Honourable Duke o' Argyll'. 'Yes, no bother to me, that job' I thought. 'Dog, come here the now with me, we have a job to do.' The wee dog took one look at me, lay down on his belly and covered his nose with his two paws!

Spying to see if the coast was clear, I lifted the latch over the gatepost with the intention of letting out one sheep. I meant to put it back when I was sufficiently trained, but nothing ever turns out the way you intend, does it? Especially when you haven't a clue what you're doing. The weighty gate lifted me off my feet as it swung open, and for a moment the sheep looked at me like I was nutty, all except four who bolted the minute they saw the open gate. With every bit of strength in me I pushed shut that iron menace just in time, before the rest of them got the same idea as their mates. The big problem being, how would I get them back? There was no way I could open that gate to put them in without the whole lot of them scattering across the brown bracken, purple heather and dark green forest.

I don't know who got the biggest fright, me, the sheep, or Tiny! As I surveyed the situation I thought the only thing to do was try to keep an eye on them until, hopefully, I met the shepherd coming back. That is, if he was coming back.

Now, I don't know about you folks, but whenever I saw sheep in a field they were always standing chewing the grass, but not these wild woollies. No, they were for a donner down the road.

So there you have it, then: my dog and me were sheep stealers! I suppose you're wondering, 'Why did she not go back through the woods and leave the beasts to the open moor?' Well, I'll tell you why, because the craturs might have gone walkabout and found themselves down near the campsite where there was not only plenty of grass to chew, but plenty big dogs who might just have liked the look of them to chew! And if that happened, who had been wandering in the place that day? Yes, yours truly! I would have been leathered for a crime of that magnitude, nothing surer. No, I was stuck with the sheep until somebody took them off my stupid hands.

I'm not sure if it was the hunger pangs; then again, maybe I was beginning to lose my concern for the sheep. Anyhow, I made my decision. I would abandon them after all, turn tail and head for home. 'Come on, Tiny, let's go,' I said, but the wee dog wasn't paying heed to me. His ears were up, nose madly sniffing at the air—something had disturbed him. Then I noticed the reason for the dog's behaviour. Coming round a bend in the road was the man with his four collie dogs. 'God, I'm for it now,' I thought, 'here's the very person I hoped never to see.'

As the shepherd got closer, I noticed he was a lot bigger than he looked earlier from my viewpoint at the top of the hill, and the nearer he got the bigger he grew. Lordy, Lord almighty, what a monster! I noticed the size of his forearms—lumps of beef would be how I'd describe them! 'Hello there, mister, how are you doing this fine day?' I called out. 'Never you mind how I'm doing, where'd these sheep come from, eh?'

As my eyes darted from the giant's cloth-capped head to his tackitty-booted toes, I knew that one thing was certain on that fateful day, that he wouldn't hear the truth from me! Maybe if he was a mite smaller, but no way was I about to take a chance. 'Oh, you'll not believe it, sir, but some bracken bairns were playing over by the sheep's pen, and as sure as I'm standing here this day, the wee devils let out the beasts. I shouted at them and warned if thon sheep got free lurchers would tear them apart, but they kept on, being right wee wildies.'

God forgive me, if my mother had heard how easy that lie came pouring from my mouth, she would have disowned me for sure.

The shepherd looked puzzled, and said, 'You mean to say weans got the heavy gate open? Well, the wee middens.'

As the big man thought about his sheep scattered all over the moors his face went red with temper, and his brow gave the appearance of four tattie drills stuck together. Worst was his nose. What a size of a thing—the only way to describe it was that it was as if he'd been hit square on with a shovel. However, it looked as if he believed me. I was on a roll, praise be. I continued lying,

'Don't you fret yerself over the rest of the sheep, because I pushed the heavy gate shut while my wee dog growled at them and they stayed put. He's a braw sheepdog you know, mister.' The man's collies just sat there eyeing up my Tiny, probably wondering what he was! Then, at a word of command, they rounded up the escaped sheep and in no time had them back in the pen with the others. 'Thank you kindly, lassie,' said the shepherd, 'for doing me that good turn. Now, what's your name, and whereabout did you come from? I suppose you'll be a tinker bairn here for the bracken-cutting.'

'No, I am not here for the brackens. No, I am certainly not a tinker, we are traveller folk,' I shouted. One thing that really angered me was that word 'tinker'. For a moment my pride got the better of me and I forgot who I was raising my voice to, so quickly apologised for my behaviour. He laughed and asked why folks should feel ashamed of being a tinker. Then he told me his great-grandfather was one. 'A very able lad he was,' he said. 'People would look for him coming, because without his skilled hands many a pot lay broken.' He went on, 'If women folks didn't see a yearly visit, then knives, forks and spoons got the worst for wear. So, lassie, remember everybody has a use. But never mind that, have you had any dinner, lassie? I don't think you have. Come back to my house and the wife will give you some soup.' The biggest man in Argyll smiled, and his face looked totally different, kindly-like. We walked back cracking away like good old friends. 'We've no wee ones our self, bairns that is, except the lassies here,' he said, pointing at his four dogs. 'That's Win, and that's Peg and the two playing with your wee spyug are Blacky and Nell.'

'My mother has her fair share of women too, with eight of the blighters incuding me,' I said.

What a laugh he gave out at my remark. 'All those women in a tent, good grief, your poor father must be driven mad!'

'No, no, man, we don't bide in a tent, we live in a bus. We're posher than that, I'll have you know.' My bus had taught me a sin, one of pride.

The man laughed even louder, and said, 'With all those daughters my father would be demented, no matter where we lived,' and I had to agree with him on that one.

Soon the house came into view and the dogs ran on to alert the wife of our arrival. 'What's this, then, Dougal?' said the woman, who was as big as her man, and just as bonny, 'a lost wean?'

'Na, lost sheep, wife.' Her husband told her about my heroism, my false heroism that is.

'Come you in and get a plate of soup, pet, I'm thinking you deserve it.'

I didn't half feel guilty, but after washing my hands at the outside well, then tucking in to a braw plate of chunky vegetable soup, finished off with a giant scone and melted butter, my only thought was—crime pays! Tiny was given a bit of cooked rabbit that disappeared down his throat quicker than a haddy slides down a seal's.

Soon it was time to go home, sadly, because I had become quite attached to those friendly folk. The grandfather clock dominating their lobby was striking four, and if I didn't get back pronto then Mammy would have the search party out.

Dougal's dogs, one by one, jumped into the back of an old jeep while I sat in the front, Tiny on my knee. After a final goodbye to the big man's wife with promises to visit next year, we headed down the narrow hill road. 'Mammy's mouth will be dry whistling on me. You don't mind telling her what I've been up to, do you Dougal?' I asked, beginning to think a welcome was the last thing I'd get from her when I got back.

'Don't you worry your wee head, I'll tell her she's got the best bairn in the whole of Scotland.' He laughed, then said I was a braw bairn and wished he and the wife had a family.

'Steady on, big man, even I know she'll not have you exaggerating to that extent.'

As we got nearer home I was beginning to feel a right wee cheat for putting the blame on those invisible bracken bairns. I suppose it's called 'conscience', but it was fair eating away at me. We arrived back in time to see a search party consisting of my older sister Janey, her new boyfriend (I can't recall his name) my Daddy and one or two local lads who just happened to be beach-combing nearby.

'Jessie, for God's sake, lassie, we thought you were stolen or something! Where the hell have ye been?'

I had never seen my Mother look so worried, or angry, so I shoved Dougal the giant in front of her to do the business. I sat on a rock at the water's edge and listened as Dougal sang my praises to everybody.

When he had finished, Mammy came over and looked into my eyes with her 'is that true?' stare. I knew there was no way I could lie to her. So, out came the truth, accompanied by a flood of guilty tears.

Tiny, my partner in crime, sat at my side as if to say, 'If you're in hot water, then so am I.'

Dougal came over and stood towering above me, then said, 'Do you know the story of the jail and the judge who threw weans like you in prison alongside the lunatics?'

'Aye, him who lived hundreds of years ago.' I said, rubbing the tears from my eyes with the edge of my cardigan.

'Well, perhaps nobody told you, but the present judge, his great-great-grandson, punishes folks in the same way, and tomorrow sits in the courthouse to deal with sheep-stealers.'

'Oh, please, Dougal, don't let on! I'll work at your house, any chores you or your good lady need doing, only please don't tell on me.' My heart leapt a mile in my chest as fear gripped me.

The big shepherd put his hand on my shoulder and said he knew all along that I was the one who had let the sheep out. I asked him how he knew. 'I saw you watching me from the top of the hill before I went away, and as there were no other bairns for miles then it had to be you.'

I asked him why he didn't row me in the beginning.

'Because you had the decency to stay and face me. That meant you cared.'

Those words said, the big shepherd looked at my mother, gave a wee wink, then told me never to lie like that again. I promised him I wouldn't, and to avoid the taunting of my sisters, ran down the beach to lick my wounds, Tiny at my heel.

After a good crack with my parents, Dougal waved goodbye and set off in his old jeep with his four collie dogs, and oh, how I wished I'd never set eyes on them—well, perhaps for the rest of the day at least.

That night the big shepherd and his wife came back to join the bracken folk and us. As the campfire crackled away, we all sat round with the rest of the bracken bairns singing and cracking. And guess who was the centre of conversation? Aye, the 'Shepherdess and her wee dug', who had learned a valuable lesson: you can't pull wool over a wool man's eyes!

25

KIRKCALDY

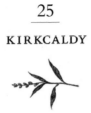

In summer, the traveller was free. With no rules or ties to bind or imprison, we were like birds in flight. However, there was a government, and they stated that 'all nomadic children should be schooled'. I liked Crieff school, but my parents would not return to Crieff, their favoured winter ground. Daddy had found another place. Come with me to Kirkcaldy.

§

Kirkcaldy was not to my liking. This East Coast town in the Kingdom of Fife would have to work hard to win me over. I didn't take easily to the smell of her life's blood: linoleum. It found its way into my nostrils and onto my skin. Nor did I care for the coal-black faces of her men that I would see every day. Those hardy lads who worked beneath the earth's surface to fill fire-scuttles, and could still smile in spite of it!

Within her boundaries I ceased to be a true 'traveller'. Where were my hills? My glens? This place was alien to me, a Perthshire traveller. Although she was home to many of my own kind, they seldom went on the road. The women gave up hawking and the skill of fortune-telling, which was handed down through generations, to work in the linoleum factories, while the young men joined the scaldie boys in the coal mines, never again to deal the horses or lift tatties or clear the vermin from acres of grassland. It became evident to me, as the days turned to years, that my own kind found 'self denial' an easy thing. No, I definitely did not like this place, but I, like my kin, grew to tolerate her rugged coastline with coal-dust for sand. What I did learn to appreciate, though, was her people, genuine folks with a working-class background second to none. There were open doors and smiling faces, and people were seldom judgmental. Perhaps this generosity of spirit was the reason why many travellers left the road and settled here.

I knew one thing that day in the late autumn of 1959, when we pulled onto the Gallatown's Lennie's Yard next door to Andrews' coal depot in the north of the town, that would be our wintering ground for many more seasons. I heard my father say to Mammy, 'I've found us a place to winter for years to come.'

High walls, excluding us from public view, gave a privacy my older sisters had longed for, and here, more precious than gold dust, was a toilet, one that flushed. For my parents this was a good place to live, because Daddy's sister Maggie and Mammy's sister Lena were already settled here. Auntie Maggie was mother to my torturing cousin Joey (remember the slow worm?). Auntie Lena was married to Tommy Reekie and mother of fourteen of the happiest kids I had ever met. I can say, in all honesty, what they lacked in material wealth they certainly made up for in love. We'll spend some time with them later.

Within days we were schooled, me at Sinclairtown primary and my sisters in Dysart infants school. Mona left us because she fell out with Daddy over some lad she was seeing, one he didn't approve of, while Janey and Shirley got jobs in the town.

That first winter we acquired electric lights. Gallatown football club shared the yard with us through their changing rooms. A nod and a backhander to the handyman allowed Daddy to wire into their meagre electricity supply. Now, far be it from me to say Daddy would ever willingly put our lives in danger, but on this occasion let me tell you how he did just that!

I can't say what wakened me, whether it was the incessant rain battering the corrugated roof of the lean-to beside the bus, or Tiny whining to get out. I lay for ages, before whispering for Daddy to let the dog out. No answer from him, so I decided I would have to do it. Sweeping my hand across the floor to find a pair of shoes I stood up, only to be knocked abruptly back onto my bed. 'Stay there, lassie, and don't move.'

It was my father.

'Why? If the dog doesn't get out soon he'll soak the carpet,' I said, a little confused at my father's reaction.

'Look at the glow, Jessie, the bus is glowing!'

I opened my half-sleepy eyes, rubbed them and stared. 'God almighty, what is it, a space ship?' The entire bus was engulfed in a bright blue haze. My heart began to beat loudly in my chest, as one by one the younger girls awakened to the same phenonomen.

'I think I know what it is, but I hope I'm wrong,' said Daddy in a whispering voice.

My mother had risen and sat on our bed, gathering us up like a hen whose chicks are about to be gobbled up by the wily fox. Daddy told her to keep us away from windows and on no account to touch anything metal. I curled my toes off the floor, knowing that, somewhere down there in the dark, were rows of brass screws.

For a moment there was silence, then Daddy said, 'If I don't get us out we might all fry.' Saying that, he threw himself at the door. Sparks formed under his fingers and ran up his arm, but there was no turning back. I can still smell the burning flesh of my poor father's hands as he wrenched open the door. He was thrown several feet in the air, as if invisible hands had shaken him like a rag doll. Mammy screamed, so did I, and we ran out through the opened doorway to see him lying, Tiny beside him, both unconscious on the wet gravel. The blue haze was gone, but sparks and a hissing sound came from an exposed cable thrashing on the ground. Mammy told me to watch over the girls while she got help from a lorry driver, sleeping unaware in his cab round by the front gate. He threw several empty coal bags on the hissing cable, while Mr Andrews, the coal merchant from next door, and his wife helped Daddy, who was by now groggy but conscious, into their car. What a close call, that night!

Next day he came home from hospital. Apart from a badly burned hand and broken ankle, he was none the worse. The lorry driver, who broke the changing-room door off its hinges to get in, fixed the electricity.

Poor wee Tiny, although none the worse for his ordeal, did look awfy sorry for himself. Mammy bought him a string of beef links (sausages) all to himself. Well, if he hadn't started whimpering then we might all have been fried brown like our hero's treat. Seriously, though, we were very near being burnt to death that night. When Daddy got the power back in his hand, he made sure the job was done right the next time, by burying the cable, properly insulated, deep beneath the ground.

One thing I remember about our modern brightly-lit bus was how dull the moon looked as I gazed up from my little bus window during cold frosty nights! Before the electric light my moon was the brightest light I knew.

§

Let me now take you down to Laurel Crescent, near Victoria Hospital. Midway up the street, in a sprawling house, dwelt Mammy's younger sister Lena. Sharing her life, as I mentioned, were fourteen kids and her man (an only child), Tommy Reekie. I say this with the utmost sincerity: never had I spent time with a happier bunch. The front door was never locked, and visitors were given a row for knocking. They just stood at the open door and shouted 'hello'.

Lena or Tommy would, if they heard them, shout back, 'come in whoever you are, but only if you've blown yer nose and are clean and honest.' People who knew them just walked in and helped themselves to a cup of tea from an ever-boiling kettle. If, on the other hand, a debt collector came a-calling, then he or she was wasting their time. Their call was never answered, so after a long wait they just abandoned their visit. On the kitchen table sat a massive pot. Each day it was filled, either with stovies or chunky vegetable soup. A bread-bin brimming with crusty loaves accompanied the pot, and this was their staple diet. No biscuits, sweeties or puddings. Needless to say, they had the bonniest teeth in all Kirkcaldy.

Bairns leapt up and down on the two biggest settees you'd ever seen. The infant pram, which sat by the window in the living room, was always filled with a sleeping bairn.

Auntie Lena loved singing. Tommy played the accordion. So usually when supper was over and pyjamas donned, the house boomed with singing and laughter.

Some summers they came with us to the Berries with the biggest tent (purchased from an army store) you'd ever seen. Auntie Lena would throw back the tent door, peer inside and call 'Are you all in bed?' Of course half of them would be missing, either playing in the nearby wood or routing about some place. Did Auntie Lena know that half her brood was missing? Of course she didn't, because the truants paid one or two of their brothers and sisters to imitate them.

26

ONE COLD NIGHT

Soon we were into the dead of winter. It was late at night, a storm had threatened all day and I lay in bed freezing, unable to sleep.

'Mammy,' I whispered, so as not to wake my three younger sisters. 'I am freezing to death lying here, is there a pair of Dad's socks for my feet?'

A quiet snore from my mother told me she was asleep and it seemed selfish to wake her.

This was my thirteenth year, and I had pestered Daddy to have my own bed. All four of us lassies used to sleep like sardines in the big bed, but we were growing, and nights were filled with toes stuck in noses and elbows rammed in ribs. Sleep was the one thing we didn't do. So here I was in my nice single bed, actually more like a bench than a bed, and, on this bitter cold night, I was sorely tempted to sneak back in beside my siblings. Each turn of my body allowed more cold air in to share the bed with me in my wynceyette goonie, which, incidentally, I had worn for more years than I could remember. I thought of rolling myself up in the blankets and lying on the floor, but there was a mousetrap under the table somewhere. I cringed at the very idea of a contorted wee mouse and me lying together on the floor, so I continued to shiver where I was.

My persistent turning about in bed eventually wakened Mammy. 'Can you not sleep, pet?' she asked. 'Is the bed ower cold?'

'God, Mam, the cheeks of my backside are like two frozen

stones on a dyke, and my feet have long since been replaced by icicles.'

'Aye, I'm feeling the cold myself, Jess, and with your father visiting Granny Riley at Pitlochry I miss his old bones lying beside me.'

'Aye, poor Granny, I hope she gets over the flu soon,' I said. Here was I fussing over a wee bit cold, and her struck down with the dreaded influenza. Granny was in her seventies and quite frail. A simple sneeze sent the family to her bedside in a state of deep concern.

Sadly, this time my dear old Granny did not recover. Within three days of that cold December night, she passed away. Perhaps this was the reason this particular tale is more vividly remembered.

'Och, you're a poor wee cratur right enough,' said Mammy. 'Come on, you and me will sit down by the stove and warm ourselves, there's just enough heart left in the fire, it only needs a poke.'

I watched as my Mother silently and quickly put a little coal on the wee three-legged stove; then, to my delight, she poured some milk in a saucepan for cocoa and sat it on the top to boil. She draped a tartan rug round my shoulders and gave me Daddy's thick grey army socks—not ones from the War, just socks bought from the Army and Navy stores. While I popped them on my frozen feet, she poured the bubbling cocoa into two big mugs.

In no time at all I'd forgotten how cold I was as we sat there, hands cupped round our cocoa, staring at the red glowing embers of the wee stove.

'The wind's whipping up a cracker of a storm by the sounds of it,' said Mammy.

'It'll snow for sure,' I added.

'This weather reminds me of a tale your Granny Riley told me once, about an ancestor of Granddad's. Do you think you'll bide awake long enough to hear it, Jess?'

'Aye, that I will, Ma, but do you think, seeing as Daddy's away, you'll let me sleep in the big bed with you?'

'We'll see, we'll see. Now drink the cocoa before it goes cold.'

Now, let's begin.

§

Old Flora and Hamish Johnston farmed a wee holding in a remote part of Glen Tilt. Long years working the soil was beginning to take its toll, and where once both of them laboured, now most of the chores were done by Hamish. They had one son, a giant of a man by the name of Joseph. Flora had lost three children, all girls: one was stillborn, the other two died in infancy. That was many years ago. Joseph was now forty, and as the old woman watched her son striding up the hill road, she wondered if she would live to see a grandchild.

Unlike his father, Joseph's heart lay in forestry. He made his living amid the woods of Atholl and, as often as work permitted, spent most of his spare time visiting his parents. He built a small but sturdy wooden shack in the wood several miles from his parents' farm, and here he spent the long summer months working timber on the sprawling north Perthshire estate.

Joseph waved to his mother as he caught sight of her standing in the doorway of the wee white cottage. 'How are you keeping, old wife?' he asked, lifting her up in his big arms.

'I'd be doing a lot better if you didn't just squeeze all my ribs together, my big brute of a son.'

'Well, I'm fair glad to see you, Mother, fair glad right enough. What's for dinner, and where's the old man?'

'He's away into the village for some flour and an odd thing or two, he'll not be long.'

His mother looked at her fine son and he knew what was coming next.

'I was just saying to myself as I watched you coming up the road, laddie, it would be nice if you could find a wife. Is there no lass caught your eye yet? A bunch of bonnie bairns is what you need. That is, before it is too late.'

'Now, Mother, don't you start that again, I'm fine the way I am.'

He turned and said, 'I'll away down to the village, maybe Father has need of a hand.'

Flora smiled as her son strode off to avoid any more awkward questions, muttering to himself, 'I wish that mother of mine would leave things as they are.'

As Joseph reached the outskirts of the village, he saw his father talking to some folks. Getting closer, he saw it was a man, a girl and three wee lads.

Hamish, on seeing his son approach, said, 'Here comes my lad, he'll help carry your belongings up to the house. These folks have come all the way down from Kingussie, Joseph, and I have promised them a bite to eat and a bed for the night.' This was quite a common event: Hamish was renowned for his generosity, and, regardless of who they were, if a person was in need of help, then he never hesitated to offer a hand.

Joseph smiled at the bedraggled travellers, picked the heaviest of the packs, and walked on back to the wee house, wondering where they would all sleep. He failed to notice the lassie behind him, who was trying to keep up with his long strides.

'Hello, I'm Helen, and who might you be? You wouldn't be a two-legged Clydesdale pony, now would you?'

Joseph laughed as he realised his long strides must have been hard for this five-foot-nothing trying to keep up with him. 'Och, I'm sorry lassie, I mean Helen, I do tend to go a bitty fast. I reckon it's to do with working the forest. Oh, and my name is Joseph.'

'That's a gentle name for a giant.' Her face lit up with such vibrant beauty he felt a flush of red fill his cheeks and turned away, not knowing why.

Flora shrugged her shoulders when she saw the visitors. If she'd a penny for every time Hamish went into the village for a bag of groceries and came back with some needy soul in tow she'd have a fortune. So, as always, she made the family welcome, although it would be a tight squeeze. Nevertheless she managed to make up enough beds, then set about preparing her wee house for their night's sleep.

The man, a tinker to trade, told his hosts that his dear wife had recently died in childbirth. With tear-filled eyes, he went on to describe how, from first light on through until the next day she struggled to give him a fifth child, but it proved too much and she was weakened beyond recovery. 'My beautiful wee woman closed her eyes, never to open them again. I laid our dead infant in her arms before she died. To pay the doctor I'd to sell the cart and pony. So I made a makeshift stretcher to carry her body from Tomatin to be buried among her own folk up at Kingussie.' The man went on to say they were heading down to winter at Stanley, where he would work for a farmer he knew.

Flora's heart opened to the sad family as she remembered how she herself had almost died in failing to bring a bairn into the world alive. 'We would be more than pleased to ask you to bide awhiles here. At least until the end of the month. You can help Hamish fix a fence or two, and there's the cowshed, it needs tending.' Flora went on, 'Our only son, big Joseph here, works in the wood and has little time to do as many chores as he'd like, so with his father coming sore with age, I'm sure your help would be well appreciated.'

The tinker looked with kindness at Flora, then at Hamish, before saying, 'Thank you kindly, folks, but without my horse I'd never make it before the first of the snow.'

Hamish, who was listening to the man and could tell he was an honest cratur, said, 'Now, how does this sound to you, my man? We've an old gairn over yonder on the braeside. She's been retired for a year or two now, but I dare say there's a bit of power left in her old legs, and she would get you to Stanley before the weather changed. God, I've seen her carry many a stag off the hills in her day—aye, she has powerful legs, that old lass. Now, what do you say?'

Joseph, who was deep in conversation with the bonny sixteen-year-old Helen, said he'd be pleased to make a cart for the family if they took the gairn.

The tinker, who had never been shown hospitality of this meas-ure in all his life, could not refuse, and thanked his generous hosts most kindly.

That was settled, then. For the next few weeks, the tinker fam-ily lived with Flora and Hamish, while Joseph, with a great deal of company from Helen, built the cart. The old woman crocheted gloves and socks for the wee lads as their father helped Hamish fix fences and make watertight the cowshed and hen-huts for the coming winter.

As the weeks passed, the old woman noticed something she thought never to see: her son was becoming increasingly drawn to the bonny Helen. The pair had the same likes, laughed at the same things, and sat well into each night simply chatting and being together. They became closer, and soon Joseph could think of nothing else but the young tinker lass. He was falling in love! And that love was met with returned love. When the time came for the family to depart, Helen asked her father if she could stay with the kindly folk and help the old woman with the daily chores. 'Father,' she said, 'the lads are a fine size now, you won't be needing me, will you?' She went on, 'Surely you can see how crippled Flora's fingers are?'

The man could see his daughter would be well looked after, so without argument he agreed to let her stay. However he too knew, as Flora did, that the lassie's real motives had more to do with Joseph than the old woman's chores.

Soon the day arrived to say farewell to the visitors. Helen's father took Joseph aside and said, 'Have you something to ask of me? Are you not asking for our Helen's hand. After all I might never pass this way again.' He continued, 'Now, man, I know you're not that much younger than myself, but I've seen the way the lassie looks at you; and given that I don't know kinder folk than you and your family, well, if it's my blessing you want, you have it.'

Joseph, being a man of few words, could only manage to say, 'I'll take the greatest care of your lassie, I swear to you. Not a hair on her precious head will be harmed. For none could love her as I do.'

The tinker family bade farewell to their Helen, leaving her in the tender caring home of the hill farmer's son, twenty-four years older than herself.

The following spring, while daffodils and willow trees bloomed in their midst, the big woodsman took the bonny Helen, now seventeen, to be his bride. She was like a breath of fresh air as she sang and skipped about the farm, feeding the hens and milking the cows. She made new curtains for the wee windows of the old farmhouse and filled them with vases of sweet-smelling meadow flowers. Flora and Hamish could not have been happier with their new daughter-in-law. Meanwhile Joseph was busy rebuilding his old shack into a proper home for his Helen.

Soon the new home was ready, and the newly-weds waved a brief goodbye, promising to visit in a while. 'Before the summer's end,' said Helen, as she kissed and thanked the old couple for their kindness.

'It is we who should be thanking you, lassie. Now remember and keep your promise to visit us,' were old Flora's parting words.

During the next few months, the old woman became more and more confined to the house, venturing only as far as the wee wooden gate at the end of the garden. She would stand there staring down the road, looking for the couple to come calling as they had promised, but autumn was upon the land and so far there was no sound from them. Hamish reminded her that obviously they were busy. 'Can you not remember how you and I were, away back when we got wed? Michty, lassie, we never had enough hours in the day.'

'Aye, man, I suppose you're right, it's just that I feel my strength is getting awfy low.'

Hamish could hear the weakness in his wife's voice and became increasingly concerned for her state of health. He began to check her in the night to see if her breathing was fair. Deep within his soul he began to think their time together was waning rapidly away. Hill folk were hardy craturs and accepted Nature's ways, but nevertheless, loss of their loved ones was as painful to them as to any other body.

The misty month of November came and went, and still no sign of the couple. Even Hamish began to worry. 'I'm sure if there was anything the matter we'd have heard it before now, lassie,' he assured his wife.

Flora smiled at her husband. 'If anything was wrong, husband, I'd have felt it,' she said.

She was right, because within hours, on that very day, a familiar voice was heard on the wee path leading up to the house. 'Hello, Mother, hello, Father, it's us! Is that kettle on the stove? For me and this mother-to-be wife of mine have an awfy drouth.'

'God bless us and save us, Hamish, did you hear that?' cried Flora, hardly able to stop herself from throwing open the door and hobbling into the open arms of the happy couple.

'When, when, tell me now, are we to see the happy day?' The old soul was by now crying tears of joy as she held both their hands to her chest.

'I told you she would be like this,' said Joseph to his Helen, 'She always went on about grandchildren, didn't you now, old yin?'

'Aye, son, that I did.' Flora was running her fingers across Helen's abdomen, tears freely flowing down her wrinkled cheeks.

Helen and the old woman went into the house to talk about the coming arrival of the first grandchild and the things that women do, while Hamish and Joseph cracked over the farm and the new house.

The baby was due in March. 'Spring babies,' said Flora, 'make the healthiest weans, because they have the summer to thrive in.'

The couple's visit did Hamish and Flora a power of good, and they stayed for several days before heading back to their house in the woods to settle for the winter and to prepare for the new baby.

Flora didn't tell them about her deteriorating health, and in fact neither did Hamish. Such was the couple's happiness it would have been wrong to say anything to spoil it.

Flora spent the winter knitting wee mittens and bootees and bonny tiny cardigans with such pleasure that it did her the power of good. Sad to say, though, the tide of time can not be held back, and by January's end she lost the power of her legs and was confined to bed. She knew her time on earth was fast closing, and with her every prayer she asked her God to grant her the joy of seeing the new baby.

§

As I listened to my mother I found it impossible to stop the tears that were fast rolling down my cheeks from finding their way into my cocoa cup. Drying my eyes with the corner of the tartan rug draped over my shoulder, I asked my mother why she chose such a sad tale to tell me. Mammy smiled, and said that life could be sad sometimes, and now that I was a young woman, then perhaps it was time to hear such tales. 'Any road, I'm not finished, do you want me to go on or not?'

I knew that the sleep I had so desperately yearned for earlier would surely escape me if I didn't hear the end of this tale. 'Yes, Mammy, of course I do!'

§

March was striding in like a lion! Swirling ice-cold winds had been blowing up a fearful storm. Helen felt a pain deep in her lower back. It was early morning and the same pain had awakened her several times in the night. 'Joseph, it's time, love, the baby is on its way.'

The big man leapt up with such suddenness that the sight of his naked body made her laugh out loud.

'You may well laugh, lady. You're not the one whose wife is having a baby.' His choice of words made them both laugh until another sharp pain brought home the reality of the situation. 'What will I do, my love?' Joseph asked, kneeling beside his teenage wife.

'I'll be alright with you at my side, husband—women have babies every day, so surely it can't be that bad.' She bit her bottom lip as another pain travelled through her.

By midday Helen's labour pains were coming with much more

severity than before, and it was obvious to Joseph that if the baby didn't come soon he would have to get help. The mother-to-be began to fret as she remembered her mother's last birth. Did she not sit with the dear soul until she died, aye, her and the baby. 'Joseph, for God's sake fetch your mother. Please go now or I fear I'll not make it.'

As pain followed excruciating pain without any sign of the baby's arrival, they both knew that if this birth did not kill Helen, then it would almost certainly kill the baby.

'How can I leave you like this, what if you need me?'

'Just go, Joseph, for the love of God. I need her more than I need you. Go, Joseph, go!'

Leaving his wife as comfortable as he could, he took off through the forest, taking every short cut he knew, to fetch old Flora, unaware that his mother was bedridden. The thickening snow greatly hindered his progress, but within an hour and a half the desperate man was knocking on his parents' door.

Instantly Flora knew there was something wrong, Joseph looked so frightened.

'Mammy, the lassie is in terrible pain, the baby's not coming, and I am frightened that she'll not make it.'

Hamish closed the door behind his son and put an arm around his shoulder as he beckoned him to sit at the fireside; then he shook his head and said, 'Mammy's ill, son. In fact...' But before another word passed his lips the old woman prevented him from saying any more. 'Get my coat and shawl, and a pair of your breeches, Hamish, to keep my legs warm.'

Hamish knew that if Flora did what she was proposing it would be the end of her, but he also knew that she would have it no other way.

Sitting up in bed she pretended to be smitten by flu. She said, 'Joseph, I've lost the power of my legs with this damned flu, do you think you have the strength to carry me on your back?'

'Mother, you never made me this size for nothing, of course I can.'

Hamish kissed his wife. As she bade him goodbye, she said, 'Keep the kettle on the boil, old man, I'll be needing a cup of tea when I get home.'

Hamish looked into the face of the woman who had shared most of his life. He held the thin, weak hand that hung limp beneath her coat. 'I love you,' he whispered, kissing her at the same time. 'Thank you for everything.'

The old man watched his wife and son disappear into the swirling snow, then closed the door to wait alone.

Each step the big man took became harder, both for him and for Flora as she fought the pain in her aged body. But this journey was not for him, nor his mother. It was to save the life of his precious Helen.

At last they were at the door. What would they find? Flora's past experiences told her that, given the time the lassie was in labour, the baby would almost certainly be dead! If Helen herself were still alive, then the fight to save her from death would indeed be great.

Praise be, she was still fighting, but she was hanging by a thread. On seeing Flora, her fear gave way to hope. She kissed the old woman's hand and managed a weak smile. Flora felt the swollen abdomen, then said to the lassie, 'Now, my bonny Helen, when I say push, do as you're told.' Turning to her son, she said, 'Joseph, the heat in your wife's body will make her faint, keep her as cool as you can. Whatever you do, keep her awake!'

It was now midnight. Helen was beyond exhaustion and Flora was almost giving up the battle. Joseph, unable to watch any longer, went outside and fell to his knees on the freezing ground. He put his face in his hands and cried, 'Lord, if you're somewhere out there, then save my Helen. I think you've taken the bairn and no doubt you'll have it among the angels by now, but give me my wee Helen, please, Lord.'

'Joseph, come ye in here, man.' Flora's voice sent a shiver through his body, and he froze at the thought of what was behind the door. Then he heard it—a baby's cry! Yes, there again, a wee bit louder this time. He rushed in, and the sight before him was, in his own words, 'A miracle'. Mother and baby were both alive. With the help of his very own beloved mother the pair were going to make it. Helen was drained of all colour. Tears came freely as she held out the tiny bundle, a girl, to meet her new Daddy. 'Flora, how can we thank you for all you've done?' she cried. The old woman smiled, and said 'Let me hold her for a wee minute'.

Joseph gently put his precious bundle into the old woman's arms. Flora looked at her first grandchild through tear-filled eyes, then softly kissed the tiny cheek.

'You are Granny's wee miracle, that is what you are, a gift from God.'

'What name will we give our wee lassie?' asked Joseph to his wife, but Helen had fallen asleep exhausted. He turned to Flora, still holding the baby, and said, 'Well, Mammy, you'll be happy now. In the morning I'll fetch Father, and you can both stay here awhile with us, to share our joy.'

Joseph's words never reached his mother's ears. Peacefully holding in her arms the longed-for baby girl that she herself had never had, and was now at long last gifted to her son, she died!

Joseph lovingly tied his mother's body to a wooden stretcher and, for the second time, made the journey back to his father.

Hamish told his son that a gentle wind had brushed against his cheek while he was sitting at the fireside. 'It was Flora, your mother, she came to say goodbye.'

They buried her beside the infants who had died so many years ago.

When Joseph returned home to his wife and child, the snow was almost gone, melting under a warm spring sun.

'Can you think of a better name for our bonny wean than Flora?' Helen asked her husband.

'There's no better name in all the world,' he replied.

Joseph and Helen went on to have five more healthy bairns. Three big lads just like their father, and two wee stotters, the spit of their mother.

§

The fire was out as Mammy finished her story. It was turning cold again, and we needed our beds, but I had to ask one more question before prising my backside off the wee stool.

'Was I a hard birth, Mammy? Did you have any bother bringing me into the world?'

'As a matter of fact, my lass, you were a breech. You decided at the last minute to come into the world the other way round, bum first.'

These words opened a floodgate of questions, but from the look my Mammy gave me, they wouldn't be answered that night.

'Race you to bed, old yin, last one in is a scabby cat!'

Slap!

'You can sleep to the front, where Daddy sleeps!'

27

ARRAN SUMMER

Cousin Anna could hardly contain herself as she ran into the bus. Bursting with excitement, she grabbed me by the shoulders, stared through eyes as wide as pools and said, 'We're going to little Scotland, Jess, all of us this summer! I can't believe it, can you?'

I hadn't a clue what she was talking about. Before I had time to think even a single thought, Daddy came in at that moment and enlightened me. We were going to the West Coast island of Arran, beautiful Arran! He had been busy, my Dad, and secured spray painting jobs at several farms and hotels. So it looked like we were to holiday on an Atlantic island, sitting next to my Scotland. If there could be anything to tarnish my delight, however, then Daddy's next statement did it!

'We can't take the bus, though, so tents it'll have to be.'

'Why not? We can't leave the bus, not here in the yard. It'll be lonely, someone might break the windys.' The thought of not being with my bus brought a lump to my throat.

Daddy said the ferry didn't take buses, and our Janey wasn't going because of a job she'd just secured in Kirkcaldy, so she'd be staying behind. That was all right then, tents it was.

Within a fortnight, we were all standing on the quayside at Ardrossan, vans loaded with camping equipment to last the summer, watching the mighty *Glen Sannox* ferry coming into dock. I'd never been on a boat of that size; it was like a wee village.

'I bags the seat beside the driver. Come on, last one on is a scabby cookie!'

'Jessie, you stupid pudding, ships don't have drivers, they have rudders!' shouted Anna, pushing past me.

'Well, wherever he sits, I bags a seat beside him.'

Auntie Jessie grabbed us back into line and said, 'Listen, you two, calm down, you're like dafties let out for the day from an asylum. Folk will think us travellers have wild weans.' She flashed her sharp green eyes as if to say, 'If you don't behave, then it's the back o' the hand.' She had big hands, did my auntie, but never used them to hit any of her children. We knew this, but what she did do was tell Mammy, who on the contrary had wee powerful hands, and never hesitated to use them.

As we all stood on the top deck, faces into the warm wind, I felt like a tourist abroad. You know, the ones in the cinemas, Ava Gardner in Africa or Marilyn Monroe sailing away with some fella, somewhere exotic. I remember feeling rich, not with wealth, but the richness that comes through freedom, the traveller's freedom.

My young sisters were playing skip-slap. Let me think, how did it go again? Oh yes, I know, it goes like this: 'eesie osie, mannie's nosie, eesie osie oot!' Skip, then slap, then 'eenerty feenerty, fickerty feg, eel, del, domineg, irkie, birkie, starry rock, an, tan, tooslie Jock!' Then one skips forward as the other slaps hands and continues, 'black puddin, white troot, eerie oorie, your oot'. As the big boat gave a gentle sway our Mary skipped and fell. This prompted Auntie Jessie to raise her voice yet again. 'Sit down the lot of you, people are staring!'

An elderly lady, who had been enjoying my sisters' play, told our ever watchful aunt that it brought back memories of her childhood in the Angus glens. Then, sprightly as can be, she showed us her version of eenerty feenerty. She couldn't half shift those old bandy legs. Yes, this year's summer jaunt was indeed going to be a cracker.

We were bursting with excitement as we shuffled and rooted through the ferry, and only a stern 'Don't touch!' from an angry steward who caught us shinning down a thick rope tied round a red and white tyre calmed our shenanigans.

Having searched unsuccessfully for the rudder-driver, Cousin Anna and I skipped down the gangway at Brodick, convinced the poor soul was stuck deep under the ship and guiding it along the ocean's floor. Several boxes of groceries later, we set off to find a suitable camping spot. Cousin Wullie didn't share the journey with us; he was expected to join us later on in the week after taking ownership of his first motorbike. This was his seventeenth-birthday present from Auntie Jessie and Uncle Wullie (of Jake the Adventurer fame).

The sun was hot for early May, prompting Uncle Wullie to bring forth one of his long-range weather predictions, with a wee verse thrown in for atmosphere.

> *When the sun gives heat in the bonny month o' May,*
> *It will shine through the hawthorn pink and white,*
> *Red berries, foustie hay.*

And do you know this, folks, that is exactly what it did, because from that day until we sailed back home, not a single drop of rain did we feel on our faces. From May to August's end, we had lovely, tar-melting sunshine.

As we drove along the coast road, more and more delightful camping spots came into view. 'Oh Daddy, look at the waves coming onto the beach, this will do.' Then another just as appealing inlet brought forth more ooohs and aaaahs. Then we saw it: our heavenly campsite, big enough to take vans, tents and washing lines. It was off the road in a sparsely-wooded area, with plenty of unspoilt grass to soften our sleep. A few flat rocks provided fine seating, with a place to put a safe fire for cooking. Most important of all, there was our very own swimming pool: the blue-green waters of God's own Atlantic Ocean. Heady scents from azalea and rhododendron shrubs growing wild in the wood would lull our slumber, while a fresh salty sea spray would awaken the senses come morning light. Could anyone ask for better?

After helping pitch tents, Anna and I squeezed into the year before's cossies and joined the jellyfish, which looked for all the world like rolled-up chiffon scarves floating on the sea's surface. Bobbing in the lukewarm water within the rock pools and kicking aside stringy threads of green seaweed, my cousin and I hugged each other. We were thirteen, almost grown-up. Life felt terrific, we would never forget Arran.

That night, as we lay in our camp beds, hair still damp, we dreamed of happy days ahead, whilst the big folks sat sharing a drop of tea with the island's local policeman. He had noticed our arrival at Brodick and, as most bobbies did, decided to give us a check-up visit. The fact that there were no baddies on Arran meant that nothing ever happened to need his attention, so a mug of tea and a crack round our fire became part of his day.

The next morning we were welcomed by a warm sun which seemed to shine just for us. 'I'm going dooking, anybody joining me?' I called, pushing a leg into a sandy, damp swimming costume.

'Hey, ma lady, you're going for milk and rolls, that's where you're going,' called my Mother. 'So get the legs into a pair of dry shorts—dooking, indeed.'

Anna laughed, saying, 'See ya later'. Auntie Jessie grabbed her mermaid daughter before she plunged into the waves, saying, 'And you can go with Jessie. Bring back the day's papers to see if the world is still turning.'

We both reluctantly slipped from our cossies, donned vests and shorts, then made our way into the town. En route we left the road to skip along an ancient harbour-wall, long since deserted for a new one. The crystal-clear water was filled with many kinds of sea life. Silkies (seals) and various colours of jellyfish shared the harbour with four giant basking sharks. 'Look at the fatness of yon brutes,' said Anna, adding, 'I've heard tell they are gentle creatures and couldn't hurt a fly.'

I peered down at the great beasts. 'They look as if they're dead. Are they real?'

Anna, having lived most of her life on the East Coast, Aberdeen to be exact, knew a lot about marine life. 'Yon brutes live their whole lives appearing dead-like. I've a pal who told me when she goes on holiday to Nairn she swims under them!'

'Don't believe that,' I said, unconvinced that anyone with tuppence-worth of sense could be so stupid or brave.

'Polly McPherson is her name, and next time you visit I'll take you to see her yourself. I'd seldom seen our Anna get rused, but the more I pooh-poohed the more she was determined to prove me wrong.

'Right,' she said, 'let's get in.'

'In where?' I asked, confused.

'In the water and swim under yon bellies. I know Polly would never lie, her being a minister's daughter, so let's see if it can be done!'

Without another word, my cousin stripped naked and dived in! I stiffened like a poker watching the water engulf her thin frame. As quickly as the ripples formed they just as instantly scattered, leaving Anna's head inches from the shiny black sea monster. 'Watch this,' she gurgled, then before I could find one word of protest, she was gone beneath her water companion's underside. Emerging at its other side and pushing her dripping hair from half-shut eyes, she called out to me, still open-mouthed,

'Come on, scaredy breeks, get yourself in. Polly was right, they're so big they don't even know I'm here.'

I can only describe my next actions as madness. Purple shorts and grey vest lay discarded on the ancient harbour wall while I found myself diving to join our Anna in the soft green water to swim below the basking sharks! Holding my hand she guided me under, then up. Twice, three times we swam. The gentle beasts, obviously unaffected by our presence, did not move; we even went as far as tickling their bellies with our toes. I think that moment was one of the most marvellous of my entire life. I felt half-fish, half-girl as the water filled my ears and a shark rolled his lazy eye to glance briefly at my form passing through his domain. All thoughts of the family waiting hungrily back at the campsite for milk and rolls were gone from our minds as we hurriedly donned our clothes. 'That was immense, I shall never forget,' whispered Anna. She never did, but then, neither did I.

'In future, if a bully gets me beat, I will know I've done something greater than they shall ever do!' I threaded my arm through Anna's and added, 'Let's keep this as our forever secret.'

'To tell no one until we die, right Jess?'

And to my knowledge this has been our secret until now, the swim below the sharks.

On our way back from the shops, after a wee blether with the shopkeeper's wife, we heard loud music coming from the shore. This sent our curiosity into overdrive. Following the noise we came upon a long black sort of floating barge. On the boat a dozen or so lads were all rushing about, some singing to music coming from a trannie, others jiving to it. Others were laughing and shouting as they poked and pulled at ropes on the strange flat surface of the vessel. We watched them for a minute or two, when suddenly a loud siren sound had us clinging onto each other in fright. Before we could imagine what it was, the lads stopped what they were doing and disappeared down a hole in the middle of the boat-thing. Within seconds it sunk out of sight, taking the unfortunate laddies with it.

'Oh my heavens, Jess,' said Anna 'what kind of monster was that? Do you think they've all drowned?'

'I don't know, but best tell the men. It might be a lifeboat job, come on.'

We arrived back as the lid was dancing on the big black kettle.

'Another minute and I'd be searching for you two,' said Mammy sternly. 'Do you know that kettle has dried out twice? Why are your faces blood-red, and why is your hair wet?'

'Never mind that, Mam, there's a boatful of lads drowning out in the water!'

'Aye, Auntie Jeannie, we think they'll need rescued,' panted Anna.

My father came round from behind a large rock and told us the boat was an American submarine, and that they were based nearby. He added that we would probably see a lot of these strange-looking ships while on Arran. Our Shirley, emerging from the sea, heard Daddy and rushed away excitedly to tell Cousin Carol there was talent in the shape of Yanks.

If anyone mentioned Yanks, Elvis came to mind, and the two lassies, being madly in love with the King of Rock, had no doubt a visit to one of these U.S. vessels had to be a priority. My father reminded them that only cheap woman frequented navy ships, and if he found them within a mile of one, then the 'back o' the hand' it would be!

Both girls, though, were nineteen and he knew there was little he could do if that was the way they decided to go. 'During the war...' he started to say, but before another word left his lips a screeching sound had all of us turning on our heels, to see Cousin Wullie straddling his new shiny motorbike, riding full-throttle towards the campsite.

'God almighty, here's our Wullie on his bike, and the daft goat hasn't a clue how to ride it!' exclaimed my uncle.

'Aye, and it looks awfy like the ragie doesn't know where the brakes are either.' At Shirley's words the red-faced laddie ploughed straight through his parent's tent, coming to a halt halfway through ours. 'Braw bike, eh, folks? Now lets get a cup o' tea and then rebuild the tents.' That was our Wullie, a big, daft, soft-hearted laddie.

No one said a thing, because that was how it was with our cousin. He never swore or fought or said a wrong thing against a living soul. Give him a guitar and let him sing and that was Wullie.

So as that day headed to an end, Anna and I had swum with the sharks. The older girls were enlightened about the talent close by. Our tents had been rebuilt and the little ones lay sleeping, toes black with bursting tar bubbles. Wullie serenaded us all to sleep with his rendition of the King's 'Love Me Tender'. Here's to tomorrow.

$$\mathcal{S}$$

Apart from Daddy keeping eyes in the back of his head to defend the older girls from the Yankee talent, our island existence remained idyllic. The men worked hard at spray-painting, while the women kept an eye on us lot slipping in and out of the ocean. When the men were not at work, they too enjoyed the greeny sea pools lapping at our canvas doors. Young Wullie spent his spare time either serenading the curious seals who came in with the tide, or polishing the new love of his life, his very noisy motorbike.

I will now digress slightly and tell you a tale of Devil worship, told to my mother and me as we spent the day hawking on our Arran isle.

Anna declined Mammy's offer to go with us that day because she'd a sore head with too much sun, so a book in the tent was to be her lot. I didn't fancy going either, but she couldn't go alone; anyway, Shirley would only babysit the three smallest ones.

'We better get off, Jess,' said my mother, taking off her apron and tying it on a tent rope. 'Uncle said it would thunder before the day's end, so best not go far,' she added.

'Aye, I think he could be right, there's a sticky heat this morning. You can almost feel the heavy air,' I said, remembering how hard I found it to sleep the night before.

A half-hour later we were standing outside a wee picture-postcard cottage, with a low thatched roof and tiny windows. White-painted walls were crowded from every side by red, yellow, and purple rhododendrons. 'Look, Mam, your favourite flower in all the world.' She saw the little snowy-white flowers of lily of the valley and tears welled in her eyes. They grew all around the roots of azaleas like small companions to their delicate blooms.

'Oh, do you know why I love these bonny flowers so much, pet?'

If I'd a penny for every time she told me I'd be rich, but I knew how she delighted in the telling, so I said, 'No, Mammy, why do you?'

'The night before Daddy went to war, he walked me down to the wood at the end of the Bobbin Mill in Pitlochry to where the lily of the valley grows. Holding my face in his hands, he said, "If I never come home to you, my bonny Jeannie, then come here and sit amidst the birch trees and valley flowers. Close your eyes and put all fear away from your mind. If you listen I will call to you through the breezes blowing up from the River Tummel. Promise me now."'

My mother went on to say that, as she lay in her bed and listened to enemy bombers droning in the night sky above, she filled her thoughts with her man and the valley flowers. It got her through, she said.

'Is this not the bonniest wee cotter house, Jess?' Before I could answer, a frail-sounding voice from within a bush had us turning to look—a little thin-faced lady, secateurs in one hand, basket in the other.

'Good-day to you both,' she said, removing a dirty green glove from one hand and pushing it out to shake my mother's. 'You're no' from here. I know everybody round about for miles.'

'Aye, that's right, missus, we're travelling folks spending a few weeks on the island, and a grand place it is.' My mother was politeness itself when hawking. 'Can I interest your kind self in a bit or a bob from my basket?' Sitting down on the cottage step, she gestured to the old lady to have a look. Leaning on one knee she rummaged through the basket. 'How much?' she asked, holding a piece of Irish lace and a card of six red buttons. 'I've been looking for this colour of button to finish a cardigan.'

I can't remember the price asked for, because it was never relevant to my Mother. What she really wanted was to tell the lady's fortune or read her tea-leaves, either way she made a great deal more from that.

'I tell you what, why don't the both of you come in and share a pot of tea with me. I've been out in this garden far too long, and I've a drouth half way down my thrapple. Oh, and before you ask to tell my fortune or read the tea-leaves at the bottom of my cup, don't bother. Its ninety-five I am, and if you know of anybody who cares at that age about a future then I'd like to shake their hand.'

Mammy laughed at that remark, and said yes, we'd be grateful for a cuppy, but would sit outside and take it. Far too clammy being inside today.

'No, come away in to the cool of my wee cottage,' said the old lady.

I asked her, with such a low roof and tiny windows, surely it would be boiling inside.

She assured me the walls were so thick they served to keep the place cool in summer, warm in winter. Then she told us a sticky gingerbread was cooling on a wire rack on the kitchen table. 'You'll not say no to a bit of treacle toffee, lassie, I dare say now.'

That did it—my mother loved ginger cake and I was equally addicted to the browny-black toothache sweetie.

Inside Mammy removed her thin headscarf and wiped her brow before tying it round her neck. It certainly was cooler inside, with an air of garden freshness. We both sat down on pine chairs with bowed backs. 'Now,' said Mammy, 'are you sure I can't tell your fortune? Age matters not and you look healthier than myself.'

The old dear laughed out loud, displaying a toothless mouth and a chunk of gingerbread. 'If I open my eyes in the morning then it's a surprise, never mind what the future holds.' She laughed again, more of a cackle, and I held my breath thinking she might choke.

Mammy, being the professional that she was, said, 'Everyone has a future, wife, even if it's a flickin' of a lamb's tail.'

But our host would have the final word on it and said, 'Lassie, the only thing I have to look forward to is a wooden box. Now tell me, where are you camped?'

Mammy pressed her back against the hard chair and said we were outside Brodick, two miles to be precise, sea on one side, wood on the other.

All of a sudden our host's eyes widened in their sockets and her face went death-pale.

For several seconds nothing was said, then sitting forward in her chair she asked in a whisper, 'There wouldn't be a large, bell-shaped rock nearby?'

Mammy looked at me, obviously puzzled and confused by our host's instant change of mood, and said, 'You're the explorer, Jess, have you come across such a rock?'

I had no hesitation in answering. Of course I had. It was as big as an elephant's head. 'Aye, Mammy, surely you've seen it. Did Uncle Wullie not think it was a beach standing stone, like Stonehenge or the Orkney ones?'

'This rock you mention, wife,' I asked, 'why has it put the fear o' death into yourself?' She paid no heed to my question; instead, turning to my mother, she grabbed her hand, held it tight in hers and warned her that we must go back, pack up and move at once. Mammy rose to her feet, and said, 'We'll be going nowhere until there is good enough reason.' She went on to tell this disturbed old islander that she'd been chased by countless numbers of landowners, farmers, policemen, angry drunkards and so forth. 'Now, if a stone was all that threatened our peaceful haven on Arran's shore it would hardly make us move so much as a dish, never mind pack up and go.'

'There's a hidden danger to you all, especially little children. Have you any?'

When Mammy told her she had a six-year-old the woman shook her head and screamed, 'For the love of the dear Saviour, I beg you, leave that evil place!'

Whatever it was that held our old friend in dread, one thing was certain, my Mother had to find out. How could she expect everyone to move the campsite without good reason?

The old woman, bent with stiffened bones, rose silently from her seat, put the kettle back on the shiny black range, cut another few slices of gingerbread, arranged them on a little plate and handed me a large chunk of treacle toffee. 'Right,' she said, looking at us both, 'this story has never passed my lips before to another living soul. Take heed at the calendar over by the brass horse tack.' At once my mother and I scanned the wall, eyes falling on an old calendar hanging from a painting of two Scottie dogs.

'Now, lass, tell me what is today's date,'

'Twenty-first of June,' I said.

'Yes, the eve of the Summer Solstice,' said she, sitting back on her dark green armchair of faded brocade. Pushing a small frayed cushion into the small of her back, she began.

§

Kate Rathlin never set foot on Arran, so why is her curse here, on that very rock a hand's throw from where you now stay? Well, the world first heard of her appearing one cold night at a Romany campfire in Ireland, during the early part of the fifteenth century. No one knew how she got there, or where she hailed from, but gypsies accepted strangers with a warm hospitality and seldom questioned the lonely visitor. Soon, though, it was to their dismay they gave her a friendly place at the fire, because within no time she was bullying the women and bossing the men. An ugly woman who stood six feet tall, with a belly too fond of strong drink, she became feared and hated by her unwitting hosts. One night, while she lay in a deep sleep after days' drinking, they silently packed and moved away, leaving her lying near a lochside.

Word spread across the land to avoid Kate Rathlin, the violent drunkard, who some say must have been a child of Satan! Being fairly young she longed for companionship—of the opposite sex, of course—but with her ever-growing reputation this came only from people of her own kind. So it was to the rat-infested underworld of low lives she found herself more and more drawn. One dark night, while in a black mood, she throttled the life from a fellow who took more than his share of the demon bottle. After realising her awful deed, she took herself as far away from that town as her wretched legs would travel.

No one heard of Kate from that day, and soon it was thought she was dead. But this was not the way of it. In the depths of a bleak moor near Ireland's rugged east coast she continued to simmer her hatred of mankind. The desolate and savage regions of her new home claimed the woman as their own, and soon she found new companions: the thunder which rolled across lowering dark skies, fierce winds that forced her back to straighten and the shadows she befriended when the sun's light faded. They gave her strength; she felt better, stronger than she'd ever done. But oh, how she longed for beauty.

One fateful night thunder rolled and lightning gleamed across the sky. With shadowy friends dancing in a frenzied fury round about, she threw her hands up towards the charged elements and demanded that 'You, Lucifer the Prince of all Demons, you of darkness, keeper of Cleopatra's Asps and Pandora's Box, give me a body no man can resist!' In a deep mood of despair the wretched woman fell onto the sodden ground and there she lay in troubled slumber until a shrieking seagull awakened her. It was dawn, and all around nothing stirred amongst low mist and wet grass. Slowly rising from her grassy bed, she glanced briefly into a rain-filled hole. A reflection stared back at Kate Rathlin of such beauty that she turned instantly to see who stood behind her. There was no one! Again, deeper into the pool she looked, this time almost touching the water with her nose. Yes, it was herself, but how, when? She drew a finger across the reflection, instantly distorting it, but the water stilled, and yes, she of great beauty was there. The Lord of Darkness had heard her prayer and answered it! Ugly Kate Rathlin was gone, and in her place was a creature more beautiful than she herself had ever set eyes on.

For the rest of that day she did nothing except find pools of water to gaze upon this new-found beauty. That night, exhausted, but with more happiness than her miserable life had ever before afforded her, she lay staring up at the star-filled heavens, eventually falling into a deep sleep to dream dreams of love and marriage.

'Daughter, awaken,' called a voice in the night. 'Rise and heed me.' Kate rose up and stood like one possessed. 'You are pleased with my gift?' The voice spoke from every darkened inch of the night as if it were the dark itself which spoke.

'You have given me life, Master, I am forever in your debt.'

'I will need payment, my sweet loveliness. Will you do my bidding?'

She did not, for one moment, hesitate. 'Anything, anything,' she called out.

'On the eve of Summer Solstice, when the day is at its longest, bring me a sacrifice. A child no older than seven years and no younger than seven months. Continue to do this indefinitely, and your beauty will never fade, nor will you age!'

For the next fifty years, children all across the country disappeared from their beds in the dim light of the year's longest day, when a beautiful rich lady just happened to be visiting.

Kate went from town to town beguiling men by the score. The moment eyes fell upon her beauty they were enslaved. The Devil kept his bargain, and she hers.

Fate, however, was planning an end to those fiendish deeds, and this is how it happened. A man of great power and wealth met Kate at a fine ball one night and invited her to dinner. This grand fellow was guardian of his late cousin's twin boys, aged five. When she laid eyes upon them, her instant thought was, 'How rich a sacrifice, my Master would indeed be pleased if I brought him, not one, but two fine specimens.' With the help of a six-foot deaf mute of immense strength, she stole the boys while the household slept. Using four swift stallions and a black coach (provided by her Master), the children were brought to a deserted beach nearby. Then, as the hour of solstice approached, the Devil took his prize.

Now, as I said, fate waited. In the rocks by the shoreline where the fiends were, lay an old tramp who witnessed that terrible deed. He had in his miserable life seen many bad things, but nothing as awful as this. Fearing for his safety, he held his tongue and stayed hidden, then waited for the woman and her deaf companion to leave before escaping as fast as his aged legs could go.

Several months later, after a foul night of ale-drinking, the old tramp found himself spending the night in a bleak jailhouse. Another like-minded vagrant shared the cell. The night was cold and long, neither could find any comfort on the wooden beds, so they spent the night talking.

It seems the other fellow was no stranger to the premises, or the judge. Come the morning, he told our friend, 'A fearsome man is the judge, because a wicked woman stole his charges, two five-year-olds. Although he employed the help of fifty men to scour the country, no sign has been found of them. His heart is sore and our sentence will be just as heavy because of it.'

The old man said nothing until standing before the judge next day. Then, in a packed courtroom, our brave fellow told his Honour of the dreadful scene he had witnessed. As word after word came from his mouth, the whole place fell into hushed silence.

A voice from the back of the crowded court called out, 'Tis the Summer Solstice Witch, I have heard of her!' Her days then were numbered, the net was set for the 'Devil's daughter'.

As she sat at some rich man's dinner table, Kate did not realise that the red wine had been drugged. And it was before the same judge from whose care she had stolen the children that she duly stood. Because the courthouse was unable to contain the hundreds who came to see a real witch being tried, her trial took place outside in the town square.

Thinking her Master would give her protection, she laughed and mocked those who spoke against her. The judge reminded her of the night she spent as his guest, and asked, 'Why did you steal and murder the innocent children?'

In answer she said, 'All belong to Him'. By this she meant her Master, Lucifer.

Yes, there was no doubt she was guilty, but what would be the manner of her punishment? Some said she should burn, others insisted she be drawn and quartered. All day long forms of punishment were discussed, but something became obvious. Who would be brave enough to take on the Devil? Who could carry out the punishment? An elderly holy man who'd been listening came forward with a solution. 'Put her to sea, where God himself will carry out the punishment!' So, grateful and relieved, the Judge agreed this idea was the best. Into a small skiff three strong men placed Kate's tightly mummified body. Before they pushed her out to sea, a plague bell was secured to the boat, warning all to steer clear of it. A calm fell across the water. All watching thought the Devil was protecting her, and fell to their knees in fervent prayer. Soon, though, the waves began to grow higher and stronger, and to the great relief of all Kate Rathlin's coffin disappeared from sight. All night long the Devil and the good Lord fought over her soul.

As the Isle of Arran came on the horizon, Lucifer swiftly carried the evil seafarer to her safe shores. But with one last giant wave the Lord lifted the boat up and threw it against jagged rocks further up the coast. Her remains were never found, but some said a strange bell rang for days on that fateful spot.

'And that spot is the rock where we are camped?' I asked.

'The very one,' answered the storyteller.

Hair rose on the back of my neck.

Mammy thanked our host, lifted her basket, grabbed my hand and said a swift goodbye. We went so fast down the little path we almost knocked a young woman from her bike. 'Sorry,' both she and my mother said in unison. 'We were in sharing tea with the old lady and forgot the time,' blurted Mammy.

The lass propped her cycle against the white-washed wall and said, to the surprise of both of us, 'I see Granny's been telling one of her tales. Which one was it?'

'Kate Rathlin,' I instantly said. How could I ever forget that name?

'Oh goodness, you mustn't let her frighten you like that,' she laughed. The lass then enlightened us about her granny's art of story-telling. There was the hill walker whom she had told that Kate haunted Goat Fell. Poor man, and to think he came all the way from Devon to climb the hill. Then there was the American couple, who went home thinking Kate stalked their hotel bedroom. 'I could go on all day,' she said, 'but I can see you're in a hurry.' With that we all said our farewells, and I, for one, was more than pleased that we had met the old dear's grand-daughter, I can tell you. If we had not, sleep would have been nigh-on impossible for me.

When we arrived back, another surprise awaited us; tents were packed up and vans on the road. 'What's this, then,' asked Mammy, 'the curse of Kate Rathlin?'

'No, the curse o' the bloody midgie,' answered my father, scratching furiously at the nape of his neck. Yes, of course it was her time. Worse than any witch was wee *Mrs Midgie*. A hundred to one, if her hunger was on her, then you became dinner!

Exhausted, we at last found a spot facing out toward the open sea with a fine breeze to keep midgie away. That night as I lay in my tent, with the door open, I watched a violent thunderstorm raging across the ocean; thankfully it never reached Arran. Before Mr Nod took hold, a nagging thought crept into my mind: just where did the name 'Kate Rathlin' find its origin?

§

Sister Shirley (Charlotte) believed her art of poetry came from Rabbie, the 'Bard', Burns. He and our paternal Granny shared the same surname. 'Rabbie was one o' oor lot!' Shirley exclaims many times. And if you read some of her works in verse and song I think you may agree. This is the poem she penned for me to accompany 'Arran Summer'.

Ouch!

If like a' campers, the bracken beckons,
Pray, dinna hurry tae bare yer wee bum.
For Ladicus Midgecus truly reckons
Tae gaither her cronies, an hae some fun.

If, fur some reason the wind should drop,
Pray dinna tarry where a midgie frolics

On yer facet she'll land and wi' help fae her friends,
She'll agonisly chew her way doon tae yer hollyhocks.

If at two in the morn when the rain is intense,
I sorely advise tae secure one's defence,
For she'll try like a bear tae invade yer domain,
And ye'll ne'er anticipate how, where, or when.

If a sheet o' pure gauze, sown up like a sack,
Disna act as deterrent tae Midecus Mack
Then dinna stay put, for ye'll feel but pain
She's much faster than you, an' ye'll lose the game.

If efter the thunder an' lightnin hae scampered,
Pray don't emerge till the sun stays tae play
This is guid sound advice fae a camper wha gits butchered
Tae feed Ladicus Midecus meals everyday.

§

Although this new campsite was breezy, it in no way made a difference to the warmth of the Atlantic. We still swam early morning and lived in our cossie skins, building sandcastles and wee villages filled with a community entirely made up of crabs. Big red ones were the police, wee green ones were women, brown were men and the tiny green ones were kids. Sea urchins, scallop shells and flat shiny stones were used as furniture. Cockles and mussels acted as family pets. This wee play village existed in tranquillity until Neptune sent his salty water racing in to claim back its inhabitants. Until, that is, the tide came in again, and we would gather up a whole new community.

After tea each night, Cousin Wullie, guitar over his shoulder, walked out to a rocky island, where he'd sit serenading the shiny silkies (seals), who just loved his music.

As I watched my mother and her sister-in-law wander off for their usual evening stroll, a thought pestered me. Why did they not swim?

I approached Uncle Wullie. 'Women are a mystery to me, lassie,' he said. 'Haven't a clue why they won't go in the water.' I reminded him that, although still young, I too was a woman. A wry smile spread across his face. 'Aye, but you haven't mastered the art yet,' was his answer.

There was not much help there, so it had me sharing a flat stone with my father, asking him the same question. 'Well, lass,' he said, 'beneath those blouses, skirts and cardigans, is a finely concealed coat of armour. Not for keeping the enemy out, but the enemy in.'

Annoyed, I asked him not to speak in riddles, and I still remember his face going uncomfortably red as he explained the meaning of his words.

'They wear a contraption called stays, or corsets to be correct, made up of bones, tight satin, miles of laces and endless hooks and eyes.'

'God, Daddy, why?' I asked, still in the dark.

'Because Betty Grable wore the blasted things in the pictures. And if thon wee waist she had was the result of corsets, then every woman between the world's two poles just has to wear them.'

'But why should they stay out of the water, Dad?'

'Have you any idea how long it takes to get the blasted things on? No? Well, the best part o' an hour.'

I felt sorry for them, and told him I was going to tell them so.

'Don't you dare, lassie. If they find out we've been discussing the secret garments then it's me who'll suffer, not you.'

Not willing to expose their secret, and put my father into Mam's bad books, my lips were sealed, but it seemed a pity that they should spend all these weeks on Arran without a dook.

Yet this situation was about to change. Call it fate if you like; I called it oor Wullie not thinking. See what you think.

It was evening; the men were quietly cracking at the fire. The older girls had sneaked away to meet their Yanks. Us youngsters were, as usual, playing on the beach while Mammy and Jessie were on a wee stroll. After learning a new pop ballad on his wee tranny, Cousin Wullie, guitar over his shoulder, was off to serenade the silkies from his favourite rock. Now, this ballad of his was on the quiet side, meaning his audience were unable to hear it—well, so he thought. So off he took himself to a more advantageous position. The receding tide exposed one or two rocks and it was from here that the maestro went to work, singing and strumming to a small band of seals who, may I add, did indeed enjoy my cousin's act. Now, I know you might think me a penny short of a shilling, but you should've seen the way they encircled him, wee wet noses sniffing the air and honking away good style. They were having a ball, and so was tonsil-warbling Wullie. What he failed to notice, however, was that at that point the back-rolling tide halted and came quickly in again! Soon his dangling size-tens were immersed, followed by the lower legs. It was not until he opened his eyes and saw the frothy water walloping onto his thighs did our lad realise something very precious was about to be ruined, namely the guitar. God, he thought, not that two-toned Elvis replica of magnificence.

A wild scream from the bold balladeer had everyone on red alert. 'Ma geetar's gonna get soaked. Da, Ma, help!'

His father called out that if he held it above his head he'd make it to the shore.

'Too risky, I'll slip for sure. Help, Mammy!' Now, when all seemed lost, six-foot Wullie needed his Ma. She heard her laddie's desperate calls from the wood where she and my mother were strolling, and like a rabid banshee her skirt was up above the knees and she was sprinting to the rescue.

Now, to be honest, the water level would only have come as far as his oxters, but when she came running and saw her precious laddie, who by now was standing on the rock, my Auntie Jessie, without a thought for herself, belly-flopped into the sea! Boned corsets and all! 'All' being long-legged satin bloomers, tweed skirt, mother-of-pearl buttoned blouse and Fair Isle cardigan. Down she sank like a ton of tatties, then gurgled to the surface, calling, 'Mammy's coming, son,' only to sink as fast again.

Now, what do you think happened next? Auntie Jessie's wee fat legs came up first, buoyed up by her ballooning, knee-length, peach satin bloomers. Her upside-down body was cocooned inside her corsets. The knickers filled like a parachute. She was in deep trouble to say the least.

Thanks be to God, though, we managed to save her from Neptune's watery grave. By 'we' I mean Daddy, Mammy, Uncle Wullie and Cousin Carol, sister Shirley, oor Janey, Anna, two wide-eyed Yanks and me. Oh, and the village bobby as well.

Wullie, holding his guitar above his head, managed no bother to get it successfully home. This was a waste of his time, though, because when we told her he wasn't shouting 'I'm getting choked', as she thought, but 'It's getting soaked', his musical instrument was hurled into the sea in a wild rage, with a scratched fingerboard and six snapped strings.

That night after the tempers were quietened, we all had a good laugh, sitting round a braw fire as two sets of boned corsets twanged and curled within the flames.

From then on my wish was granted, as our mothers enjoyed a grand daily 'dook'.

Apart from a turbaned Pakistani trying to sell us the contents of his suitcase of multi-coloured cardigans and elephant-patterned head-squares, we saw no-one else to speak of, and continued to enjoy our 'little Scotland' holiday.

Too soon it was packing-up time, and our return journey by the *Glen Sannox* ferry was a great deal quieter as we watched our haven disappear into a thick sea haar. I shall always be grateful to Arran and its folks for such a lovely summer.

Now come back to smelly Kirkcaldy with me and I'll tell you another tale or two.

28

SCHOOL BULLIES

While at Kirkcaldy, Daddy made big changes to our winter homing ground. He built an extension onto the bus in the form of a wee prefab. A front door led into a small kitchen area with sink and worktops. Later, as a Christmas present, he added a very Modern Milly contraption, a washing machine with hand-wringer attachment, a cooker and cupboard space. There was a chest of drawers, a pull-down bed, settee and, positioned in a corner, the ruination of mankind—a television set. To enhance the small house, there was a cosy 'burn anything in me' stove with two doors. Fitted carpet covered the wooden floor. The bed was my parents', giving them much-longed for privacy and us more space in the bus, which incidentally was conveniently accessible via the kitchen area. Daddy, the handyman, had excelled himself. Relatives flooded in to admire his handiwork, and Mammy, for the first time since losing out on her 'house that never was' back in Crieff, was pleased as punch.

I too was delighted with our expanding home, but only when Daddy reassured me the prefab was easily sealed and left intact while we went on our travels in the bus.

So then, as winter tightened her grip on Kirkcaldy, we lived in relative comfort, enjoying the extra space our new awning provided.

Daddy had discovered a factory in the north of England which sold Formica cuttings. This was the trendy new hard covering everyone was using to cover kitchen worktops. He rented a small shop in Rosslyn Street, and soon the stuff was selling like hot cakes. A drive down to the factory every month made certain his supply didn't run out. So over the cold winter months, as he and Mammy both ran the shop, we all enjoyed our comforts.

Changes were taking place, not only in how we were making a living, but within our ranks. Janey had been working on the buses. Mona left home to work and live independently, eventually marrying a second cousin of my father's. Shirley worked in a fishmonger's shop in the High Street, and it was whilst travelling there on the number 1 bus that a certain handsome six foot-something lad fell madly in love with my favourite sister. This later led to a blossoming romance followed by a lovely wedding. When Shirley left home she took much of its fire with her. I missed her more than anyone else. Janey was later to follow by marrying a traveller lad. Daddy had little time for this roguish lad, but he was to prove a grand provider. I liked him, he made me laugh. Chrissie pleased Mammy when she and her curly-headed laddie, plus two sons, moved to Kirkcaldy. They lived to the south of the town.

Granny Power became frail and lonely in her little cottage in the Bobbin Mill at Pitlochry, so the family clubbed together and bought her a ground-floor flat in Kirkcaldy's Overton Road. This meant she would seldom be alone, especially with Auntie Lena's cheery bunch popping in and out. Apart from the smell of the nearby linoleum factory she enjoyed her new home.

For the first time in my life, school was fun. It was a massive place with hundreds of pupils from different areas. I made a few friends. One day a girl in my class invited several of us to her birthday party. Seldom had anyone apart from travellers offered me hospitality. 'Perhaps scaldies aren't all bad,' I remember thinking, as she said her Dad would pick me up. When he drove round into Oswald Road where I stood waiting, I recall the puzzled look on his face. 'Where do you live, lassie?' he enquired.

Thinking little of it I pointed to the yard. He said nothing, picked me up and then collected the other girls.

Shirley had given me a present of a new dress she bought specially for the party. It was gingham blue, my favourite colour. That Friday night I made new friends, both girls and boys. For the first time in my life I enjoyed the company of kids other than travellers.

Come Monday morning, I could hardly wait to join them and

be part of the crowd, but no-one prepared me for the treatment my so-called 'friends' were about to dish out.

Mammy had bought me a new satchel because of the extra books I needed for exams. It was real leather and one she really could not afford. I proudly hung it over one shoulder, showing it off to my friends. 'Where did you steal that then, Tink?' hissed one lad, wrenching my new bag from my hand and throwing it over by the gates, where a row of metal dustbins was lined up. Everyone else laughed, and as I retrieved my precious satchel it didn't take long for the bubble around me to burst. The father must have told his daughter she had invited a tinker to her party, the one who lived behind a high wall in Lennie's Yard.

From then on, I hid until morning bell sounded, and left as it rang for school's end. My school life became a nightmare. Nobody would be seen talking to me. One lad named Derek did, and got a bleeding nose for his trouble.

I didn't bother my parents with bully worries, because they would have told me to get them sorted out, but I did mention things to big Joe Macallum. He was the husband of Auntie Maggie, my father's sister. 'Jess,' he said, 'you're a wee lassie who shouldn't be worrying about useless cowards with drunkards for parents. Here's how to deal with them.' I listened, desperately hoping he'd banish these cruel kids from me by saying he'd wait on them and pull a few ears in a side alley or something. But no such solution; there was a better way. 'Ask one of them to come to your party. Not a birthday, but a coming-home one. Get closer and make sure he or she hears clearly. Say Uncle Axie is getting out. If they ask you who he is, look puzzled, then say, "Have you not heard of the Axe Murderer who chopped up three woodsmen after one of them cheated at a card game?" Go on to say he is your favourite Uncle and will be happy to meet your friends.'

After a week of sleepless nights I eventually found the courage to approach a bully, asking him to come to my uncle's coming-home party. Imagine my surprise when he ran off goggly-eyed to tell his mates. Lo and behold, it worked. They believed me, and for the duration of that year I was left in peace. The autumn would bring them back, but that was a spring and summer away. Perhaps I'd find another way to ward them off?

Daddy didn't mean to leave for the road so soon, but a visit from two council officials hastened our departure. They insisted he dismantle our prefab because there wasn't the necessary planning permission—not to mention the water and waste pipes he'd added to the already overloaded Gallatown football club's changing hut. Mammy was glad to be going, because she'd spent all winter cooped up in the wee cold shop, fingers swollen and sore from cutting the sharp-edged Formica.

Daddy carefully dismantled his makeshift home, storing it in a warehouse within the yard. Several days of maintenance followed on my old bus before he coughed and spluttered back to life. It was a warm April and already little heads of apple blossom were pushing out from their branches on the trees in the park, scattering a hint of spring fragrance. A stirring in my belly of tiny butterflies brought an excitement only a traveller would understand as I positioned myself near the front of the bus.

As he drove onto the open road my father laughed as Mammy put her arm on his shoulder, saying her usual 'Where to now, Macduff?'

He leaned back into her chest, saying 'Brigadoon, here we come!'

With Shirley, Chrissie, Janey and Mona walking their own paths, it seemed so still and quiet without them. Usually, on taking to the road, they'd stand in a circle, holding onto each other for balance, then burst into song. Shirley wrote her own songs, and we'd laugh as she performed one written for that particular journey. We laughed because it was usually full of swear-words and comical innuendos. Yes, of all my sisters, she was the one who I'd say made me happy.

Come with me; spend the summer, the last one, with what's left of our family in the old bus.

29

MAGGIE-ELLEN

Daddy said he'd heard that Auntie Jessie and Wullie were heading out from Kelty. 'We'll meet up and travel awhile with them,' he told Mammy, adding that they'd be grand company, seeing as the lassies were away. Before they arrived, this is what happened to us while waiting on them.

My fascination for 'midden-raking' wasn't a child thing. It didn't desert me at youth's birth. No surprise, then, to find our visit to Kelty in Fife had me straining at the reins to join the rats in the nearby coup of goodies.

Granny Power told me last time we spoke, 'You'll catch something rummaging through folks' discarded muck, my lass,' then muttered under her breath in Gaelic as she handed me a pair of red rubber gloves Auntie Ina (Mammy's youngest sister) used. These navvy tools were issued to workers while using the awful-smelling Jeyes Fluid disinfectant, a certainty for ridding germs from the busy kitchens and bathrooms of the Atholl Palace Hotel in Pitlochry where she worked.

She would say, 'I'm stumped ye've no caught a disease from an auld "yookie" [rat]'. This added comment was followed with a history of the Black Plague and the Grey Plague. She even managed to remember a Red one as well! Then, finally, her parting words were, 'Dinnae drink your water near a midden burn! That's where the rats drink theirs!'

Granny's problem was she had dozens of grandbairns and loved us all too much. Thoughts of harm to any of us brought out her mothering-hen instinct. If love has a limit, no one told my Granny.

'Jessie, where are you going?' shouted Mammy, tying a sturdy rope between two silver birch trees growing in the wood by our Kelty campsite.

'To check out the midden,' I called back.

'That's what you think, lady. I need eggs, milk, bread and a quarter of tea, so take the basket, get some money from Daddy and bolt down to the wee corner shop, now!'

'Mammy, did we not pass the empty bin-lorry as we came in? That means it was just emptied, so the midden will be full of goodies,' I protested.

'Full of rotting rubbish,' said Daddy, positioning the wash-hand basin in its tripod near the bus door.

'Och, there could easy be a treasure sitting on the coup waiting for me to find it.'

My father pushed a hand into his trousers' pocket, took out a pound note and said, 'Your mother asked for tea, eggs, milk and what was it?'

Grabbing the money I lifted the shopping basket. Before storming off I called back to my father as he poured water into the basin, 'Bread!'

'Aye, that's it, bread,' he called back, 'food of the Gods!'

I must have flown down to the wee shop, for, in the flicking of a lamb's tail I was back—minus the bread.

'Jessie, I couldn't have been any clearer, and it's not like I asked for a mountain of messages. I've not a slice of bread in the place, lassie!' Mammy was instantly annoyed.

'I'll give you a loaf, Jeannie. I bought too much at the baker's in Cardenden,' said Big John Young's wife, Maggie-Ellen, who had moved onto the site a week before us.

These traveller folks had known our family for as long as I could remember. She hailed from Paisley, and was fairground stock, while Big John was a Fife dealer. They had one son who everyone knew as Joe-Toe. For the love of me I have no idea what that meant, perhaps Joseph Thomas?

Mammy accepted the kind offer of bread, allowing me the freedom to rake the midden. 'Take the rubber gloves with you, Jess, better be safe than sorry,' called my father, waving them in the air.

'They're too big, Daddy. I would need hands on myself like a twenty-stone Irish navvy.'

'Well, in that case,' called my mother, while busy brushing sticky wullies from Renie's hair, on account of her falling backwards into the offending plants growing near the riverbank, 'you can forget the midden.'

With dogged reluctance I took the gloves from Dad and ran off to partake of my greatest pastime—routing amongst other folk's rubbish.

Within half an hour I returned, blood dripping from a gaping wound in my right hand.

Horror upon horrors, I had cut myself while ramming my glove-less hand into a box of broken cups, discarded no doubt from some old biddy's china cabinet. Three hours later I came back from the cottage hospital, sporting a hand swathed in thick bandages. Worst was the swollen bum where the ancient nurse rammed a thing like my mother's knitting needle into my poor wee hip. 'That's to stop you getting lock-jaw,' she told me, adding, 'What the hell were you doing in among midden stuff any road?' Turning to Daddy, she said, 'You're needing a word with this lassie of yours,' handing him fresh bandages, saying it was a deep cut but not needing stitches.

Mammy said she was black-affronted at me, and how would she face folk while hawking. Then she broke my heart in a dozen bits by forbidding me to rake a midden ever again! So, readers, that was how my dreams of being the richest scrappy in Scotland came crashing down. All those dreams of owning a fleet of scrap lorries across the land. Lorries with the Queen's stamp of approval emblazoned on their doors. The trouble with my mother was she had no ambitions.

Next day I had removed the best part of the bandages from my injury, allowing more freedom to my hand. Saying that, what were my capabilities? Not dishwashing or rinsing knickers, fetching water or messages.

A voice from an open car door answered my question. 'Come with me, Jess, I only need a one-handed lass to help carry my swag bag.' It was Maggie-Ellen. She was going hawking in the country, which meant a lot of footwork. Everyone knew the dear lady had corns and calluses, probably from tramping up and down long farm tracks and telling fortunes for more years than any one could remember.

Well, I enjoyed hawking, so why not? After getting my mother's permission, I was sitting alongside Maggie-Ellen in a big shiny Buick, as Joe-Toe drove us away into the countryside.

This tale comes from that time. The day my friend Maggie-Ellen, a genuine fortune-teller of the highest esteem, cursed a farmer's prized bull!

Her swag-bag, the dear lady's treasure chest of jewellery, was not filled with gold and silver, but cheap tinny baubles that she sold as an added attraction to a punter thinking she was buying a bargain. As I lifted it up one thought entered my head, 'Ye Gods, what a weight of a thing, no wonder she needed someone to carry it!'

Maggie-Ellen and I left Joe-Toe at a farm road entrance. He drove off, saying he'd come back round twelve and would bring mutton pies for our dinner.

As we walked up the stony track, she asked how my hand was. Apart from a slight throbbing it was fine.

'Well, if the swag gets heavy, carry it over your arm, that'll prevent you from using the one hand all the time.'

Who was she kidding? This bag should have been on a donkey's back, never mind my arm. She told me her Joe-Toe always carried it. But he said he felt like a sissy walking about with a woman's bag.

Maggie-Ellen was a mystery. Everybody for miles knew the strange powers my companion possessed. Many a tale was whispered of her ability to tell one's fortune with uncanny accuracy. No one dared cross her. No one, that is, who knew her.

As I stopped to adjust my sandal strap I looked at her walking in front, a fairly tall figure, round about five feet nine. Long, black-to- greying hair piled up and secured by gold-coloured combs gave her an appearance of being taller. Unblemished, smooth, olive skin and a once-slender figure meant that, even at my age of fourteen, I could easily tell that, in her day, she was indeed a strikingly beautiful woman. More telling than all her other features, though, was that dark, mysterious look, the look of a genuine Gypsy! At the time of my tale she was over fifty.

As we turned the umpteenth bend, at long last a farm house loomed into view.

'Thank God for that, I was beginning to think we chose the wrong place,' exclaimed Maggie-Ellen.

Making our way towards the house we both turned towards a

field on our left. The biggest bull we'd ever set eyes on stood staring and snorting at us from over the gate. 'Look at the goolies on that beast, I bet there's a million offspring he could easily count!', laughed my companion.

'Aye, poor beast, thon goolies are dragging off the ground. It must be right sore at times, especially jumping a dyke!' I added.

'Jess, if you weighed the same as him, lassie, I hardly think you'd be able to jump over yer Granny's thimble. Come on, let's get and see if we can find a bob at this place!' she said.

Although I'd heard others talk about Maggie-Ellen's work, I had never seen her in action. I'm grateful for my cut finger, because this day's events allowed me at first hand to see a true teller of fate at work. It was an experience which has stayed with me all the days of my life.

Adjusting her coat buttons, fixing a loose hair-comb, and asking me if her lipstick was still red, she knocked three times on the farmhouse door. No answer. She knocked again, louder this time, followed by a gentle, 'Hello, is anyone in?' Still no answer. I said there might not be anybody in, further reminding her that farm people seldom care to deal with strangers at the door. Ignoring me she knocked again.

'Jess, go and look through the wee window at the side of the house.'

I felt annoyed at her insistence. 'Perhaps there is nobody in. Do you not think we waste our time?' I said, as I reluctantly did as she asked.

'There is a bad thing here, I sense entrapment. Look through the window, we've not much time.'

I didn't understand a thing she said, but it made me feel uneasy just the same. I stared through the small window, and although a net curtain hindered my gaze I did catch sight of a young woman sitting at a table. I tapped gently on the glass. She instantly stood up, came over and opened the window. 'What do you want?' she asked.

Before I had time to answer, Maggie-Ellen was at my side. 'Lassie, I've come to help. Pack a bag quickly,' she told the young woman.

The next thing I can only describe as indescribable! The young woman opened the door and called for us to come in while she packed.

'What's going on?' I asked my companion, still totally stumped at the reaction from the woman. After all, had we not just met her? Was she not a complete stranger?

Within no time the lassie stood in her kitchen, suitcase in one hand, small vanity-case in the other.

'Now, listen to me,' said Maggie-Ellen. 'I feel he is not far. In fact the beast comes up the road, but don't you fret, me and the lassie here will keep him from you.'

'What in hell's name is going on?' I asked, for the tenth time.

At those words the woman began to tremble, tears instantly filled her eyes and ran freely down her face. 'I'm dead now, he'll kill me for sure. Help me, gypsy, please.'

'Are you ready? Have you all you need?' asked Maggie-Ellen. The frightened woman nodded in answer. 'Well, lassie, this is the only chance you're going to get. Come now.'

I was still utterly stunned at what was taking place.

On opening the door my mouth dropped, for standing feet away from us was a six-foot tall, heavily-built man. His eyes narrowed on seeing us. 'Where the hell are you going?' he shouted at the frightened woman. 'Get yourself back in there or it's the stick I'll give ye!', he added, before turning to us, hissing through clenched teeth, 'And you, filthy gypsies, you can go now, or else.'

He lifted his crook and brought it down inches from my legs.

I lifted the swag-bag, swinging it at him and narrowly missing the side of his face.

Maggie-Ellen straightened her back, squared her shoulders, stared the offending gent in the eye and said, 'You are a vile, evil man! I give you one warning, let us go without hindrance or on your own head be it.'

'The day I bother about the likes of you will be the day hell freezes over. Now, see the bull at the gate over yonder—do you want me to set him on you?'

'I see the brute,' answered Maggie-Ellen, keeping her gaze on the wicked man, 'but he doesn't stand at any gate, he lies in his own dung!'

I couldn't believe my eyes. The broad, healthy bull we joked about earlier lay as dead as stone at the foot of the iron gate.

'Oh, my God, my prize Charolais, what's wrong, what's up with you?' the man cried, clambering over the gate to get to the departed beast.

'Let us be gone from here, it won't take him long to make chase,' said my fellow traveller, holding my arm and pulling the young woman away at the same time.

In no time we were standing at the road end. Joe-Toe was already there, and I can tell you, I wasn't half relieved to see him.

'Just drop me off at the bus stop,' asked the still-shocked woman, 'I'll get a bus.'

'Don't you think the seed growing in there needs its father?' asked Maggie-Ellen, patting the woman on the abdomen. These words brought floods of tears.

'I think you may be right,' she smiled, drying her eyes. 'He lives in the village of Cardenden. If you take me there, I'll find him. And thanks Maggie-Ellen, for keeping your promise. Here's something for your trouble.' She slipped some money into her hand.

'Will the wild man come looking for you?' I asked her.

'God, I'm pretty certain the loss of his prize bull will have knocked the stuffing from him. No, he'll not bother me again,' she said, thanking me also for my help.

We watched the woman run off down the road to, hopefully, a new life.

As we ate our cold mutton pies, I asked my friend what the day's events were all about. 'I think you owe me an explanation,' I said to Maggie-Ellen.

She told me that the day before, she had found the poor soul crying at the side of an old dyke near the farm. The big-mouthed man whom we'd had the run-in with was her brother. Ever since their parents died he had been using her more or less like a slave, forbidding her to go anywhere. One day, a young lad came looking for work. They met and fell in love, keeping their romance secret for over a year. The brother had recently found out. He beat her and forbade her from seeing him again. Maggie-Ellen, on hearing of the young woman's predicament, promised to help. You know the rest. And there was me thinking my friend was a psychic extraordinaire.

'But,' I enquired of my companion on our way home, 'one thing puzzles me.'

'I know you're going to ask me about the bull. Well, that's for me to know and you to guess.'

So, then, that was the only answer she gave me. I never knew if the old bull went naturally or otherwise. One thing I do know, that young woman never told Maggie-Ellen she was pregnant, so how did she know that?

Traveller women who have the 'gift' never disclose their secrets, not even to their own daughters! They say if an individual is to be clairvoyant, then they will know from within from an early age.

My own mother, no matter how many times I asked her about it, refused point blank to say a thing apart from, 'If you tell people good things, and keep the bad from them, then what harm can be done?'

§

We met Auntie Jessie and Wullie, then travelled to the Berries where, as usual, a great time was had. I do not have a tale to tell of this occasion, except it was there for the first time in my life I fell in love.

If you have read the books of Betsy Whyte then you will know who I speak of, because my first love was her younger son, William. I followed him around like a doe-eyed pup until he gently sat me down on an old dyke and disclosed he loved another.

I was heartbroken. There was I, hopelessly in love. I cried my eyes out while I told him so. Betsy's laddie, being a true gentleman, said I was far too bonny for him, then kissed my flushed cheek before strolling off to pick the morning's berries.

I spent many happy hours with Betsy and her man Bryce that berry time. It was with them I heard many happy tales of their young days on the road. Little did I know her life story would one day be read by the whole world in the form of her renowned books, *Yellow on the Broom* and *Red Rowan and Wild Berries*. She was a lovely travelling lady whom I am the richer for meeting.

§

We left Blairgowrie that summer at the Berries' end and headed to Glen Shee.

30

ARMADALE MARY

'Where to now, folks,' asked Daddy, 'is it west or east?'

Uncle Wullie said he wouldn't mind a donner up round Brae-mar, he hadn't been there for ages. 'Do you know there's ancient pine there that grow so high they kiss clouds, and the burn water so cold at its source only the Gods taste it. Them, and travellers like ourselves, of course.'

He came from that part of Bonnie Scotland did my uncle, and beamed with pride when describing it. If anyone happened to disagree with him, then he proudly reminded the said body that a great Royal once fell in love with it at first sight, then wryly asked, 'Well, tell me, why did Her Majesty build Balmoral?'

No one could argue with that, for Queen Victoria indeed said, and I quote: 'There is no place on earth so majestic as my Deeside.' She and Uncle Wullie have long since passed away, but I know they would have had no doubt that this part of Scotland would forever retain her beauty and remain 'Royal'.

'Fine, Braemar it is!' answered my father, as he adjusted the wee velvet cushion behind his back on the driver's seat.

I am eternally grateful to my Uncle Wullie, because if he hadn't suggested going east, then my meeting with Mary would never have taken place, and a valuable lesson in life might not have come my way. This was, never to judge a book by its cover.

On one of the many snake-bends on the road from Blairgowrie to

Glen Shee, I noticed a bent old woman. Her appearance sent shivers up my spine. I dived to the back window to get a good look at the old witch's features before another bend took her out of view. We stopped up for the night in bonny Glen Shee.

'Did anyone see the old biddy with the heavy bundle on her back? We passed her by about mile or so back at the Spittal.' I looked round my relatives for a response to my query. Auntie Jessie frowned before answering me.

'Don't you be thinking on yon old witch. I've seen her many a time, on plenty roads. Big Wull Macdonald had a run-in with her over a dead hen. He said she was using it to hex some poor farmer who chased her out of his barn.' This was typical of my Auntie Jessie; if she didn't know a person then she gave them a character, and always one of a dubious nature.

'Och, she's only a tramp,' said Uncle Wullie, blowing into the newly stick-piled fire to give it a heart. 'Keeps to herself and never bothers a soul.'

Cousin Anna laughed as she said, 'Maybe yon big heavy pack is full of bairns' heads, Jess, so you better watch in the dead of night that an old, bony-fingered hand doesn't reach into the bus and pull you out!'

'Aye, by the lugs, no doubt!' This remark from Daddy brought on hearty laughter as everybody gave my larger than normal ears a second glance.

Mammy saw my face turn bright red, smiled, and told me there was nothing wrong with my ears; then reminded me to fetch the water from the burn. 'It's half an hour gone since I asked you, my lass, to get water for the tea. Now be off with you, or it'll be me grabbing the lugs!'

The burn water was crystal clear. Removing the top from the water can, I plunged it into the deepest bit and drank my fill. It was so cold and sweet I helped myself to another cupful. As I leaned over the pool a reflection joined mine in the mirror of the water. I stood up quickly, and standing behind me was my witch-cum-tramp!

'Well now, I hope you haven't frightened away my supper,' she said, pointing at the fast-moving trout darting to and fro among the smooth stones at the either side of the burn.

'Oh, sorry,' was all I managed to say.

'Never mind, lassie, I wasn't hungry any road. Are you part of those tinkers camped by the March dyke?'

Had she not called us tinkers I might have felt a sense of fear. Instead my hackles rose at her remark, bringing anger instead. 'We are travellers. Are you a hexy witch?'

She glowered at me. I took two steps backward and wished I'd held my tongue.

Saying nothing, she undid the broad leather strap placed round her head that held secure her weighty pack. 'I'm no witch, but I tramp the roads, so that makes two of us. Now you'd better fill your can and be away with you. I'm back-sore and feet-weary and the last thing I need is a snottery-nosed tinker scaring away my supper.' That said, she placed the heavy pack on the ground.

'You said you weren't hungry, and you're the one with a dirty nose, it's ingrained. When did that old wrinkled face last see a drop soap?'

'Why, it's a while since I had words with sic a fiery bairn. What do they call you?'

Mammy's whistle brought our uneasy conversation to an abrupt end. Screwing the can lid tightly I started for the campsite, saying in answer to her question, 'You tell me yours first.'

No answer did she give me, just muttered something under her breath, sat wearily down, removed a small pouch of tobacco from a pocket in her long black skirt, and began filling an old clay pipe with the stem half broke.

As I walked away she called out, 'Mary, my name is Mary,' then pulled a sad old face down onto her chest and covered her head with a black shawl.

As I hurried back with the water-can, thoughts of my encounter, albeit of an unfriendly nature, made me feel drawn to this tramp named Mary, and I just had to find out a wee bit more about her background.

As soon as supper was over I was sitting on the humpback-bridge crossing the burn where she settled for the night. 'Where are you from, Mary? I'm Jessie, by the way. I want for you to accept my apology. I'm right sorry for being cheeky to you earlier on.'

She looked me up and down, then pulled the black wool shawl from off her head, saying, 'Usually I tell nobody about myself, that's how I prefer it. Are you an Angus tinker—oh, sorry, I mean traveller!'

'No, we're from Perthshire. I was born in Aberfeldy Cottage Hospital. A Dr Yellowlees brought me into the world.'

'Yellatrees, gey funny name, is it not? Are you sure the good doctor was called that?' she asked teasingly.

I moved nearer, reminding myself that the older you are the harder of hearing you get.

'My mother said he was her favourite doctor at bringing bairns into the world, and as she had nine babies she would know, don't you think?'

'Michty, I think she would. Did they all survive? How many of each kind were they?'

My new companion seemed genuinely interested, and I was more than keen to tell her all about my mother's attempt to swell Aberfeldy's population.

'Eight lassies, including myself, but sad to say she had a wee laddie who never survived.'

'Oh, that was a right shame. What happened to the infant?'

'Well, my mother seldom speaks on it much, but during a bad measles scourge, she lost him. John,' I continued, 'My folks gave him the name of my father's best pal in the army, because he saved my daddy's life, he did.'

My new friend settled herself back against her bulky pack and asked if I'd tell her how Daddy's mate saved him.

'Well,' said I, very happy to tell this tale, which I knew off to a tee, on account of my father telling it on many a cold winter's night with my sisters and I huddled round his feet, as wee Reekie turned our faces bright-red from the heat of her coal-stapped body.

It was nearing the end of the war and thoughts of victory were on the soldiers' minds. Daddy and his mate Johnny Slay, who served with him in the Black Watch, transferring to the REMEs and then finally the Tank Corps, were advancing through the Black Forest in Germany. At long last the allies were beginning to see an end to six years of hellish war. The Germans, who'd been in retreat for three weeks, rallied and were soon pushing British and American troops back the way they came. Daddy's tank took a direct hit from a severe mortar bombardment. He and Johnny escaped with little injury, but their officer, a young man from Bedfordshire, was killed instantly.

The Germans had dug deep pits throughout the forest. Daddy

thought it was to bury the dead hastily , but wasn't sure. Anyway, in the darkness the two comrades fell into one of the pits and couldn't get out. Down in the pit filled with corpses and rainwater, the pair clung together as enemy soldiers scanned torches over the forest floor searching for survivors, who without doubt would have been shot. Several times during the long night my father slipped in and out of exhausted sleep. Johnny, obviously the stronger, held Dad's head above the blood and water filling the hole, saving his life.

Early morning saw friendly troops descend upon the half-dead duo, retrieving them from the pit of death. Daddy promised Johnny, 'When I have a son he'll have your name, that's a promise!'

A minute or two's silence followed. Then Mary said, 'I had a son, Andrew I called him, after his Dad. Curly blonde hair he had, the bonniest bairn in Armadale, I'd go so far to say in all of Skye.'

I looked at my old companion, and a solitary tear rolled down her wrinkled face. She fumbled in her skirt pocket, pulled out a piece of rag, wiped her face and then, before putting it back, blew hard upon her nose. 'My wee curly-headed Andra, who'd have thought such a bitty wean would grow to six feet. As broad as he was tall, my laddie was. The navy, that's where his heart took him, just like his father, sailors the both of them.'

I didn't need adulthood to tell me this old lady's son had passed on, but dare I push her to open a long-closed heart to tell such a story? However, without any prodding from me she opened her sore heart and said, 'Both of them, my two men, husband in the first war, son in the second. Their ships were sank and they, God bless them, are buried on the ocean floor. Entombed in salt-eaten metal and rotted wood, my precious laddies never came home to our wee cottage in Armadale on Skye.'

Slowly I closed the distance between us and gently touched her shoulder. She drew back as if in some way a comforting hand was denied to her in her solitary world.

She continued, 'I had no relative to turn to, or neighbour. My home became like a tomb. I spent more time outside than in, even when winter snow and wind froze my bones. It was towards the mighty ocean I gazed for comfort. For it was she who held them in her watery depths, in a grave I could not tend.

It was one day while staring out at the vast ocean I made a deci-sion to leave my island home, go to the mainland, and find another life. This I did, but my heart found no peace, and soon the life I live today became my lot, tramping the roads.'

I closed my eyes with shame and thought on my Auntie Jessie's words of witch, evil, mad—just a few of the adjectives used to describe this heart-broken, lonely old woman, who'd been dealt more than a fair share of bad luck!

'Look, lassie, the sun sets and I haven't even got my hap up yet.' Mary had unburdened herself more than she meant to, and quickly changed our conversation.

I said nothing as I helped her pull her bed and bivvy from her pack. No pile of severed heads rolled out, only the necessary things to keep body and soul intact.

'I'll get a puckle sticks for your fire. The nights are fair drawing in. Mary, you'll sleep better with a wee fire at the hap door!' I wanted so much to help her, she seemed so vulnerable.

'Aye, I'll accept your help, lassie. Then I'd be grateful if you'd let me be. There's a long road ahead of me tomorrow.'

'Oh, and where are you going?' I asked, before adding, 'We're going over the Devil's Elbow to Braemar. Come with us, Mammy would be pleased, I'm sure, to take you.' I had become concerned, worried about this sad old woman. It didn't feel right she should be uncared for. I took hold of her skeletal hand. 'Please, Mary, I'll take good care of you, and I never make promises I cannot keep.'

Her look softened at my concern. Touching my face, then turning towards the high hills on our right, she said, 'Do you see those hills away up yonder? There's a sheep track will guide my feet into Glen Muick. From there I'll visit Braemar, so if that's where you'll be then we will meet again. And if it's not to be, bonny lassie, remember how vast the Heavens are. If we don't meet in this life it's certain we will in the next.'

No words passed between us as we busied ourselves, she building the small deer-skinned hap, me lighting a fire.

After chores were done she held out a piece of dried ham. I refused, saying she shouldn't share what little she had, but thanked her just the same.

'You away home now, pet, for I'm sure your folks will be worrying, and as for me, well, I can hardly keep my eyes open.'

'Oh, Mary, you can't be serious about climbing up thon high hills. Anyroad, you'd need a powny to carry your heavy pack!' I pleaded again for her to come with us.

That comment brought a hearty laugh, as she said she'd had a heavier pack in midwinter and managed fine. I could see my old friend had a will of iron, and no amount of pleading would make her change a set mind.

I hugged her. She smiled and thanked me, saying the last person who had done such a thing was young Andrew, the day he set off to defend his country.

She crept inside her tiny abode. I ran home to my family, my happy cheerful family.

In the early morning I decided to surprise her with sandwiches and milk for the hill journey, but when I got to the grassy bank by the humpbacked bridge, she was gone. The flattened grass and patch of burnt ground was all that remained. Panic filled my chest, I scanned the hillside, called her name: 'Mary, Mary, I've got some food for you. Please don't go without a decent goodbye!'

It was as if the mist that shrouded the hillside had swallowed her up. But if she fared well in the glen and didn't get sick or something, we'd meet in Braemar. This thought consoled me. I had became fond of her like a third Granny. She should have a family; I had to see her again.

But before we left the wee glen snuggled at the foot of the high mountains, the notorious Devil's Elbow had to be negotiated.

'No way in this world do I sit in that bus while you drive it pointing towards God's heavens,' shouted Mammy at Daddy, 'and neither do the bairns!' With that said, she ushered us in a line to climb up and round the hairpin bends of the road. Truth is, no-one could blame her, because this stretch of narrow road was near on vertical. Uncle Wullie had a Bedford van, a lot smaller vehicle than our bus, and crept up without rolling backwards or stalling. Well, my dad feared no road, regardless of its width or gradient, and as this was the only way to Braemar, then upwards and onwards it was.

'You coming, Jess?' he asked me.

'Can I, Mammy, please?' I pleaded with her, saying that when the Links Market Fair came to Kirkcaldy she let me go on the divebombers.

'First sign o' the bus rolling back you jump out, do you hear me, lassie?' she warned, then walked on up the way, my three younger sisters in tow.

It seemed to take forever. I remember every nail-biting inch of tarmac; every chug, chug and spurt from the engine's gut brought my heart into my throat. At the bend itself I sank my nails into the back of Daddy's neck, prompting him to shout, 'Go and take a seat, lassie!'

I even forgot about old Mary, such was my experience of sheer terror. What a relief to feel the bus level off as the deer fence running round the foot of the Cairnwell Mountain came into view. Daddy pulled the bus onto a heathery layby and set up a wee fire. I spread a tartan rug on the heather, disturbing a red grouse who let me know how annoyed he was by almost choking on a guttural scream, as he reached for the misty sky with outstretched wings.

(Note: The Devil no longer bends the road to Braemar into a fierce elbow. It has been replaced by a wider and straighter road. It is far better for the driver, but to me personally the old road seemed more in tune to the terrain of that part of Scotland.)

§

Although we stayed in Braemar for more than a week, the old woman failed to arrive and I never saw Armadale Mary again.

Sometimes, when feeling despondent with life, I thought she might have slipped on a rocky outcrop in some desolate spot, or died of the cold on a high snow-covered hill.

Perhaps, while driving round a bend on a lonely road, a weary long-distance lorry driver thought he hit a lone deer, and she was thrown into a deep ditch to die of her injuries. But my mother re-minded me that imagined scenes were just that, and that my dear old friend probably passed away in a kind farmer's warm barn, who then saw to it that she was given a decent burial. Now she was probably happily surrounded by her son and husband.

Whatever happened, and wherever you are, Mary, I would like you to know this—I named my first son Johnnie!

31

THE BEST TABLET IN THE WORLD

W e said goodbye to our relatives, who went up to visit friends at Brora in Sutherland. We headed west to spend a week on the coast. Here's a tale of sweetness for you. Also a story of evil and revenge. 'Why?' Well, this is life, is it not?

§

I am the country's best butter-tablet maker! I can sense you think me a wee bit swelt-headed. Fine, think what you like, because it just happens to be fact. Ask anybody who has tasted my tablet and they'll tell you the same. Reaching the heights of this culinary, sugary delight, however, was not achieved without a wee bit of an obstacle or two, to say the very least! Read on.

Edie (Edith) Dalrymple and her mountain of a man, Barry, acquired a field on the west coast somewhere twixt Irvine and Ayr. I remember hearing that he won it during a card game with a landowner. The deal was signed before the gent sobered up, and being a man of honourable seed he could do nothing about it. Barry owned several palomino horses. After a spit and slap day at Appleby Fair one year, he'd allowed his heart to rule the head, and ended up with five more ponies than he needed. Still, though nothing took precedence over his love of Edie, these dappled beauties came a close second.

The grand pair, who for reasons unknown were never blessed with bairns, were renowned, so before long the field where the horses roamed was filled with travellers who happened to be passing by. It was well-known throughout the circle of the wandering folks that a welcome awaited at Big Barry and Edie's.

Barry was in his element, surrounded by little yins clambering to sit upon a pony. Older kids, those who didn't yet have the knowledge, were taught to saddle and harness. The ones who did were allowed the freedom to gallop and canter within his field of equine delight. So if you have a memory of a green pasture down on the coastline filled with travellers and coloured horses, then you're probably remembering the wild hospitality of two of God's finest.

Local villages were more than grateful to the pair because of the rising trade they brought, especially when the site was full. Barry, being the gentle giant that he was, had no problem with any would-be troublemaker, because a firm hand round the back of the neck was all it took to rid the site of the offender. This meant local bobbies had no need to visit. Yes, peace reigned amongst the travellers who pulled on to spend a while by the sea in the sandy field of Barry and Edie Dalrymple. There was no charge (but if you felt the need to part with a bob or two, then Barry didn't refuse) even although he'd built a block with toilets (hand-emptied) and one sink. Two taps supplied running water, one at either end of the field. The awful task of emptying the latrines was done by whoever had the most bairns or the fattest wives. (Only kidding, I can't enlighten you on that one. Sorry!)

So here we were, then, mingling with friends and relatives after a long summer. This would be our final stop before heading back to Kirkcaldy for the winter and school. Yuck!

It was a Sunday and Mammy had lifted a stern finger, warning us to stay out of the bus. Had she not spent the morning polishing and cleaning? This meant one thing—Auntie Anna and Uncle Robert were calling in. Mammy made some soor scones, which were fly-protected under a clean muslin cloth on a plate near wee Reekie. He had a grand glow, our warm stove, and Daddy thought it a waste not to use it. He just wanted a cosy feet-up, but she insisted the bus stay empty and clean until the visitors had gone. Renie, like Janey, was horse-daft. She'd found a brute of a horse and could not be prised from it. The other girls were playing on a slide made of corrugated roofing, while I followed a smell, one that had filled my nostrils the best part of the morning. A hot, sweet aroma, which made me think, whatever it was, it would be damned tasty! Like a bloodhound I wandered round the site, sniffing the air, until I got the smell in my nose and throat, throwing my taste buds into turmoil. What could this be?

'Hello, Jessie, have you come to help me make Barry's favourite sweetie?'

I was standing outside the open door of Edie's caravan. Inside, a great black pot sat on her stove, bubbles blobbing gently at the surface.

'What a marvellous smell, Edie. Show me what you're doing.'

'Come in, lass, I'm making Barry some Scots tablet.' I went up the high step of their caravan and sat down beside the bubbling pot. Around the narrow seat the smell rolled, engulfing me in its snare. I was being hypnotised. I sat transfixed as Edie stirred a long-handled wooden spoon in circles within the black pan. 'Always stir clockwise. Never go the other way, you'll annoy the de'il,' she informed me.

'The devil? Why should he be interested in a boiling pan?' I enquired.

'He'll guide you away from the straight and narrow if you stir even the porridge round agin the clock.'

Those words made me shiver, and even to this day I feel the same tingle if I accidentally find I've circled my spoon the opposite direction from the flow of natural time. I feel stupid telling you that, but it's just one of those things.

Anyway, after half an hour she dropped a little of the now-brown fluid into a cup. 'Hold that, Jess, and wait a minute while it cools.' I sat staring, as the droplet formed a ball lying at the bottom of the cup, no bigger than a pea. Edie buttered a tin tray, then laid it on a tea towel. 'Is it a wee ball yet?'

I nodded.

'Right,' she said, 'this is the secret of making tablet taste divine.' Taking her pan carefully from the stove and sitting it gently on a thick wooden chopping board (Edie had all the mod cons) she began turning the spoon hell for leather! Round and round she went, like the devil himself was fast on her heel. 'Look, do you see the mixture change colour?'

I stared in at the forming tablet, like a whirlpool it was. Edie's forearm was bulging like her man's and for a moment I thought it would burst. The smell was swirling round too and into my mouth and nose.

'Do you see the tablet changing?'

Yes, it certainly was. What was transparent seconds before was now sandy-coloured and thickening. 'Did you put butter in it?' I asked, 'I can smell butter.'

'There's the best part o' a cow's mornin' offering in there and a good pint of it as well, melted together with a full bag of sugar, lass,' answered Edie, before pouring the finished mixture into the tray. As I sat and watched the tablet solidifying in its rectangular bed, Edie offered me a drink of lemonade, saying it would take up to an hour before the sweetie was edible. This brought a huge feeling of disappointment and I didn't think I'd last that long. She told me to come back later, but I felt the tablet might either get eaten or stolen, so making the excuse that I'd nothing to do I stayed where I was—on guard, so to speak. She smiled, perhaps reading my thoughts. We cracked a while and our blether took on a conversation about Crieff. 'Do you know the story of Baby Bairn?' she asked, running a knife lengthways across the hardening tablet. I told her I had no recollection of the tale.

Edie asked my age. When I said I was a teenager, she said that was a good age to hear this tale. We sat cupping our lemonade, and here, reader, is the harrowing story of Baby Bairn, which I tell to you word for word as Edie told it to me.

§

A popular campsite for the Perthshire travellers was a place called Lady Mary's Walk, on the banks of the Turret river which flowed opposite the lower end of Macrosty park. Across a bridge spanning the burn, a path leads to an area which used to hold up to a dozen or so families. This filled to capacity around the tattie-howking time in October. The main railway line from Perth to Oban ran through the campsite. Old folks talked of the friendly train staff who would throw sweeties to the bairns as the train trundled loudly along the track. Wee laddies used to run alongside the engine as the driver pulled on the whistle, much to their delight, though not so to the angry mother who had just got the wean to sleep.

At this time the tatties hadn't yet started, so there were only a few families on the green. One was a family consisting of a mother with two grown sons and a daughter of sixteen years. The lassie, though grown in body, had the mind of a five-year-old; 'a simple wee cratur' was how folks described her. They said it was sad seeing the lassie playing in the sand by the burnside, and thinking how unfortunate that this poor thing would never know the joy of getting married or having a family, because she would never grow up. She had the body of a woman, though, and for this reason her elder brothers watched over her like a hawk. Her mother called her simple child 'Baby Bairn'. Although conscious of her daughter's disability she never fussed over it, and was just grateful to the Almighty for her bonny lassie. And what a beauty she was, with long blonde ringlets cascading down her back, touching the ground when she sat on the grass. She had blue eyes as big as saucers and skin like the elusive pearl. Travelling folks who knew the family said she had the face of an angel, and all who saw her remarked on how she could brighten the dreichest day.

Soon, as the tattie time drew near, others arrived on the green. Everybody more or less knew each other, and before long the place was full of cheery folk, eagerly awaiting the chance to make enough money to see them through the long winter ahead. Apart from the tattie-dressing there was no more work on the farms until the planting in the spring. The bairns all had to be schooled, so extra money was needed for clothes and sturdy shoes.

No-one saw the lone man arrive on the green and pitch his small tent. He must have come during the night. He had with him a bike and khaki-coloured haversack, and that was all. Travelling folks did not shun the stranger, nor did they judge him, but they were always mindful of his lone status and kept a wary eye on him when he was near the bairns. He did not seem to cause any problems, however. In fact he seemed a decent enough man, and after several days was welcomed at the campfires.

Soon the tattie-lifting was in full swing, and everybody was busying themselves, taking advantage of the unusually mild weather enjoyed that particular autumn. Weans eagerly awaited the friendly train workers for the free sweeties thrown from the old steam train as it trundled past the campsite, while mothers cooked the big pots of stovies for the hungry workers coming home from the back-breaking tattie-lifting.

The lone man had struck up a friendship with the two brothers of the simple lassie, spending his nights at their campfire. He seemed genuinely fond of the girl, spoiling her with gifts of coloured ribbons for her hair and bracelets. She called him her uncle, and being childlike in nature she trusted him as she did everybody.

The tatties that year had been very good, and the farmers were pleased with the yield, so everyone received a bonus. The two brothers were not ones for drinking, but with their mother's approval they took a dram from the kindly stranger whom they had befriended. The mother had no objection to her laddies having a dram or two, so after making sure her precious lassie was asleep she bedded herself down for the night. Soon her boys bade their friend goodnight, and apart from the sound of a lonely hooting owl high in a nearby tree, the happy campsite fell into a welcoming slumber.

Just before dawn the old train headed by on its journey north, and that was when the demon showed the real reason for his attention to the simple lassie. With the cunning of a fox he sneaked her out from the tent, her muffled protests disguised by the noise of the passing train, did to her what is unspeakable, and killed her.

A woman filling her kettle from the burn found her. The blood was splattered across the autumn grass and down over the sand, where the lassie used to build sandcastles at the burnside. The mother's screams were heard for miles, as the sight of her bonnie wee lassie's body was indelibly imprinted on her mind. The two brothers knew only too well what had to be done. They would find the beast before the law did and mete out their own punishment. Travelling folks had little respect for the law, and if retribution was to be made then the victim's relatives carried it out.

They packed a haversack and set out after him, ensuring that their distraught mother was in the safe hands of folks who promised they would take care of her. People say the lads found the monster a mile north of Comrie, washing himself at the burnside. One can only imagine what form of justice was dealt to that man, the devil who had robbed them of their baby sister, at the hands of those two heartbroken young men.

'What did they do to him, Edie?' I asked her.

'Let's just say that good breath was wasted in him, pet,' was her reply.

They say that the poor mother, filled with hate, cursed his soul to the spot where he savaged her lassie. Moreover, from that day a tree at the fateful site bore in its trunk an uncanny resemblance to a man's face, and neither leaf nor bud grew on that tree since!

'Good God in heavens, Edie, that put the thought of the tablet out of me right enough. Why did you tell me such a tale?'

'Well, being a travelling lassie, and one who is not far from womanhood, it does no harm to be wary of strangers and not so trusting. Now, I think this sweetie is ready for tasting.'

Baby Bairn would come into my thoughts and dreams again, but not today—I had some tablet to eat. What a delight for the gods it was. Never have I tasted such wonder. Edie gave me a square before putting the rest in a biscuit tin. The piece was far too little to satisfy me; I just had to have more, but how? I wasn't a thief, or forward enough to do an Oliver Twist and ask for more. No, the only thing to do was to make my own.

I was only too aware of the gleaming bus awaiting its visitors. There was no way under Heaven's fluffy clouds that Mammy would allow the desecration of her bonny wee stove, but I had no choice— my taste-buds were in total control.

Sneaking in I checked the press to see if there was enough butter, milk and sugar, and there was. The big jam pan was plonked on the heat and off I set—my first attempt at tablet-making. Soon the bubbles began to plop on the surface, and the same aroma I'd enjoyed at Edie's began to fill my own home; the taste-buds were doing a tango on my tongue. I kept a vigil between the pot and the door to see that Mammy wasn't coming back. She had wandered off in the direction of the caravan of Maggie Bunt, a Border gypsy. Once that pair got to yapping I knew that it would be at least an hour before the lips closed again. Swirling the spoon clockwise so as not to antagonise Auld Nick, I soon had something resembling what Edie had produced. Time to finish my task.

I dropped a little into a cup. Yes, it formed a ball. Time to remove the pan from the heat, and by God, it seemed I was going to get away with it after all!

'Now,' I remembered Edie saying, 'don't forget, when handling hot pans, always wrap a cloth round the handle.' So, with these wise words in mind, I reached over the stove to remove a dishtowel from the wee cupboard above. As I did so I knocked something out of its place and stood open-mouthed as it fell into the pan. What happened next was like a scene from a Walt Disney cartoon. The contents spewed up and over the side of the pot; hot browny liquid shot up like mini-rockets, hitting the bus roof. It spewed over everything like molten lava from the belly of an active volcano. It was unstoppable! Mammy's neat and tidy cushions and curtains, arranged just so for her expected visitors, were spotted with tan-coloured drippy blobs. And still the eruption continued, sticking to the Tilley-lamp, covering the back window and running down the Paisley-patterned seats— it missed nothing. Never had I seen the place look so awful; I was dead for sure. This was out of my control. Flying like a banshee I tore across on my wee legs to fetch Edie; she would know what to do. We all met together at the same time—Mammy, Daddy, Edie, me and, who do you think? That's right, our visitors.

Edie laughed (she was the only one) when she realised what had happened. 'You silly lassie. You've knocked enough baking soda into the pan to make puff candy for Scotland and all her neighbours!'

Not only had I learned the art of tablet-making that fine Sunday, but I had made puffy into the bargain. Two treats for one day, wouldn't you say?

Well, after things were cleaned up, the visitors gone, and one of my ears near pulled from its socket by Mammy, I took the time to remember the tale Edie had told me. As I lay in bed I told it to my mother. She said she too remembered that crime, and that in the papers at that time there was a report that 'a headless body, thought to be a vagabond' had been found a mile or two from St Fillans at the mouth of Loch Earn. Could it have been the killer? It may well have been. Travellers say that the brothers buried his head beneath the roots of the cursed tree, so that his spirit would look on the spot where he took the life of the beautiful and innocent Baby Bairn.

Recently I told members of Perth and Kinross Council why the tree with the imprint of a contorted face had a history, and without a word they sent someone to cut it down. It is now a small bench for weary walkers to rest upon. I walk down there. I get weary feet. But it'd be a cold day in hell before I rest on the twisted soul bench.

We bade farewell to the couthy folks of Ayrshire, and before finding the road for Fife, we spent several days in Perthshire. Daddy's sister Lizzie lived in Muthill, a tiny village south of Crieff, and it was there we headed.

In the area of the 'Sma' Glen' I remember falling asleep to the whining of the engine, and rain pelting off the roof. Several sharp bends on the old road wakened me. The window wipers fought hard against the ferocious rain, prompting Daddy to find a lay-by to rest things down. Mammy wiped condensation from the window nearest her and stared out. 'Oh dear,' she said, 'is this not the Grey Lady's field?'

'It's the only spot big enough to stop for the night,' answered Daddy. 'And I need to investigate a grinding sound I heard from the engine.' Mammy's eyes widened as she turned to look at us. She said that when she was a lassie, traveller folk never stopped at the roadside next to the 'Grey Lady's' field, and here we were, right in the very spot. I was curious.

The story goes that after Culloden a young woman hid her husband in a cave near their tiny cottar house, but the English Redcoats put the lad to the sword after discovering him there. She believed the soldiers would never have found the cave, had a tinker not told them where it was. The distraught woman, before ending her life by hanging on a rope tied to the rafters in her home, cursed every travelling tinker. A shepherd tending his sheep heard her curses as she hung from the rope. He immediately went to her aid, only to find an empty house. So the curse of the Grey Lady was born.

The rain stopped, leaving a mist-shrouded glen. If ever a place had an air of haunting about it, then this was it. Mammy gave me the kettle, telling me to fill it at the burn. I remember a feeling of icy coldness as I looked back at the mist creeping over the bus; in an instant it was gone from view. As I knelt down to fill the kettle, something brushed against my face. Leaving the half-empty kettle in the burn I stood up to see who had approached me. Thinking Mary was playing tricks, I swung round to see, but there was no-one there. Feeling hair rise on my neck I swiftly retrieved my kettle and started making my way back towards the bus, but try as I might I could not find where it was. My heart was pounding so much it was the only sound I heard. Then I saw her: a woman had appeared from nowhere and was standing feet away from me! I froze. Water soaked my socks and shoes as the kettle fell and spilled. She towered over me, wispy grey chiffon like the mist itself shrouding her thin form. I was at her mercy, unable to move. I watched as she knelt down at the burnside, then removed a long cloak and began washing it in the water.

Ignoring me, but obviously aware of my presence, she folded the wet garment and laid it on a flat stone. Then very slowly she got to her feet, swaying all the time. I stared, still unable to move and terrified, as she spoke cryptic words in rhythm: 'You shall meet him on the Samhain. If he throws not the silver coin then the Kelpie shall take him away.' With that, she circled round me with a swishing scream and was gone. Fear shot through me, and taking to my heels, not knowing where I was going, I ran and ran.

'Jessie! Jessie! Wake up, lassie, you're dreaming.' I opened my eyes to see my mother leaning over me. We were still on the road, rain still pelting off the windows, as Daddy called to us that Muthill was in sight.

'Thank heavens I was only dreaming, but what a strange dream.' I told everyone, including Auntie Lizzie.

'You had a Banshee dream,' she told me. 'It should have meaning. Let me know if anything comes of it, lassie.'

Something did come of it, but that's later on in my story. I hope you stay with me.

Dreams...

We are the messengers of life,
The passing strangers in the night.
In flights of fancy we may seem
A yellow road of sheer delight.

We set the rhythm and the tone,
The mind to stretch in many ways;
We touch the soul, the heart, the bone,
We are the masters and the slaves.

We are the guts of life's machine,
The passion of forgotten time,
We are the blankets or the ice,
We are the names on parchment signed.

We are the aches, the hurt, the blight,
We are the angels or the freaks,
We can delay the planned awake,
Then take great care before we speak.

We are the keepers of each thought,
To each one's own in deepest sleep;
This strong desire to dream alone
Does help the Lord one's soul to keep.

Charlotte Munro

32

SCOTIA'S BAIRN

Back at Lennie's Yard, Daddy positioned the bus in its usual stance. Out of storage came the prefab, and with or without planning permission it was soon sealed onto the bus. Water and electricity were plumbed and plugged in and we were ready to face another winter.

Several times I heard Daddy say he felt the bus was getting dodgy, and perhaps this winter might be its last. I couldn't face a truth like that, so I blotted it from my mind. Mammy didn't want to run the Formica shop because folks were not as keen on it any more. This pleased him, as the road to England could be hazardous in bad weather. Anyway, he had had bad bouts of bronchitis the previous winter and was happy to stay at home. The Fordy had long since been scrapped. My mother cried that day because she'd grown so fond of the wee van that resembled a frog with a swollen head. It was replaced by a more modern version, which Daddy used to eke out a living painting the odd farmhouse or two.

The thought of going back to school bullies brought me out in a sweat, and I was relieved that I qualified for two weeks' exemption to go tattie lifting. Farmers in the area employed fourteen-year-olds because they were short of adult workers to gather in their crops. Two weeks, however, is hardly any time at all, and soon I was imprisoned within high walls surrounded by my cruel torturers.

Apart from running the gauntlet with these degenerates, I enjoyed some school subjects to an extent. Art was always my favourite. Mr

Heggie, the art teacher, felt my portrait of an American Indian merited public viewing, and so entered it into an exhibition run at that time for schools in the area. It impressed several experts and my old craggy-faced squaw hung for a time in an Edinburgh art gallery. Just thought I'd mention that.

Cookery was another fun subject, and guess what, I passed my recipe (well, Edie Dalrymple's, to be honest) of butter tablet on to the cookery teacher, who said it tasted better than hers. So there's two contributions a travelling lassie left at Loughborough Road School in the early sixties. What impressed the headmaster, and he invited my parents in to tell them, was my flair for writing magical tales. I had written an essay about a dying princess and the heroic efforts of a gypsy lad to save her. Our English teacher gave us the assignment of no more than five hundred words on any subject we liked. I got totally lost in my tale, and before I knew it had notched up five thousand. When I presented my effort to the teacher she took one look and said 'Take it away, it's far too long.' I was shattered, given that I'd worked well into the night, and as I walked down the corridor my eyes welled with tears. Mr Rollo, the head, asked why the sad face. Taken aback by such concern, I dropped my satchel at his feet, my essay pages sprawling over his highly-polished shoes. While he helped gather them up, I told him in a whisper why the sad face.

'Leave the story with me for a day or two, I'd like to read it,' he said.

Next day his secretary gave me the letter inviting my folks to see him. He asked that I be there, and when I think back on how proud they were it makes me feel so warm inside to think their wee travelling lassie could please such a prominent person.

'This girl has great potential as a writer,' he told them. 'I don't usually do this, but if you want there are certain teachers who could help further and nurture her abilities.'

Daddy thanked him, saying if that was what I wanted then by all means please to go ahead.

As I looked at the three faces staring at me and waiting for a response, I went quite red and mumbled that I'd think about it.

'Come back and discuss it with me, lass,' Mr Rollo said, as he shook my parents' hands in parting.

Of course I'd no intention of going to college or taking extra lessons; all I wanted was to travel! So I never saw the inside of his office again, but I must admit he was a good man. One thing he, the cookery teacher and art teacher overlooked, though, was that their attention was turning the bullies into jealous fiends. Sleekit kicks beneath desks had my shins permanently black and blue. Wicked jibes, pulled hair and elbowed cheeks had become my daily dose, and with each day something deep within my weakened, terrified brain was stirring. How long would I be prepared to take this? When, if at all, would I snap? One day I'd show them, but not today.

Mammy had taken to hawking again, because Daddy's bronchitis was worsening and they argued constantly about his smoking. Doctors told him his lungs were very weak, and one said that within five years he'd be a goner. This did slow him down somewhat and he cut his smoking to a few a day.

Granny Power was into her eighty-fourth year, and everybody took turns sitting in the evenings with her. I remember one foggy night whilst I was there. She was in her chair by the fire and I was at her feet. Granny loved brushing my hair, and while I sat nestled against her legs I felt a shiver run through my spine. The brush fell from her hand. When I turned to see my dear old Granny, she was deathly pale. The rose had left her cheeks, and even I could see something was wrong. She gently stroked my hair, asking if I'd fetch her shawl from the bedroom, before saying she needed Mammy. I felt she shouldn't be alone and told her so. She took my hand, brushed it across her lips and repeated her request. Something inside said I had to obey. As I walked up the road to fetch my mother, I had a feeling I'd never see my beloved Granny again and I was right.

That night, circled by her family, she slipped peacefully away. (Love you.)

For the next few weeks relatives came and went, visiting us and talking over old times. Travelling people do this after a loved one goes; they try to keep the memory of the departed alive for as long as they can.

Thankfully, as a result of a fortnight of tonsillitis following Granny's death, I was freed once more from my school tormentors.

§

Remember my dream, where the Banshee spoke a cryptic phrase to me? Let me disclose an incident to you. See what you think.

Several times that winter night kids came a-calling—'Guisers, welcome the Guisers.' Halloween brought painted faces and weirdly-dressed bairns singing songs, reciting Tam o' Shanter and doing somersaults. We moved the seats back to make space for our bath filled with apples for dooking, then we strung some string from the bus-door to a nail hammered into a kitchen shelf, on which we tied sticky treacle scones. Soon the wee prefab was packed with dripping wet-haired faces and black-mouthed bairns having a grand party. It was almost eleven when Mammy wound things up for the night. By the time we'd cleaned up, midnight was upon us. My younger sisters were bedded. I was about to go to bed myself when a loud knock at the door made me leap from my floppy slippers. Thinking teenage guisers were prowling, Daddy called out that we were in bed. The caller knocked louder and wasn't going away, so my father opened the door to see a stranger standing there. 'I'm looking for Patrick,' he said.

'No-one here by that name, lad, but there's a lorry-driver sleeping in his cab round at the gate might know,' answered my father.

Mammy joined Daddy and jokingly told the man that it was the first day of November and by tradition he should throw a silver coin in our door to make sure enough money came into the house during the coming year. The stranger, horrible man that he was, spat and said, 'Tinks look better in oblong boxes.'

Daddy slammed the door in his face, refusing to speak any more with such an uncouth person.

Mammy made light of him, saying, 'The things you see at a prefab mouth fair lowers the tone'.

No sooner had she spoken when a loud screeching of brakes from the main road had us throwing on coats and dashing out to see what had happened. A baker's van was rammed into a lamppost. Trays of breadrolls were scattered at the open rear doors, and lying in a crumpled heap, lit up by the van's headlights, was the rude man whom we'd encountered minutes before.

The Banshee's dream came true!

'*You shall meet him on the Samhain [Halloween]. If he throws not the silver coin then the Kelpie shall take him away.*'

The Kelpie, as folklore teaches, was the ancient death-horse sent by the devil to bring a soul home. In our stranger's case it had taken the shape of the bread van.

He'd been killed outright. The driver sustained no more than a slight bump to the head. And who was Patrick? He was the lorry-driver sleeping unaware in his cab. He later told my father that the stranger was his girlfriend's ex and he was out to get him.

So, reader, watch for dreams where a tall woman wearing a wispy grey shroud enters into your sleeping mind and leaves a message of dread.

§

Well, Christmas came and went. Ne'erday brought resolutions: Mammy's going to stop dying her hair lilac and Daddy has thrown the fags to the back of the fire. Shirley, Janey and Mona have all added to the family by one baby each.

The 10th of March, my fifteenth birthday, had passed and by law I'd almost finished with school. I'd leave come the Easter holidays. If it hadn't been for the bullies, my last days at school could've been happier. However, something a lot worse broke my heart. Daddy had been giving away bits of my bus-engine. The first time in my entire life I ever screamed at him was when he gave a man the dynamo and cylinder-head, because he was giving away the heart of the engine. Without these parts my bus was dead! Nothing hurt me more: not measles, mumps, chicken-pox or my sorest bout of tonsillitis, or, come to think of it, bullies.

Daddy said the bodywork was crumbling and the windows were cracked. No, the bus had to be scrapped!

I went to school that morning feeling as if I'd been at a funeral, and try as I might the feeling wouldn't go away. It was the day of prize-giving, and although I was presented on stage with three certificates I still felt despondent.

Making my way home, lost in thoughts of losing my summers, I failed to hear those oh so familiar voices echoing behind me until they were on my heels. 'Tinkie, Tinkie, cold bum. Yer Mammy cannae knit. Yer Daddy's lying drunk in the auld village nick!' They went on and on with volleys of curses, followed by disgraceful lewd innuendoes. I hurried my pace, and turning the corner, standing upon the humpbacked railway bridge, stood three lassies, leaving two lads at my rear. 'They're determined to get me before I leave this day,' I thought, as the fear they'd put me in for four years returned. One lad came up behind, wrenched my leather satchel and threw it over the bridge. 'My bag,' was all I could think, 'My precious bag that Mammy bought me.' I thought on her hawking street upon street, legs aching, doors slammed in her face, fat, roller-headed women parting with pennies to hear their fortunes. My tender loving mother, with the little money she saved, bought, through the greatest love, that satchel!

Butterflies in my stomach turned to hulking buzzards until I felt they would burst out my chest. Hands began shaking, mouth and throat went parched dry. My eyes stared through red pools, almost leaving their sockets. There weren't five kids in my presence. There were five rats needing scoured from the Earth. I don't remember much from then on because I snapped. Years of torment, losing my bus, no future in travelling, brought forth a demon I didn't know I possessed. Handfuls of hair sprouted from clenched fists, every nail was imbedded with skin and blood, great waves of strength swept my being and with every blow I rained down screams of 'Bastard bairns!' I only came to, so to speak, when a black-faced miner grabbed me, saying they had all ran away.

They ran, those evil youngsters who'd made my life a misery for so long, ran! I could hardly believe it.

The miner's mate retrieved my satchel from the track after a goods train had trundled over. It must have been blessed, that wee bag, because it hadn't even one scratch.

There were a few rips and tears on me, however, and I was glad to find the family out when I got home. Having the bus to myself, I lay down on the courie doon and sobbed until my eyes were swelt sore like balloons. By the time the family arrived, my broken heart was hidden and I told no-one about the bullies. Many years later I wrote these words to those people who tormented me.

SCOTIA'S BAIRN

Yes, it may be said you are 'better' than I, your peers have obviously blessed you with a grand home, fine clothes, the best schooling, good food etc.

I, on the other hand, saw life from the mouth of a 'tinker's' tent.

But I have felt the breath wind of John o' Groats.

I have seen the hills of Glen Coe clothed in purple heather, heard her mountain tops whisper a thousand curses on the murderers of the Mac-Donald bairns.

The ghosts of Culloden brushed against my cheek as I sat on a rock seat, watching heaven's lightning streak across the land to the sea beyond.

Can you say you've tasted the first ripened strawberries of Blairgowrie?

Sucked on rasps until their red juices filled your taste-buds with flavour fit for the Gods?

Is there a time in your life you've washed in the early morning dew, in a field flowering with cowslip, pink clover, and wild daisies?

Did you ever swim below the belly of a giant basking shark?

Have you sung to a curious seal?

Have you heard the weasel's whistle pierce the eardrums of a hypnotised rabbit?

Seen the fear in the eye of the Monarch of the Glen as the stalker's finger pulls back upon his gun?

Did your protective parents tell you tales of the feared Fian Warriors of Glen Lyon?

Do you know how old the Yew Tree of Fortingall is?

Have you ever listened to a deaf child sing a beautiful Scottish ballad, music and words unwritten?

Have you tasted the morning milk from the cow before she suckled her calf, or tasted the freezing waters of a burn at its source?

Have you ever watched the dolphins follow the Lord o' the Isles *as she sails majestically from Oban to Mull?*

Saw a fight to the death between two Traveller warlords ruled by their fore-fathers, adhering to the rules of their clan?

Have you seen the Banshee washing shrouds at the river's edge in the thick ghostly mist of a lonely glen?

Have you held the hand of an old woman as she breathes her last breath and stretches her body for the last time?

I am a Child of the Mist, what are you?

I am 'Ethnic', you are the accepted. I tell a tale of your ancestors, you are taught not to!

Would you converse with a road tramp?

*Does a 'Tinkers'' encampment fill you with excitement, or do you draw
back in disgust?*

*Do you give thanks for each breath God gives you, or do you take life for
granted?*

*We are different, you and I: I am the wind in your hair, you are the voice
of mistrust.*

*I am the blue of the Atlantic as she thrusts her watery fingers into Scotland's
west coast.*

You are the gate that stops me from entering the forest.

*I am the grouse in the purpled heather, you are the hunter who denies me
my flight.*

*I am the salmon as she leaps to her favourite spawning stream, you are the
rod who would end my epic journey.*

*I am the seed of all who went before me. I am from the brave ones who hid,
not burned the tartan. I am from those who spoke the Gaelic in secret places.
I am part of the 'true Earth', the sea, the sky—*

I am 'THE SCOTIA BAIRN'.

§

Soon the month of May, when we usually were well on the road,
passed. Shirley moved from her wee house in Mackenzie Street to
the new town of Glenrothes. 'Come and live with us, Jessie,' she
said. 'You can get a job in the local paper mill; there's money to
be made.'

Daddy had already made up his mind about scrapping the bus and
bought a second-hand Eccles, a four-berth caravan. Two beds, one
for him and one for the lassies. My home, the bus, was gone.

'You go and live with Shirley for a while,' said Mammy. 'If
it's not what you want then Dad will come for you.' I think my
parents recognised how attached I'd become to the travelling life,
and knowing there was no future on the road, this was their way of
severing me from it.

I did get a job, at the Fettykil paper mill in Leslie, the neighbour-
ing village to Glenrothes. I made three pounds and fifteen shillings
a week, of which two pounds went to my keep. Even to this day,
on thinking of the place with its hot, vile smell and towering walls

lined with giant rolls of uncut paper, not to mention the clattering whirling of massive machines, I cringe. It was awful. Thank God for the older women who, knowing how unhappy I was, took me under their wings and made the job human.

I had, for the first time in my life, a bedroom. Shirley looked after me well enough, even though she suffered from a bad back and had two children to look after. But, oh God, how I missed the road and my bus. One Sunday I cycled the seven miles to Lennie's Yard. I was curious—was he still there? Yes, he was, but I would have done better not to seek him out, because the scrap-man had removed his wheels and the door was half-open. I looked inside, disturbing several pigeons who flew screeching by me. I went inside and sat down on the torn faded Paisley-patterned seat. I remembered all those years of fun, laughter and tears. My heart tore in two and I wanted to curl up in a ball and sleep forever.

How old he looked, the silvery chrome trim was hanging from his side, paint flaked from every exposed corner. A long, jagged crack in the back window went from top to bottom like the one in my heart.

We were dying, he and I. He facing a scrapyard, me leaving the road. They told me, the wise ones, my life was just beginning, but if that was so, then why did I feel like I was witness at my own funeral?

Wee Reekie's lum had hit too many trees, and was all but gone. No more to warm Mammy and me as she sat telling the tales that are scattered through the pages of this book, or to put the red back into my father's cheeks after a freezing day gathering rags from cold doors.

I closed my eyes to blot out reality and went back in time. The bus was all shined up. The curtains were tied back with little bows. Daddy sat behind the wheel, ready for the open road. Mammy leaned gently on his shoulder, running a hand through his thick black hair and whispering lovingly in his ear, 'Where to now, Macduff?' Rolling up his shirt sleeves, wrapping an arm round her waist he'd answer, 'Brigadoon, here we come!'

Fragrant lily-of-the-valley toilet water wafted from every corner. Sisters giggled with excitement, wondering if the same handsome laddies they'd canoodled with the previous year would be returning to the Berries come July.

Wee Tiny was eager to impregnate as many bitches as would wander by his nose searching for a suitable mate.

The big black kettle was suspended from its chitties, always on the boil.

I thought of Inveraray's ghostly Jail and the surrounding bracken-covered hills. Friendly farmers who'd spend an hour cracking round our campfire, and not-so-friendly ones who threatened us if we failed to leave their land. West Coast beaches with hidden caves and jagged rocks, stirring me to write tales of witches and seers.

I so wanted things to be as they were. To hell with growing up. To hell with a career, husband, children, a grand house. I had no thoughts on a future. The past suited me just fine. The bus, with both security and freedom, had conditioned me. I was afraid of the wide world. I would never fit into the pattern of things. What kind of place could I live in happily without the sea, the swaying branches of a Caledonian forest, my migrating birds, wild horses, Jake the Adventurer, mongrel dogs, tramps of the road with hearts of gold? This was my world.

Many years have come since that Sunday morning, and I have learned one thing. Circumstance. We are all victims, pushed along on a road of many bends. Of course, at fifteen I never knew love would lead me to a lovely man and to have three good kids. Nor did I foresee the many friends who came and went in my life. Heartache, without doubt, misses no-one, and I have had my share. But how else do we appreciate the sun, if we do not stand in the rain?

I am, and till death will always be, a Scottish traveller, but a change in the way my country regards its nomadic people is forcing them to deny their roots and give up the culture that was so well handed down through generations. I have experienced this in my own family.

The ethnic minority of my people is being cleansed from the roads of Scotland. There is just no place left for the likes of Charlie, Jeannie and their bus full of bonnie lassies!

GOODBYE OLD BUS, YOU WERE A STAR.
THANKS FOR YOUR COMPANY.

…and thank you, reader, for allowing me to share my journey with you.

Glossary of Unfamiliar Words

baggy—minnow, small fish

bissum—impudent, worthless person

cadgers—hawkers, itinerant dealers

chavie—friend

chitties—stand for a kettle, tripod

coorie doon—snuggle down, cosy bed

coupies—rubbish collectors

deek—see

donner—wander, stroll

dross of strength—power, vigour

fee-ed—hired for a period

gadgie—man, fellow

gairn—small horse

girning—whining, grumbling

goonie—nightgown

hantel—crowd of people

hap—covering, shelter

hornies—police

lowy—money, fortune

luggy—container with one or two handles (used for collecting berries)

manshie—wife, woman

menses—hospitality

moich kier—madhouse, asylum

moich—mad

peching—gasping

ragie—silly, weak-minded person

routing out—rooting about

rugger—tough, sturdy person

rused—agitated, enraged

scaldy—settled folk

scranning—starving, hungry

skleff—thin, flat

sleavers—slavers, saliva

spug—sparrow

stardy—prison

swingeing—whining, complaining

thon, thonder—yon, yonder

throng—thrawn, contrary, obstinate

wayn—cartload

yookie—rat